CASES *in* RETAILING

ROBERT LUSCH
University of Oklahoma

PATRICK DUNNE
Texas Tech University

SOUTH-WESTERN College Publishing
An International Thomson Publishing Company

Developmental Editor: Alice Denny
Production Editor: Holly Terry
Cover Design: Michael Stratton
Marketing Manager: Stephen E. Momper

SF63AA

I(T)P

International Thomson Publishing
South-Western College Publishing is an ITP Company. The trademark ITP is used under license.

1 2 3 4 5 D1 9 8 7 6 5
Printed in the United States of America

Library of Congress Cataloging-in-Publication Data

Lusch, Robert F.
Cases in retailing / Robert F. Lusch, Patrick Dunne.
p. cm.
Includes index.
1. Retail trade--United States--Case studies. I. Dunne, Patrick M. II. Title.
HF5429.3.L87 1996
658.8'7--dc20 95-16259
CIP

ISBN No. 0-538-84791-3

TABLE OF CONTENTS

PREFACE

Cases in Retailing was developed because we were constantly hearing from professors teaching retailing courses that there was a lack of case material that could be accessed in one convenient place. At the same time, it was generally felt that many of the cases included in retailing textbooks were simply too short and simplistic. Often, these cases were more case vignettes of one page or less. What professors seemed to be telling us was that they wanted material that was more challenging to their students and that they could use to illustrate some of the more complicated and sophisticated management issues that retailers face. We would also occasionally hear from a professor who was teaching cases in a retailing course who was having trouble finding a retailing casebook. Consequently, the casebook we set out to develop consisted primarily of moderate to long cases with a few short cases. On average, the cases are 8 to 12 pages in length and address a variety of retailing issues and concerns.

Not surprisingly, the feedback we received on the desired industry setting of the cases was quite varied. Those teaching fashion merchandising wanted almost exclusively fashion-oriented cases. While those teaching retailing at community colleges generally wanted a fair number of cases on small independent retail operations. Many faculty believe that too many cases in the past have focused on department stores and they urged us not to concentrate on these retailers. Other faculty emphasized the importance of franchising in the economy and the need to not ignore this line of trade. In short, the more we talked to potential users of a casebook we learned that their needs and preferences were quite varied. We decided to cover a wide variety of industries and issues in retailing and include 21 cases. Most teachers will use 8 to 10 cases per semester in a retailing course, thus they have a high degree of flexibility in selecting the cases to use. At the same time, we believe the casebook, if used for a cases in retailing course, has a sufficient number of cases to allow it to be the primary book for that course.

All of the cases in this book are about actual retail firms, many of which the student will readily recognize. In a few cases, we disguised the name of the retail firm for proprietary reasons. This is done in such a fashion as to not destroy any of the pedagogical aspects of the case. We are pleased that we have been able to cover such a wide variety of lines of retail trade to include apparel retailing, office supply stores, food/grocery stores, fast food franchising, department stores, convenience food stores, direct marketing retailers, drug stores, craft/gift stores, discount department stores, and retail banking. The cases are on such well known companies as JCPenney, Wal*Mart, Circle K, and Spiegel--E Style.

Although the cases in this book have been contributed by over twenty authors, we have made an effort to standardize the writing style and writing level. Although addressing complex issues the cases are written with the student in mind. We avoid the use of unnecessary jargon and try to simply state the issues and circumstances confronting the retail managers in each case. This is not to suggest that the student will not need to dig to find the data or key issues, but rather that he or she will not get ladened with an overly burdensome writing style.

Finally we would like to acknowledge each of the contributing authors for their assistance and interest in this project. This is a much better book because of their contributions and we are very appreciative. At Southwestern Publishing Company, we would like to thank Holly Terry for her efforts in helping us bring this book to market. Finally, we are indebted to Grainne Krasovic for her diligent efforts in preparing the final manuscript for production.

Robert F. Lusch
Norman, Oklahoma

Patrick Dunne
Lubbock, Texas

DEDICATION

This book is dedicated to Marion Bachrach, Nancy Leubner, Robert John Dunne, and Maureen Dunne who have all been a source of support and wisdom.

Robert F. Lusch
Patrick Dunne

E STYLE: REACHING THE AFRICAN-AMERICAN WOMAN*

By Marilyn Lavin, University of Wisconsin--Whitewater

"In today's fragmented marketplace, where there is no single, monolithic consumer, we have to recognize the diversity of consumer attitudes and fashion requirements." This statement by John J. Shea, the vice chairman, president, and chief executive officer of Spiegel, Inc., reflects retailers' growing recognition of the importance of ethnic and racial minority markets. *E Style* catalog, a joint venture of Spiegel and Johnson Publishing Company's *Ebony* magazine, is an effort to meet the special needs of one ethnic/racial minority consumer segment, the African-American woman.

The African-American Market in the 1990s

As late as the 1980s, few major retailers made special efforts to reach the 31 million African-Americans who make up 12 percent of the U.S. population. A number of factors account for this neglect. The African-American market is relatively small when compared with the nation's 80 million Baby Boomers or its 53 million Senior Citizens. The African-American populace has not grown as dramatically in recent years as has its Hispanic counterpart. African-Americans, unlike Spanish-speaking ethnics, do not represent a linguistically distinct segment of the population. In addition, lingering racial stereotypes that portrayed the majority of black Americans as impoverished, as well as retailers' past success with strategies that ignored the racial differences of their customers, contributed to the slow recognition of the importance of the emerging African-American market segment.

By the 1990s, however, many retailers could no longer ignore the major changes occurring within the African-American populace. Between 1980 and 1993, the aggregate purchasing power of African-Americans grew from $127 billion to $270 billion. Moreover, data gathered by the U.S. Bureau of the Census indicate that two-thirds of African-Americans have incomes above the poverty line, while 14 percent or approximately 2 million black households earn more than $50,000 annually. The Census data also show that in 1992, 67.7 percent of African-American youths completed high school as compared with 51.2 percent in 1980. The percentage of blacks with 4 or more years of college education rose between 1980 and 1992 from 8.4 percent to 11.9 percent. Finally, black participation in white collar and craft occupations increased from 23.7 percent in 1983 to 26.8 percent in 1992, data that offers further evidence of the growth in African-American upper and middle classes.

While a sizeable number of African-Americans advanced in economic status and educational attainment, Americans became increasingly aware of the cultural diversity of their nation. As a consequence, the "melting pot" model, which puts forth the expectation that ethnic and racial minorities will ultimately be absorbed into a single, seamless society, began to give way to the "multicultural" theory -- which stresses the limits of group absorption and the resiliency of ethnic and racial identification. The growing acceptance of cultural diversity within the social order of the U.S. undoubtedly contributed to the willingness of ethnic and racial groups to emphasize their particular heritage and to distinguish themselves from the nation's mainstream. The acknowledgment of the existence of differences among the nation's peoples also legitimated retailer efforts to assist ethnic and racial consumer markets that may wish to maintain separate identities within American society.

Purchasing Patterns of African-Americans

Exhibit 1 displays selected data reported by the Bureau of Labor Statistics in its Consumer Expenditure Survey for 1991. Those data show the average income of African-Americans is well below the national average, while the mean household size is considerably larger than the national norm. The data also indicate that black households purchase goods and services in a manner that is somewhat different from the spending patterns of other segments of the population.

---

* Used with permission of Marilyn Lavin

According to the Expenditure Survey data, 41 percent of African-Americans, as compared with 68 percent of the remainder of the population, are homeowners. Black households devote proportionately more of their incomes than do other households to housing, food, utilities, personal care products, and tobacco products; but less to household furnishings and equipment, health care, entertainment, and insurance. In absolute dollars, African-Americans spend more than other groups on clothing, footwear, and laundry and cleaning supplies.

Although the spending patterns of African-Americans are somewhat different from those of other Americans, a number of studies indicate that blacks have positive attitudes toward shopping, and may even be more willing than contemporary consumers to spend. Soft Sheen Products, Inc., a company specializing in black hair care and beauty aids, found that African-American women even in the 1990s continue to "use shopping as a social occasion" and that they are "avid consumers." Nielsen Marketing Research in Northbrook, Illinois reported that African-Americans, like other U.S. consumers, make about 15 shopping trips per month. Finally, Stillerman & Jones, shopping-center consultants in Indianapolis, found that blacks spend $51.21 on each trip to a mall, which is 5.1 percent more than the average for whites.

Product Dissatisfaction

In recent years, African-Americans have increasingly indicated that a wide range of products do not adequately fulfill their specific needs, and a number manufacturers have responded by developing new offerings. For example, the complaints of black women regarding the limited range of colors and ill-fit of pantyhose led Acme-McCrary Corporation to launch Essence Hosiery, the first upscale line for African-Americans. Mattel designed Shani, a doll with skin tones, hair styles, and fashions that reflect the diversity of African-American women to address the concern that the blond, blue-eyed Barbie undermined the self-esteem of young black girls. Pleasant Company addressed the same issue by adding the Addy doll to its American Girl Collection. Addy, which retails at more than $80 and is the heroine of a complementary series of books that describe her escape from slavery and adjustment to freedom, is one of Pleasant Company's most successful products. Among other companies that have responded to the particular preferences of the African-American market are Kentucky Fried Chicken, which sells "soul food" at selected locations; Tinkerbell Cosmetics, which designed "The First Play Makeup for Black Children;" and National City Bank in Louisville, Kentucky, which offers checks featuring the pictures of noted African-Americans.

The fit, color, and style of clothing has been a particular source of dissatisfaction for African-American women. Jeans are a major source of complaint; those that fit at the hips tend to be too big at the waist. African-American women also argue that brighter colors such as yellow and orange are more flattering to darker skin tones than are the more neutral shades favored by Caucasian women. Finally, African-American women favor dressier styles. The *E Style* catalog, a joint partnership of Johnson Publishing Company's *Ebony* magazine and Spiegel, Inc. was designed to address the problems black women voiced about clothing selections.

The *E Style* Partners

E Fund. The *E Style* project brought together two corporations with different and critical competencies--Johnson Publishing Company, Inc. and Spiegel, Inc. The former is a black-managed business with a special understanding of the needs of the African-American market; the latter is a leading multi-channel retailer of fashion apparel and home furnishings. Lori Scott, a Spiegel spokesperson, commented that the combined effort of the two companies provides "the industry's best possible vantage point for identifying what African-American women are looking for when it comes to fashion." The name *E Style* was chosen to reflect the importance of the Johnson-Spiegel partnership; "E" is for Johnson's *Ebony* magazine and "Style" is for Spiegel.

Founded in 1942, Johnson Publishing Company, Inc. is a diversified enterprise with publishing, cosmetic, and broadcast entertainment interests. The company publishes three magazines targeted at the African-American market: *Ebony*, a monthly general interest magazine founded in 1945; *Jet*, a weekly news magazine founded in 1951; and *EM*, a monthly men's magazine founded in 1985. The company also owns several cosmetic and beauty aid lines: Fashion Fair

Cosmetics, which are marketed in the U.S., Europe, Africa, the Bahamas, Bermuda, and the Virgin Islands; Supreme Beauty Products, which feature Duke hair care products for men and Raveen hair care products for women; and Ebone' Cosmetics, a line of skin care products sold through mass retailers throughout the U.S.. Johnson also has a book division that publishes the work of black authors. In addition, it produces the *Ebony/Jet* Showcase, a weekly, nationally-syndicated television series; as well as the *American Black Achievement Awards*, a nationally syndicated annual special begun in 1978. Johnson also sponsors the *Ebony* Fashion Fair, the world's largest traveling fashion show that, since 1958, has contributed more than $40 million to charity.

Spiegel's origins date from 1865, when Joseph Spiegel founded a retail furniture store in Chicago. In 1905, the company began its mail order division, and started to offer clothing through its catalog in 1912. Spiegel currently issues more than 80 catalogs including: the Spiegel catalog, the "Big Book," published twice each year that features men's and women's clothing, home furnishings, and electronics; *Apart*, a catalog of sophisticated European career clothing; *For You From Spiegel*, a specialty catalog of larger size women's apparel; *Together!*, a collection of value-priced casual clothing; *Eddie Bauer*, a series of men's and women's casual wear and home furnishings catalogs; and *Newport News* and *JRT*, moderately priced specialty catalogs. In addition to its direct mail businesses, Spiegel operates more than 300 full-price and off-price retail stores located throughout the U.S. and Canada. The company is involved with Time Warner Entertainment in *Catalog One*, a cable television channel, and in the development of an interactive television channel. Spiegel also has a number of subsidiaries including First Consumers National Bank, Cara Corporation, and Spiegel Acceptance Corporation. In the mid-1970s, Spiegel identified working women as its target market. The company continues to focus its efforts on this group--employed women, with a median age of 41, and an average household income of $51,000. In 1993, Spiegel's revenues amounted to $2.6 billion.

Although neither Johnson Publishing nor Spiegel has provided the exact terms of the companies' *E Style* association, Spiegel's president, John Shea, has reported that "it basically is a licensing agreement." Under the terms of the agreement, Spiegel ran a program of advertisements in *Ebony*, and the magazine provided its subscriber list to the catalog retailer. The latter action was a "first" for *Ebony*. According to Linda Johnson Rice, president and chief operating officer of Johnson Publishing, "We have never given our subscriber list to anyone before. This is something we really believe in." A profile of the *Ebony* readership is shown in Exhibit 2.

Research for *E Style*

E Style is an attempt to respond to the distinctive fashion tastes and clothing needs of the African-American woman. To accomplish those purposes, Spiegel and *Ebony* conducted two years of research before launching the catalog. Those efforts relied upon traditional techniques to ascertain African-American women's attitudes toward clothing, although they also employed innovative methods that assured that the clothing produced for the new catalog would fit the intended market.

Spiegel first conducted telephone and mail interviews with more than 800 of its current African-American customers. It then held nine focus groups in several major U.S. cities; participants in those discussions included persons on Spiegel mailing lists, subscribers to *Ebony*, and black women believed likely to be patrons of the catalog. Those efforts reaffirmed the African-American women's desire for brighter-colored, dressier, better-fitting apparel.

To improve the fit of the planned catalog offerings, the *E Style* Technical Team measured 16 body points of 1,300 African-American women volunteers. The areas measured included: bust, waist, high hip, low hip, cross shoulder, front waist, back waist, thigh, inseam waist height, knee height, arm length (both wrist to wrist and shoulder to wrist), total rise, wrist circumference, and neck circumference. When the measurements were completed, the results were compared to Spiegel sizes that follow the standards set by the fashion industry for Missy sizes 6-16 and Women's sizes 16-24. As expected, that comparison revealed that the proportions of the African-American woman's body are somewhat different from those set forth in the guidelines that determine the sizing of clothing produced for the general market of women.

Promotion for *E Style*

For a number of years, Spiegel has advertised in magazines that have large circulations among their target markets of working women. Those ads generally feature an item sold in the company's "big book" and a coupon the reader can use to order a catalog. For *E Style*, print ads were also used to attract new customers. In June 1993, three months prior to the first mailing of its new catalog, an advertisement for *E Style* appeared in *Ebony*. The full-page, color ad featured an African-American woman wearing a red suit trimmed in faux leopard skin and a matching leopard skin hat, the outfit that was also on the cover of the first *E Style* catalog. The ad copy announced "The new fashion catalog from *Ebony* and Spiegel for the African-American woman." Readers were asked to "reserve yours free," by either calling the 800 number that appeared in the ad or by returning one of two postcards inserted in the magazine. The ad generated 300,000 requests for *E Style* (based on its experience with similar advertisements, Spiegel had anticipated 65,000 catalog requests) and led Spiegel to increase the printing of the first *E Style* from 1 million to 1.2 million copies. In addition, the enthusiastic reaction of thousands of women who wanted to know the price and availability date of the fur-trimmed suit prompted the catalog retailer to increase its fabric orders by 50 percent.

In September 1993, *Ebony* carried a three-page article describing the *E Style* catalog. The text discussed the *Ebony*-Spiegel association and noted the efforts that had been made to meet the fashion and fit needs of African-American women. The major portion of the article, however, was devoted to color photographs of the clothing in the catalog. The featured fashions included jeans "with customed fit [that] is an *E Style* exclusive" and a denim jacket trimmed with kente-print fabric; also shown was a red beaded dress, a three-piece evening ensemble trimmed with bugle beads and sequins, and a pinstripe suit that was described as "ideal for the office, church, luncheons or dinner."

In addition to the advertisement and article in *Ebony*, Spiegel's main catalog carried an *E Style* announcement, and cards that could be used to request free copies of the catalog were inserted into Spiegel's other mailings. Spiegel also placed ads on cable television's, Black Entertainment Network. Finally, Spiegel announced that it would donate a percentage of every sale charged to any FCNB Preferred Charge card used for an *E Style* purchase to the United Negro College Fund.

The First Catalogs

The first *E Style* catalog was mailed in September 1993. The catalog featured clothing in the bright colors preferred by survey respondents as well as shoes, jewelry, and other accessories. The apparel styles and fabric designs reflected the strong influence of African-American ethnic heritage. Most notably, the catalog displayed fancy hats with many outfits. This was somewhat of a new venture for Spiegel, and the company's president acknowledged that "we didn't do much with hats until now." African-American women, however, consider hats to be an important accessory. Consequently, of the 65 outfits shown in the 64-page catalog, 19 included hats. Many pages of the catalog also made note of the fact that the merchandise had been resized to take account of the proportions of the African-American woman's figure.

The merchandise in the catalog was "value priced." Accordingly, dress and suit prices started at $99. In keeping with Spiegel's practice in its other catalogs, however, dresses and suits were generally shown with several complementary items. As an example of a typical *E Style* outfit, a $79 black jacket trimmed in authentic African fabric was shown with a $34 mock turtleneck pullover top, a $29 ribbed skirt, $88 suede platform booties, $29 beaded *Ebony* earrings, and a $36 "3-D cap" trimmed in fabric matching the jacket. The total cost of all the items in this ensemble amounted to $295. By contrast, in the Spiegel's main catalog for fall-winter 1993, a private-label outfit retailed for $263, one from Liz Claiborne was offered at $499, and another carrying the DKNY label sold for $1,345.

Spiegel also issued a special *E Style* catalog for the 1993 Holiday season. This mailing displayed festive apparel, but made no explicit mention of Christmas. One double-page spread, however, proclaimed: "Ethnicity. The art of a people is the heart of a people. Collect it, display it. Cherish it." Merchandise featured on those pages included a "Nubian Dancer" wall hanging, a black porcelain Santa, black cherub ornaments, and a Kwanzaa candleholder.

Announcing that the first *E Style* catalogs had been "very well received" during the fall of 1993, Spiegel issued a 64-page spring edition in February 1994. Like its predecessors, this catalog featured bright colors including red, fuchsia, lime, and royal blue. The apparel was decorated with such detailing as embroidery, beading, and tassels. Some clothing, including a baseball jacket reinterpreted in a printed kente pattern, was constructed of fabric produced in Africa. The spring *E Style* edition also contained an expanded collection of decorative home accessories for the customer who wishes to "make a cultural statement that goes beyond her wardrobe." Among the items offered were carved wooden ceremonial masks from Ghana, Ashanti fertility dolls, African-influenced art prints, and pillows and throws made in a West African-inspired "Karogho" print.

The summer edition of *E Style* presented a collection of swimwear ranging in price from $42 to $82. The catalog featured brightly colored suits and dresses, but it also offered approximately 20 outfits that were stark white or other neutral colors. The activewear shown in *E Style* was "dressy;" T-shirts were embroidered in gold, a magenta bomber jacket had seashell appliqués, short sets were made of rayon, and thongs were often decorated with beads and sequins or made of gold-colored materials. A number of items in this catalog were also offered at reduced prices. Several of the swimsuits were reduced 25 percent, and a 4-page insert in the middle of the book announced an "End of the Season Clearance Sale" on 18 items that had appeared in the Spring catalog.

The *Ebony*-Spiegel partnership is committed to the *E Style* project. During its second year, four editions of the catalog--fall, holiday, spring, and summer--are again planned. *E Style* will continue to emphasize apparel designed for the African-American woman. Customers' positive responses to the household and gift items presented in the initial catalogs, however, has prompted the catalog developers to provide additional offerings in those areas. In particular, the 1994 Holiday catalog will feature a greater selection of African-heritage related gifts, dolls, tree decorations, and items associated with the celebration of Kwanzaa.

Other Efforts to Market to African-Americans

E Style represents probably the most ambitious retail effort to meet the special needs of African-Americans. It is not, however, the only attempt to respond to this market. The success of those enterprises have not, however, been consistent.

In 1993, Marshall Field, a division of Dayton Hudson Corporation, opened an Afrocentric Shop in its flagship Chicago store, but abandoned the project after only four months of operation. The location of the boutique between women's sportswear and coats appears to have contributed to its failure. According to its manager, not too many customers were seeking home accessories, the Afrocentric's primary product lines, in this area. JCPenney encountered problems related to quality standards and timely delivery when it tried to expand its African boutiques from 22 trial markets to 350 stores. The difficulties proved so intractable that the chain ultimately closed the boutiques so that it could focus its efforts on its specialty *Fashion Influences* catalog that is mailed to 800,000 African-American households.

Stores that have succeeded with formats targeted to African-Americans include the Hudson Division of the Dayton Hudson Corporation and Montgomery Ward & Co. In response to customer demand, Hudson's established "global bazaars" with Afrocentric products in several of its mall locations. A spokesperson indicated, "That's why you're going to find a bunch of Kwanzaa cards to choose from-not two." Likewise, Montgomery Ward opened "Homeland Authentics" boutiques in about eight percent of its stores. The boutiques carry a collection of approximately 100 items from baseball caps to plastic trash cans that are decorated with colorful kente patterns. A Ward's manager commented: "We have found this niche to be profitable."

Questions for Discussion

1. Describe the *E Style* target market as specifically as possible. Use both demographic data and information about the catalog to develop your answer.

2. What kinds of retailers should be most interested in the African-American market? What kinds of retailers might not have much interest in this demographic segment at the present time?

3. Why might a mail-order catalog prove more effective than a traditional retail store in reaching the African-American woman?

4. Is *E Style* appealing to a lasting, retail segment of consumers, or is the interest in the catalog a passing fad?

Exhibit 1
Consumer Expenditure Survey, 1991 Selected Data

Item	All Consumer Units	White and Othe	Black
Number of Consumer Units	97,918	87,115	10,763
Consumer Unit Characteristics			
Income before taxes	$33,901	$35,311	$21,544
Income after taxes	30,729	31,929	20,544
Average number of persons per unit	2.6	2.5	2.8
Number of earners	1.4	1.4	1.3
Number of vehicles	2.0	2.1	1.1
Percent homeowners	63%	68%	41%
Percent renters	37%	34%	59%
Average Annual Expenditures	$29,614	$30,794	$20,091
Food	$4,271	$4,387	$3,352
Food at home	2,651	2,676	2,448
Cereals and bakery	404	412	347
Meats, poultry, fish, eggs	709	682	922
Dairy products	294	306	200
Fruits and vegetables	429	436	373
Other food at home	815	841	607
Food away from home	1,620	1,711	904
Alcoholic Beverages	$297	$314	$139
Housing	$9,252	$9,570	$6,692
Utilities	$1,990	$2,005	$1,866
Household Furnishings/Equipment	$1,200	$1,255	$760
Furniture	294	303	222
Major appliances	132	134	121
Small appliances	81	87	30
Laundry and Cleaning Supplies	$116	$116	$119
Personal Care Products & Services	$399	$404	$352
Tobacco and Smoking Supplies	$276	$282	$228
Apparel and Services	$1,735	$1,726	$1,803
Men and boys	429	431	405
Women and girls	706	706	703
Footwear	242	226	364
Other apparel/services	277	281	246
Transportation	$5,151	$5,413	$3,029
Health Care	$1,554	$1,640	$857
Entertainment	$1,472	$1,578	$620
Fees and admissions	378	410	114
TV, radio, and sound equipment	468	482	351
Cash Contributions	$950	$1,001	$536
Personal Insurance	$2,787	$2,925	$1,665

Source: U.S. Department of Labor, Bureau of Labor Statistics, Bulletin 2425, Table 7 (September 1993).

Exhibit 2
***Ebony* Magazine Demographic Profile**

Characteristics	Total	Men	Women
Average issue audience (000)	11,173	4,604	6,569
Sex	100.00%	41.2%	58.8%
Age 18-34	48.1%	47.0%	48.9%
Age 18-49	79.0%	82.6%	76.5%
Median age (years)	35.7	35.9	35.4
Attended/graduated college	38.6%	41.6%	36.5%
Employed	69.4%	80.2%	61.8%
Professional/managerial	7.5%	6.7%	8.2%
Household income $50,000+	21.3%	24.7%	19.0%
Household income $40,000+	32.8%	34.8%	31.4%
Household income $30,000+	48.4%	52.1%	45.8%
Average household income	$34,564	$37,160	32,744
Children in household under 18	54.6%	44.7%	61.5%
Married	38.2%	42.1%	35.5%
Own home	46.7%	45.9%	47.3%

Source: Mediamark Research, Inc., 1994.

REFERENCES

"African Styled Merchandise Gaining in Popularity" (1993), *All Things Considered, National Public Radio*, December 24.

Anderson, Veronica (1993), "If There's Kente, Will They Come?" *Crains Chicago Business*, 16 (11 October), 15.

Campanelli, Melissa (1991), "The African-American Market: Community, Growth, and Change," *Sales and Marketing Management* (May), 75-81

"Cosmetic Changes" (1993), *Record* [Bergen, New Jersey], (22 April), BUS sec. *Ebony,* June 1993.

Egerton, Judith (1993), "Black History Emblazoned on Bank's New Checks," *The Courier-Journal* [Louisville, Kentucky], (26 March), sec. E.

"Fashions with Pizazz" (1993), *Ebony* (September), 134-136.

Grossman, Laurie (1992), "After Demographic Shift, Atlanta Mall Restyles Itself as Black Shopping Center, *Wall Street Journal* (26 February), B1.

Legette, Cynthia (1993) "Marketing to African Americans," *Business and Economic Review* (April-June), 3-7.

McFadden, Kay (1993), "In the 1990s, Black Power is Economic," *News and Observer* [Asheboro, North Carolina] (29 August), BUS. sec.

Mediamark Research, Inc. (1994), "*Ebony* Magazine Demographic Profile" [unpublished].

_________________ (1993), "Research on Black Consumers," *Marketing News* (13 September), 1-3.

Miller, Cyndee (1993), "Major Catalogers, Niche Players Carve Up Mail-Order Market," *Marketing News* (27 September), 1-2.

Morris, Ann (1994), Spiegel representative, telephone interview, June 24.

Schlossberg, Howard (1993), "Many Marketers Still Consider Blacks 'Dark-Skinned Whites,'" *Marketing News* (18 January), 1, 13.

Schmeitzer, John (1993), "*Ebony* Good Fit at Spiegel," *Chicago Tribune* (26 July), section 4, 1.

Spiegel, Inc. (1993-1994), *E Style Catalog* (Fall, Holiday, Spring, Summer).

Spiegel, Inc. (1994), *E Style* press kit.

Spiegel, Inc. (1993), *Spiegel Fall-Winter Catalog.*

U.S. Bureau of the Census (1993), *Statistical Abstract of the United States*: 1993, No. 233. "Educational Attainment by Race and Ethnicity, 1960 to 1992," No. 735. "Persons Below Poverty Level and Below 125 Percent of Poverty Level, 1959 to 1991," No. 644. "Employed Civilians, by Occupation, Sex, Race, and Hispanic Origin, 1983 and 1992."

U.S. Department of Labor, Bureau of Labor Statistics (1991), *Bulletin 2425*, Table 7. "Housing tenure, race of reference person, and type of area: Average annual expenditures and characteristics, Consumer Expenditure Survey.

Wynter, Leon (1993), "Business and Race: Stores Have Different Ideas on African Style," *Wall Street Journal* (26 October), B1.

FIRST FEDERAL BANK AND TRUST: PART A*

By Robert F. Lusch, University of Oklahoma

Introduction

As the bank closed for the evening, Fred Wade, President, leaned back in his chair and reflected on what had transpired over the last few months. Only 90 days ago the purchase of First Federal Savings and Loan from the Federal Savings and Loan Insurance Corporation (FSLIC) occurred. The purchase was part of a program that the FSLIC had in conjunction with the Federal Deposit Insurance Corporation (FDIC) to help save failing financial institutions during the late 1980s and early 1990s. During this time period, Jay Sterling and his brothers and sisters had acquired several failed financial institutions.

Since the time of the acquisition of First Federal Savings and Loan, a mere 90 days ago, considerable progress had been made. No longer was the financial institution a savings and loan but had become a federally chartered bank. In conjunction with this change, the name was changed to First Federal Bank and Trust. Although Fred had expected that a deposit run-off of 25% would occur due to the lowering of interest rates on deposits, this had not occurred. First Federal Savings and Loan, in an effort to survive, was paying premium rates on deposits. When the acquisition occurred, one of the first things Fred did was to lower rates by almost 100 basis points (1 percent on average). Three months later, only 12.7% of the deposit base had been lost.

Instituting a New Corporate Culture

One of the biggest challenges Fred faced was the corporate culture. As First Federal Savings and Loan began to falter, the best of its employees had left for more secure jobs. Those that remained were overall quite weak. Nonetheless, Fred felt a loyalty to these 140 employees and did not terminate any of them. However, during the first 90 days, 24 left voluntarily. Fred attributed most of this to their unwillingness to adopt the new corporate culture he was trying to institute. Another problem was that some of the employees lacked the technical knowledge to operate in a full-service bank. First Federal Savings and Loan largely focused on household and consumer loans; thus, the employees generally lacked commercial banking experience.

During the summer of 1992, several months prior to the takeover of First Federal Savings and Loan, Fred read Sam Walton's book, Sam Walton: Made in America. Fred, as a longtime Wal*Mart stockholder, had been impressed with Sam Walton and his leadership style. Based on ideas in this book, Fred decided to build the First Federal Bank and Trust culture around five basic values:

1. Exceed your customer expectations. All associates should strive constantly in everything they do to exceed the expectations of customers. Only by exceeding expectations does one create satisfied customers.

2. Listen to everyone in the bank. We can learn by listening. If we listen to ideas from both our customers and associates we will have the knowledge on how to improve.

3. Appreciate everything the associates do for the bank. Recognize the associates for both the little and big things they do to help the customer and the bank.

---

* This case is based on actual data and information, however, names and data have been disguised for proprietary reasons. The case is intended not to indicate the right or wrong way to handle certain problems, but rather as a means of instruction.

4. Control expenses better than the competition. Being efficient in what we do is important to success. If we make mistakes, which are inevitable, we can better recover if we are efficient. On the other hand, if we are brilliant but inefficient, we will not prosper or survive.

5. Share the profits with associates. If we work as a team and do all of the preceding, then we should share the rewards with those that help to produce the profits.

Within 24 hours after the acquisition, Fred began to preach these values. He personally conducted multiple 3-hour training sessions with 20 employees, until all associates were trained. Fred felt that the best way to communicate values was to live by them. He realized that he was not only the message but the medium. Fred had the President's office moved from the second floor to the main lobby. His office had a glass exterior wall facing the lobby so he could constantly be aware of activity in the bank. Fred also regularly visited the branches. Every Saturday morning he would make the rounds to each of the five branches and spend about a half hour at each talking to associates and customers. During the week he was constantly writing thank you notes to associates that he recognized doing things right.

Beginning the Assault

Fred began to realize that his plan had worked--he had significantly changed the corporate culture. This was not to say there were still not problems. Occasionally, an associate had to be counseled and sometimes terminated because of their unwillingness to be part of the customer-friendly environment he was creating. Many of the disgruntled employees were not willing to work late or on Saturdays. Fred instituted 8 a.m. to 8 p.m. full-service banking on Monday through Friday, and 8 a.m. to 4 p.m. banking on Saturday. Consequently, each employee was expected to work one or two evenings per week or two Saturdays per month. Predictably, many long-time employees who were used to "banker's hours" were not happy with this schedule. But the customer wanted convenience, and according to Fred, the customer was our reason for existing.

Having built a solid foundation, Fred felt the time was right to begin his assault on the marketplace. Currently, First Federal Bank and Trust was the fifth largest financial institution in the community. Fred had two options. First, there were several smaller banks in the community that could be acquired. The key problem in this regard was that these banks were priced at two times book value, and Fred didn't think the premium was justified. He estimated that he would have to pay $ 8-10 million to acquire these institutions and that they would increase his deposit base by 30%, which would push him into the number three spot in the market. A second option was to build market share by heavy promotion directed at obtaining more deposits and increasing loan demand, while simultaneously opening at least two additional branch offices. Each branch office would cost $850,000 to open--approximately $250,000 for the land, $400,000 for the building, and $200,000 for equipment and furniture. The advertising program that Fred had in mind consisted of spending $100,000 a month for 18 months. This was three times what he was currently spending and approximately equal to what the leading financial institution in the community was spending. Fred was confident that the new branches and the accelerated advertising would boost deposits and loan volume by at least 25% within 18 months.

Obtaining Baseline Data

Fred reviewed his recommendation with Jay Sterling, whose family owned 100% of the stock of the bank. Jay was quite enthusiastic. However, he was concerned that Fred and the associates would have a problem handling the increased volume. Jay wasn't convinced that Fred had been able to fully implement his new corporate culture. Although Jay had personally observed that the associates appeared optimistic when he visited the bank, he also knew that they were aware that he routinely visited on the third Wednesday of each month. Jay wanted to know what the customers thought of First Federal Bank and Trust and how this compared to the perceptions of other financial institutions in the community.

After his meeting, Fred called Dr. Anne Morgan, a professor of marketing at a nearby university. Anne had an excellent reputation for marketing expertise and had done many market research studies for local businesses. Fred asked Anne to put together a proposal.

Anne suggested a 10-15 minute telephone interview with 1000 randomly selected head of households. She suggested collecting data on satisfaction levels with the households' primary and secondary financial institutions, the perceived performance of the primary and secondary financial institutions on 20 attributes, loan needs, word-of-mouth advertising, and demographics. Anne priced this research, including the management report she would prepare, at $15,000. After checking with Jay Sterling, Fred gave her the go-ahead to conduct the research. Within three weeks, Fred had the report to review.

Exhibits 1 and 2 provide a summary of some of the findings of Dr. Morgan's research. In addition, some of the more salient findings can be summarized as follows:

Overall Marketplace

- The market share leader is **Community Bank** with 27% of households indicating that it was their primary financial institution and 3.6% naming it as their secondary financial institution. **First Federal Bank and Trust** was named by 5.4% of households as their primary financial institution and 1.4% as their secondary financial institution. Overall, 40.7% of households have both a primary and secondary banking relationship. **See Exhibit-1.**

- Overall, 54.4% of households are very satisfied with their primary financial institution. Only 2.5% are dissatisfied or very dissatisfied.

- **First Federal Bank and Trust** leads the market in terms of overall customer satisfaction. 77.8% of its customers are very satisfied and another 20.4% are satisfied. **See Exhibit-2.**

Needs Assessment

- 80.4% of households believe their primary financial institution is doing a good job at making an effort to serve their needs.

- The largest credit need over the next 12 months will be for auto loans. 3.9% of households will definitely need an auto loan and another 21.6% may possibly need an auto loan.

- Another significant credit need will be for home mortgages. 3.8% of households will definitely need a home mortgage and 9.7% may possibly need a home mortgage.

- A third credit need is for credit cards. 3.6% of households will need a credit card in the next 12 months and another 10.7% may possibly need a credit card.

- 40.7% of **First Federal Bank and Trust** customers would find a branch office in their favorite supermarket very useful; 31.5% would find such a branch somewhat useful.

Competitive Advantage

- **First Federal Bank and Trust** is the market leader in terms of satisfied customers based on the following attributes:

    * friendly employees
    * professional employees
    * convenient drive-in hours
    * convenient lobby hours
    * quick drive-in service
    * quick lobby service
    * full-service banking hours
    * convenient locations
    * understands my needs
    * makes an effort to serve my needs
    * understandable and easy-to-complete forms
    * informative advertising

- The relative sources of competitive advantage for the top six financial institutions are as follows:

    * **Community Bank** is at competitive parity on employees, convenience, quickness, accuracy, meeting needs, and image enhancers. It is significantly below parity on pricing. In brief, it has no distinctive characteristics as perceived by its customers and is therefore vulnerable to competitive pressures.

    * **Bank III** is at competitive parity on employees, convenience, quickness, accuracy, and image enhancers. It is perceived by its customers at below parity on pricing and meeting customer needs. In brief, a significant number of customers can be dislodged from Bank III.

    * **Teachers Credit Union** is at competitive parity on employees, meeting needs, and image enhancers. It is below parity on convenience, quickness, and accuracy, but is significantly above competitive parity on pricing. In summary, Teachers Credit Union attracts the price-sensitive customer who is willing to trade off lower service for better prices on savings and loans. One indicator of this is that approximately 5% of its customers don't know the interest rate on savings and 16% don't know the interest rate on loans. For other financial institutions, about 20% don't know the rate on savings and about 50% don't know the rate on loans. Consequently, these customers will be difficult to dislodge.

    * **Liberty Bell** is at competitive parity on employees, convenience, quickness, accuracy, meeting needs, and image enhancers. It is below parity on pricing. In short, Liberty Bell is an undifferentiated competitor in the marketplace.

    * **Enterprise Bank** is significantly above competitive parity on employees, convenience, quickness, and accuracy. Consequently, Enterprise Bank is a quality service competitor. On the other hand, it is at competitive parity on pricing, meeting needs, and image enhancers. Enterprise Bank can be expected

to be a strong competitor in the marketplace. It is not only likely to hold onto its customers, but potentially gain market share.

* **First Federal Bank and Trust** is above competitive parity on employees, convenience, quickness, accuracy, and meeting needs. First Federal Bank and Trust is at competitive parity on pricing. Overall, it is the most differentiated player in the marketplace.

Relationship Strength

- Customers of First Federal Bank and Trust have a strong relationship with the bank. 61.1% of customers often favorably mention the bank to friends. On the other hand, 98.1% would recommend First Federal Bank and Trust to a friend if asked.

- Customers of First Federal Bank and Trust expect their relationship to continue. An overwhelming 96.3% of customers plan to continue banking at First Federal Bank and Trust over the next year.

- Customers of Community Bank and Bank III can be potentially dislodged. Approximately 25% of these customers would consider switching to another financial institution; whereas only 7.4% of First Federal Bank and Trust customers would consider switching.

- Although customers of Community Bank and Bank III are those most likely to change banks, these two banks (largely due to their size) are the most likely recipients of new customers as other households decide to switch banks. For households that would consider switching their primary or secondary financial institution, they would most likely switch to Bank III or Community Bank. 8.4% would switch to Bank III and 6.9% would switch to Community Bank.

Development of the Marketing Plan

As Fred pored over the 100+ page management report, he started to formulate his marketing plan. Jay Sterling was still not convinced that growth by acquisition might not be the best alternative. The premium over book value was high, but at least there would be some guarantee of what was being acquired in terms of deposits and loans. On the other hand, buying more market share by investing over $1.5 million dollars in marketing and over $1.5 million for opening new locations seemed more of a gamble. Nonetheless, Jay told Fred not only that he had to make the final decision but that his performance, and frankly his job, rested on the outcome. If Fred decided to pursue the nonacquisiton approach, Jay Sterling had put a $3.5 million constraint on the project and was insistent that at least two more branches be opened. Jay also wanted Fred to consider opening branches in a Kmart supercenter that was planned for early next year. Kmart had recently contacted First Federal Bank and Trust about such a possibility. The cost of opening would be $150,000 for leasehold improvements and furniture and equipment. The monthly lease on the 700 square foot facility would be $2000. The Kmart supercenter was to be built on the far east side where First Federal Bank and Trust was in need of a new branch. Both Jay and Fred were aware of the large increase in bank branches in discount department stores and supermarkets and felt that this could be the wave of the future.

Questions for Discussion

1. What additional information should Fred have before he makes a decision?

2. Based on the information provided, which growth strategy should Fred pursue for First Federal Bank and Trust?

3. What do you think of the feasibility of a branch office in a Kmart supercenter?

4. Suggest an advertising theme and advertising program for First Federal Bank and Trust if Fred decides to pursue the marketing strategy. Be sure to identify the major message(s), media, budget, and method of evaluation of the expenditures.

Exhibit-1
Financial Institutions'
Estimated Share of Primary and
Secondary Relationships

	Primary Relationship	Secondary Relationship
Community Bank	27%	3.6%
Bank III	24.7%	4.3%
Teachers Credit Union	8.1%	2.4%
Liberty Bell Bank	7.7%	1.0%
First Federal Bank and Trust	5.4%	1.4%
Enterprise Bank	4.8%	1.1%
All Others	22.3%	26.9%
TOTAL	100.00%	40.7%

Note: Read as follows--27% of households that have a primary banking relationship have it with Community Bank; 3.6% of households that have a primary banking relationship have a secondary banking relationship with Community Bank.

Exhibit-2
Overall Satisfaction With
Primary Financial Institution:
Top Six Institutions

	Very Satisfied	Satisified
Community Bank	35.7%	46.8%
Bank III	43.9%	41.9%
Liberty Bell Bank	50.6%	41.6%
Teachers Credit Union	63.0%	23.5%
First Federal Bank and Trust	77.8%	20.4%
Enterprise Bank	68.6%	27.1%

MILLER AND RHOADS*
By Michael Little and Gene Hunt, Virginia Commonwealth University

Introduction

Mr. Henry Coghill, general manager of the flagship Miller and Rhoads Department Store, and an employee for over twenty years, sat in the midst of an empty building preparing for the final stage of Chapter 7 bankruptcy in October 1991. Merchandise had been removed, store furniture and display cases sold, and arrangements were being made to transfer ownership of the building to its new owner, General Electric Finance Corporation. A number of questions, however, remained unresolved for him. Why had this once grand department store failed? Could the management of Miller and Rhoads have prevented the failure of this company or was it inevitable? Were there early warning signs that could have been identified? Did Miller and Rhoads lose focus of the customers' quest for merchandise, service, and convenience? If so, why? Most importantly, what strategic issues did management fail to grasp?

Background and Early Corporate Culture

Miller and Rhoads began in 1885 as a partnership of three young men from Pennsylvania with a capital investment of $3000. Although Richmond was not the first choice for their business location, it soon became apparent there was promise in this centrally located city. Richmond was recovering from the Civil War. The population of 75,000 was increasingly composed of new migrants from the rural south who were mostly victims of an antiquated plantation system. The economy of the state capital was broadly based on tobacco and other light manufacturing. Richmond eventually became a hub for transportation, wholesaling, and retailing with a strong banking and financial center. In fact, many of these attributes still hold true today.

Linton Miller and Webster Rhoads quickly established an identity for the business that contributed toward a strong corporate culture and provided an enduring tradition for customers and employees. This vision was based on a concept of "mutual integrity" that included providing special courtesies and extended services to customers, in addition to merchandise that afforded customers "better styling at money's worth." The business policies that evolved were not unlike those of competitive department stores of the day. Some of these policies and customer amenities included exchanges for any item, wide aisle design in a spacious setting, a one-price system for all purchasers, openly marked prices on all wares, and service desk convenience that included postal stamp service and later free telephone use and home delivery of purchases to anywhere within the city.

In conservative Richmond, customers were addressed by their last name and it was not unusual to see the owners of the store on the selling floor. The corporate culture was best characterized by strong community involvement. Management was encouraged to donate their time and money to community organizations such as the Virginia Museum. In one sense, Miller and Rhoads was perceived as a "public institution" because of certain traditions. These traditions included the popular Tea Room, which became a famous meeting place with a runway for modeling women's fashions, and a men's corner for discussion of business and political issues of the day. Classical and popular music were played for all. The Christmas Santa was another tradition; he originally was a professional actor and literally came down the chimney to the pleasure of capacity crowds of children and adults alike. Another institution was the author series that enriched the community each year attracting Pulitzer Prize winners and other popular writers including Robert Frost, Philip Wylie, S. J. Perelman, and Dumas Malone.

By the 1930s, Miller and Rhoads was the state's largest department store and the dominant retailer in Richmond. During this span and through the mid 1950s, Miller and Rhoads operated profitably with revenues reaching $35 million in 1955.

---

* Used with permission of Michael Little and Gene Hunt.

In summary, Miller and Rhoads' successful strategy was attributed to sound merchandising principles, knowledgeable management that anticipated consumer trends, and an image and corporate culture that was dedicated to customer service.

Growth: A New Strategy and a New Structure

Prior to 1956, Miller and Rhoads essentially was a one-store operation in downtown Richmond (446,940 square feet). Beginning in 1956 and continuing through 1966, Miller and Rhoads began an extensive 11-year expansion that evolved from the original flagship store to a 13-store operation. Many of the branches were limited to narrower lines of softgood merchandise and stores with small square footage. In fact, Miller and Rhoads' executives referred to many of the branches as specialty stores rather than the traditional, multi-line department store (See Exhibit 1).

By 1958, top management realized that the organizational structure "had reached a critical point". Several major problems had been identified. First, there was marked confusion at the departmental level in the stores concerning responsibility for sales, stocks, expenses, and profits. Second, buyers failed to give sufficient attention to the outlying stores. The average buyer was unable to effectively perform the duties and carry out the responsibilities because the workload had significantly increased. Third, the three stores outside Richmond (Lynchburg, Roanoke, and Charlottesville, varying from 70 to 165 miles from Richmond) created problems that were geometric in proportion compared to the previous single store operations. For example, stock control systems, which had been designed basically for a single-store operation, were in need of complete revision because of inefficiency. Store managers and corporate managers were also confused as to responsibilities and duties relative to the outlying stores. Finally, the key operating executive of the corporation, the general manager, was carrying a drastically increased workload with complete responsibility for buying, sales promotion, operations, and control functions of an increased number of stores.

From these problems and from the 1961 organizational chart in Figure 1, it is important to consider that the general manager of the Richmond Store was highly involved with the daily management of the branch stores; that the organization was vertically integrated with the general manager handling a wide span of control and with decision making centralized; and the merchandising (both buying and selling) was centralized in the Richmond store with major decisions made at the top of the organization.

Miller and Rhoads adopted in 1960 a reorganization plan similar to the Mazur Plan (Mason and Mayer and Ezell 1991). While major department store retailers adopted the Mazur Plan during the 1930s and 1940s, Miller and Rhoads was 20-30 years behind other department stores in their reorganization efforts. The Mazur Plan consisted of a department store organization structure including store manager, merchandise manager, controller, and promotion manager reporting to a general manager.

The need for changing organization structure was obvious and pressing. Frederick Atkins, a retail buying syndicate, was hired to assist in the reorganization. The following goals for reorganization of Miller and Rhoads were developed:

1. To clarify the responsibilities of all executive personnel from president to departmental levels in the various stores.

2. To develop a stronger approach to personal selling and sales promotion.

3. To free buyers from selling floor duties (to concentrate on buying activities).

4. To strengthen the performance of the outlying stores by insuring that adequate buying staff attention was made available.

5. To develop merchandise controls that would function on a multi-store basis.

6. To develop a framework of organization that would be capable of effectively handling the present operations and be readily expandable to meet future expansion.

It took two years to develop the plan (1958-1960) and another three years to implement the plan (1960-1963). By the end of 1962, the financial situation had not improved as a result of the reorganization. Sales had not reached the projected plans and the organization had suffered from high markdown and high inventory shrinkage (See Exhibit 2).

At this time, the store reorganization did not have an impact on performance. Neither did the operation of the smaller branch stores that executives referred to as specialty stores. In fact, Miller and Rhoads also opened a specialty clothing store, the Steven Sheppard Shop, in the 1950s. Unfortunately, this venture proved unsuccessful and was eventually eliminated. Management of Miller and Rhoads recognized that the most pressing need was to increase volume to a level that would permit a distribution of expenses over a wider base.

The Competitive Environment

Significant competition was emerging for Miller and Rhoads. Although it was prominent, it was no longer the dominant department store or retailer in Richmond. Its cross-street rival, Thalhimer's, another family-run department store, was serving a growing Richmond area as well. For example, by 1966, Thalhimer's had 19 stores with revenues over $51 million and a net income of $1.25 million.

An even more significant competition to Miller and Rhoads, and in fact to all department stores, was the emergence of discount stores. The retailing competitive environment in the 1960s was taking a new form. Best Products, a catalog showroom headquartered in Richmond, was offering products to the consumer at discounted prices. A second operation headquartered in Richmond was Ward's (later to become Circuit City). Offering major appliances and electronics at reduced prices, it was unlike other discounters in that it still provided sales assistance by well trained salespeople. In addition, other discounters such as Kmart were positioning their organizations for the future at the expense of traditional retailers.

In the 1970s and 1980s, discounters and specialty clothing store operations such as The Limited and The Gap continued to erode significant market share from traditional department stores. At this time of acquisition by Allied Stores in 1981, Miller and Rhoads had 23 stores in Virginia and North Carolina. One of its main competitors, Thalhimer's, had 25 stores in Virginia, North Carolina, South Carolina, and Tennessee. At the end of 1980, however, Thalhimer's had significantly more gross retail space per store:

Miller and Rhoads:	76,429 square feet per store
Thalhimer's:	93,833 square feet per store

Marketing

Beginning in the 1970s, and especially with the merger of Garfinckel and Brooks Brothers, Miller and Rhoads began targeting merchandising to customers with the specialty store concept in mind. In fact, Miller and Rhoads developed a split strategy of carrying a wide variety of merchandise with broad general appeal, while other portions of merchandise offerings were directed at specific customer groups. This approach presented problems. Unexpected consequences of this marketing strategy for Miller and Rhoads was the erosion of the old customer base, while at the same time not effectively reaching new customers.

The split strategy of opening and supporting both specialty and full-line department stores also stretched the company's resources. Consequently, the specialty department stores experienced an inventory turnover rate of three to five times that of the full line store. This rate required stock deliveries as often as every two days, instead of the once weekly schedule the company was accustomed to providing. Buyers, accustomed to the full-line store, had to make critical stocking decisions for the specialty store, which was much more focused on high-fashion women's clothes. Miller and Rhoads' traditional stores were accustomed to a dress that might be in style for three months or more. High-fashion merchandise of the specialty store might be in style for six weeks. To add to the problem, Miller and Rhoads' distribution warehouse was behind in the use of technology.

Despite the conversion program and rapid expansion, a 1974 marketing study profiling Miller and Rhoads' customers reported a loss of 1% (2,000) customers and 13% of its male shoppers since 1972. This same study showed that Miller and Rhoads' shoppers were better educated than the general population, were more affluent, and tended to be in the higher occupation categories. Were they losing touch with the mass market that was traditionally the "bread and butter" of the full line department store?

Like many department stores, Miller and Rhoads' merchandise strategy was targeted to the middle income segment. Similarly, as did many traditional department stores during the 1980s, the store became highly promotion-oriented. In fact, advertising and selling expenses were considerably higher than industry trends. Studies indicated Miller and Rhoads was losing a substantial number of customers to its competitors.

For example, a 1980 market study also reported a decline in the number of shoppers (exact figures were not given) as Miller and Rhoads came under increasing competitive pressure from JCPenney, Best Products, and Kmart. These three outlets' share of female shoppers were growing faster than Miller and Rhoads'. Weaknesses among both women's and men's clothes, as well as a weak market position in appliances and in household commodities were also noted. Moreover, Miller and Rhoads' customer shopping frequency had declined at the same time Thalhimers had increased.

From its founding days until 1967, the basic marketing strategy of Miller and Rhoads was that of providing quality merchandise at a fair price. An integral part of this strategy was to provide a wide range of merchandise and "free" services by being a full-service department store.

A typical full-service department store would provide a wide range of merchandise, including:

- Ladies apparel, including juniors, misses, and larger women
- Men's clothing, including young men, formal, and sports
- Children's clothing
- Shoes
- Fine jewelry
- Household goods
- Furniture
- Electronic equipment
- Restaurants
- Bakery and candy shops
- Books
- Travel arrangements
- Theater tickets

It also would provide a wide range of "free" services, including:

- Delivery of purchase
- Mail orders
- Monthly billing
- "Easy" return of merchandise
- Gift boxes

In addition, Miller and Rhoads' marketing strategy included the provision of the following special features that may develop a strong corporate culture:

- Tea Room where women would dine after shopping and businessmen could discuss issues

- Fashion shows where women could view the latest in women's clothing

- Author dinners where readers could dine and meet the authors

- Santa Claus where parents and grandparents returned each year with their children

- Large windows where merchandise could be displayed in a beautiful setting and changed with the seasons and holidays

When Miller and Rhoads began their expansion between 1956 and 1966, the strategy was mixed. The "down" Richmond store continued the "full service" strategy described earlier. The stores in the suburbs of Richmond and throughout Virginia in essence were specialty stores with a narrower line of software merchandise. Miller and Rhoads also operated a men's specialty clothing store, Steven Sheppard, that eventually was dropped.

These conflicting strategies began to cause problems for both the middle management of Miller and Rhoads and for the consumer--primarily because when one thought of Miller and Rhoads, he or she immediately had an image of the "downtown" store, which was different from the specialty, suburban store.

After the merger of Miller and Rhoads with Julius Garfinckel and Brooks Brothers Co. (GBM) in 1967, the dual policy continued. The organization continued with a narrower line of software merchandise out of the "downtown" store, with primary emphasis in women's and men's furnishings. The conflict with the dual strategies also continued. In later years, the positioning strategy for competing in chosen markets continued to be mixed at best.

Merger and Acquisition

The merger of Miller and Rhoads with Julius Garfinckel and Brooks Brothers Co. (GBM) in 1967 was hailed as being in the best interest for both companies. GBM Chairman Webster Rhoads, Jr., and President and CEO Willard O. Bent stated, "The addition of the Miller and Rhoads operating division is a major step in providing a broader base for the company's growth and development."

The leadership picture of Miller and Rhoads changed suddenly, however, in mid 1968, nearly six months after the Garfinckel merger, Webster Rhoads, Jr. died of a heart attack. Questions of leadership and management that loomed prior to the merger were even more apparent. Mr. Rhoads, Jr. was to be the last of the founding family to hold a senior management position in the department store.

The Miller and Rhoads expansion program was inactive from 1967 to 1973. However, during this period the following changes occurred:

- The company began converting its smaller stores of 25,000 to 40,000 square feet into specialty stores.

- In addition, between 1973 and 1976, 4 stores designed and built as specialty stores opened in North Carolina and 10 specialty stores offering women's apparel, fashion accessories, children's wear, and menswear were offered under the Miller and Rhoads name (1977 GBM Annual Report).

These stores were out of character with the typical Miller and Rhoads full-line department store in that they had a much narrower merchandise focus. The influence to move in this direction was clearly coming from the specialty store experience and focus of the parent company.

In its 1978 annual report, GBM stated: "The relationship between corporate management and its operating companies is based on the premise that performance is best achieved through a level of autonomy commensurate with a company's contribution to profits and its success in meeting agreed-upon goals."

There were a series of management changes in the late '70s and early '80s, but it was during the period that Charles Stanwood, a former Allied Stores executive, served as President, that community involvement declined significantly. A former store manager remembered the era in this manner:

> The new management brought a dimension to Miller and Rhoads that was uncomfortable to the company . . . The element they brought from a standpoint of management and merchandising to the company might have fit well in a large corporation, but was very uncomfortable for the familial relationships in a Miller and Rhoads type of environment: which were close, harmonious, warm, and supportive.

Simply stated, Garfinckel and Brooks Brothers were specialty store operations with primary emphasis in women's and men's furnishings. This merchandising influence prevailed in the Miller and Rhoads branch stores and new store openings throughout the 1970s, often resulting in a split strategy, as mentioned earlier. Much of the direction could be attributed to a lack of a strong spokesman with the death of Webster Rhoads, Jr., and the turnover of top executives that followed from the merger. At the same time, many of the new executives disregarded corporate culture and traditions from the family-owned era.

On November 19, 1981, Robert J. Rieland was appointed president and chief executive officer of the Miller and Rhoads division of Allied Stores Incorporated. Rieland's appointment followed a brief but stormy takeover of the former Garfinckel, Brooks Brothers, Miller and Rhoads, Inc. by Allied Stores, Inc. His appointment also followed several years where Miller and Rhoads lost customers to discount and specialty stores. Rieland (with specific instructions from Thomas Maioce, president of Allied Stores Corporation) immediately began to:

- Appoint new top management
- Renovate stores
- Delay expansion plans while Allied reviewed them
- Reduce renovation of branch stores
- Restore image and customer service
- Upgrade merchandise with better quality, more expensive merchandise aimed at a slightly higher income-bracket market
- Reduce hardgood sales and eliminate basement or discount departments

The year prior to the takeover by Allied Stores, Inc., Miller and Rhoads lost more than $1 million on total sales of $100 million. In terms of the standard retail measure of sales volume per gross square feet of retail space, Miller and Rhoads was $62.30 per square foot in 1980, where Allied Stores Corporation was $76.37. In terms of sales, Miller and Rhoads ranked ninth among Allied's 14 major divisions, but well under Allied's leading divisions: Jordan Marsh of New England and of Florida, The Bon Marche in the Northwest, and Joske's in Texas, all had sales of more than $300 million.

While Miller and Rhoads had not been profitable since Allied Stores acquired Garfinckel, Brooks Brother, Miller and Rhoads in September 1981, other members of the acquisition had done quite well. According to Macioce, Allied had carefully developed the Brooks Brothers franchise and had record earnings in 1984 with 40 stores in the U.S. and Japan. The Ann Taylor chain had grown from a $20 million business at the time of the Garfinckel acquisition to sales of more than

$100 million in 1984. The Catherine's Stout Shoppe division had $40 million in sales at the time of acquisition and had grown to nearly $100 million in 1985.

Like many other department store organizations during this period, Miller and Rhoads increased its promotional budget significantly with super sales, coupon sales; and, perhaps to its detriment, sales at Thanksgiving and Christmas, which diluted profitability in what once were non-sale periods. Finally, operation expenses also increased as stores stayed open longer and on weekends.

On May 18, 1986, President Robert J. Rieland announced plans to close three Miller and Rhoads stores in North Carolina (Greensboro, Charlotte, and Fayetteville) on June 7. This decision would leave only one store in Raleigh, North Carolina. Rieland said, "We have carefully analyzed our position in these markets and feel that we have no alternative." Each stored closed contained less than 30,000 square feet of space. The Raleigh store was slightly larger.

Strategic Issue: A New Focus

In June 1987, the Miller and Rhoads 17-store division of Campeau-Allied Corp. was purchased for $3.5 billion by Kevin F. Donohoe Co., Inc., a real estate holding company in a leveraged buy out (LBO). The Donohoe company, located in Philadelphia, owned real estate properties including hotels, office towers, and shopping malls. Mr. Donohoe was majority owner of the new company retaining 85% of the shares with remaining shares divided by the top management team and Mr. Robert Rieland, CEO.

Miller and Rhoads was the first retail acquisition of the Donohoe Co. What attracted Mr. Donohoe most about Miller and Rhoads was the quality of management, the established reputation, and well situated stores in Virginia and North Carolina. He was first exposed to Miller and Rhoads through his ownership of mall property leased to Miller and Rhoads in Richmond. At the time of the LBO, Miller and Rhoads was marginally profitable in 1987 and averaged a 1% pretax profit margin in the three previous years. Eight of the 17 stores were full department stores with the remaining stores being more specialized operations in soft lines or furniture. Mr. Donohoe was optimistic that with the seasoned management team Miller and Rhoads would be closer to the customer and have more of an opportunity to develop than it did under previous management.

Mr. Donohoe's new strategy for Miller and Rhoads was focused toward the upscale customer that Miller and Rhoads had neglected and lost in recent years. The strategy was implemented rapidly. (See Appendix A for Mission Statement and Summary of Plan). Specifically, Miller and Rhoads was targeting households with incomes over $50,000 (see Appendix C for marketing survey).

At Miller and Rhoads, top management referred to this strategy as a "Quantum Leap" for the company, according to Mr. Henry Coghill, former downtown store manager for over 20 years. Market studies in the early 1980s by Belden Associated of Dallas, Texas, identified problem areas that only worsened in the late 1980s (see Appendix B for summary of market study problems). For instance, market analysis studies of major department store customers in 1988/89 by Media General indicated customers were twice as likely to shop for Misses clothing at Thalhimer and some were more likely to shop at Thalhimer for men's clothing, cosmetics, dresses, children's clothing, housewares, and lines (see Appendix C for demographic profile of Richmond Shoppers).

Clearly, the new strategy focusing on the upscale customer was an image change for the newly energized retailer. Consequently, both men's and women's better-to-wear lines were upgraded in quality and price. For example, the men's line, which was previously eliminated under Allied management, would now offer suits at $300 to $500 and include lines such as Polo and Austin Reed. For women, $1500 skirts and $800 blouses were added to previously moderate-priced lines. Accordingly, moderate profitmaking manufacturers were dropped to open dollars for upscale vendors. Thus, cashflow during this period of change became even more critical.

Another goal included major renovation of high-traffic stores amounting to $6 million. Renovations included use of marble, mahogany, and more appealing lighting and colors for an improved ambiance to attract the new customer. Customer service would receive renewed emphasis. To this end, sales personnel were increased and redeployed while given more intensified sales training. Finally, Mr. Donohoe expected to reduce and eventually eliminate all previous specialty stores and expand up to 6 new 100,000-square foot full-line department stores in the mid-south by 1995. Although it was an ambitious plan, Mr. Donohoe was confident M and R could be successful.

In December 1988, Mr. Robert Rieland abruptly resigned as CEO for Miller and Rhoads. He was replaced by Mr. John Stokely who at the time was an executive VP for Miller and Rhoads and was promoted at the age of 36. Mr. Stokely had a strong background in finance and information systems but limited experience in retailing. The other members of the management team, however, essentially remained the same.

Decision Situation

John Stokely immediately arranged a meeting with top and middle management to review company strategy and to revive company fortunes. He believed the basic themes presented by Mr. Donohoe were necessary for the company to remain competitive. An "upscale" strategy would target upper income families, using "top of the line" merchandise. Consequently, buyers were expected to drop moderate-priced suppliers. He established timelines for major renovation of stores to fit the new image. Construction began on two branch stores in Richmond. Finally, the specialty store focus of the past was eventually phased out and eliminated.

Mr. Coghill, who also attended the meeting with top management, recalled that he and another executive questioned the decision to become an upscale retailer. He argued, why not continue to be a moderately priced department store? Stokely had his reservations as well, but he believed Mr. Donohoe, who had 85% interest in the future of the company, was determined to make the necessary changes for the turnaround.

Questions for Discussion

1. Identify and contrast the various corporate strategies used by Miller and Rhoads with their customers.

2. Discuss how well Miller and Rhoads was able to adapt to the changing environment. Analyze the organization's strengths and weaknesses as a means to respond to the changing environment.

3. Compare the changing attitudes of consumers during the 1970s and 1980s with the marketing strategy developed by Miller and Rhoads during the same years.

4. What economic, technological, and competitive forces affected the strategies of the Miller and Rhoads' executives? Did they present constraints (threats) or opportunities? What might you have done differently in response to each situation?

5. How did the organizational culture affect the performance of Miller and Rhoads? What was the relationship between organizational design and culture? How could the culture be changed to enhance its ability to accomplish its mission?

6. Compare the types of leadership at different times at Miller and Rhoads. Should there have been less managing and more leadership? Suggest changes and defend your position. In what way could Miller and Rhoads have better developed leaders for the organization?

7. What decisions about internal operating factors would have made Miller and Rhoads more productive? Defend your position.

8. Assume that you have just been appointed to a task force responsible for making recommendations on an organizational structure for Miller and Rhoads. How would you re-structure the organization? Why?

Figure 1
Miller & Rhoads Inc. - 1961
Approved Organization Plan

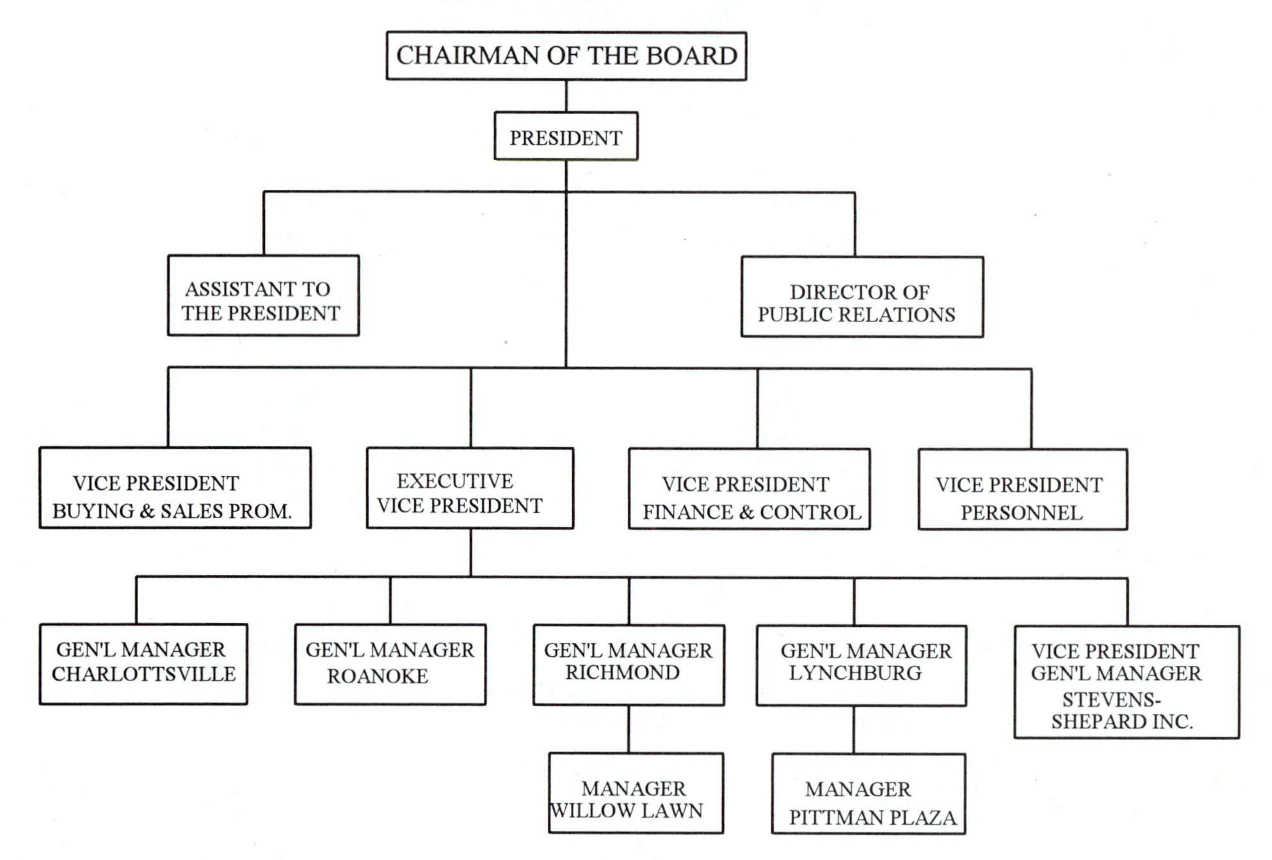

Exhibit 1
Branch Locations

Store Locations	Dates Open		Square Footage
Charlottesville	1956		42,000
Downtown Roanoke	1957		142,000
Downtown Lynchburg	1957		52,000
Pittman Plaza (Lynchburg)	1960		16,000
Roanoke-Salem Plaza (Roanoke)	1961		18,000
		(added 1964)	5,000
Willow Lawn (Richmond)	1961		25,000
Newmarket Shopping Ct. (Newport News)	1963		70,000
Walnut Hills Shopping Ct. (Petersburg)	1965		25,000
Southside Plaza Shopping Ct. (Richmond)	1965		54,404
Barracks Road Shopping Ct. (Charlottesville)	1965		54,930
Southern Shopping Ct. (Norfolk)	1965		30,740
Pembroke Mall (Virginia Beach)	1966		83,277

(Source: Miller and Rhoads Incorporated, Financial Report 1966)

Exhibit 2
Summary of Financial Data for
Miller and Rhoads Department Stores

Fiscal Year	Net Sales	Net Income Before Taxes	Net Income	Number of Stores	Steven* Sheppard	All Stores
1956	30,316,000	2,360,000	1,103,000	2	4	6
1957	35,352,000	2,010,000	958,000	4	4	8
1958	36,723,000	1,894,000	792,000	4	3	7
1959	37,523,000	2,361,000	1,160,000	4	3	7
1960	36,226,000	1,243,000	605,000	5	2	7
1961	37,669,000	1,642,000	801,000	7	1	9
1962	38,353,000	1,625,000	850,000	7	1	8
1963	40,303,000	1,475,000	742,000	8	1	9
1964	42,634,000	2,061,000	1,035,000	8	1	9
1965	47,021,000	2,123,000	1,252,000	12		12
1966	55,052,000		1,237,000	13		13

* Steven Sheppard was a men's specialty operation owned by Miller and Rhoads at this time.

(Source: Miller and Rhoads Financial Report to Stockholders, April 12, 1966.)

REFERENCES

Hower, Ralph M. History of Macy's of New York, Harvard University Press, Cambridge, Massachusetts, 1943.

Mason, J. Berry, Morris L., Mayer and Hazel F. Ezell Retailing, 4th Edition, Irwin 1991.

APPENDIX A

MILLER AND RHOADS, INC.
MISSION STATEMENT
1988

TO STRENGTHEN OUR MARKET POSITION TO BECOME THE DOMINANT STORE RETAILER IN OUR MARKETS BY OFFERING QUALITY MODERATE TO BETTER MERCHANDISE AND EXCELLENCE IN CUSTOMER SERVICE.

MILLER AND RHOADS, INC.
Required Action to Execute Original Strategic Plan

1. Credit problems must be solved
2. Representation of "Better" goods - emphasize moderate
   - Reallocation of inventory
   - Drop/Limit specific better resources, emphasize remaining resources
   - Add/Reemphasize moderate resources
3. Significant expense reductions
   - Advertising
   - Selling/Sales Support
4. Address markdown problems/Gross margin improvements
   - Clearance markdowns 1st. - timely
   - Promotional markdowns - better planning - better execution
   - Net Sales Promotion calendar/no deviations
5. Further development of Private Label

Problems

1. Poor Retail Economy
2. Went too far into better goods/starved moderate areas
3. Uneven deliveries/credit problems
4. Constant changes to promotion schedule - to drive business
   - Cost of Advertising
   - Major sales events
   - Markdowns - excessive promotional/did not drive business/did not address permanent
5. Lack of private label programs/wrong private label programs
6. Poor leadership/additions to selling staff not productive
   - Other

Positive Performance

1. Home Division continued good performance with
   - Housewares and Home Textiles
2. Enhance Image with Consumers
3. M and R Data Services - potential
4. Improvements in Customer Service levels
5. Expense savings from inception

APPENDIX B

Miller and Rhoads
Some Problem Areas
as Indicated by Survey Material

- Decline in number of shoppers 1975 vs 1980. Increased pressure from JCPenney, Best Products and Kmart
- Declining share of non-white shoppers while competitors all show growth
- Penney's, Best and Kmart's share of female shoppers growing faster than M and R's.
- Weakness among women's clothing purchasers compared to Thalhimers
- Weak market position in appliance category
- Weak market position in household commodity category
- Loss of shoppers at Downtown, Willow Lawn and Southside Plaza locations
- Inattentive and unfriendly salespeople as perceived by M and R shoppers
- High proportion of M and R shoppers are shopping less in the past 12 months
- Miller and Rhoads' shopping frequency has declined while Thalhimers' has increased

(Marketing study by Belden Associates of Dallas, Texas, 1980)

APPENDIX C

Table 1
Profile of Department and General Merchandise Store Shoppers (Richmond, Virginia) Urbanized Area Adults 18 Years or More

	Market Total	Miller & Rhoads	Sears	Stein Mart	Thalhimer	Shopped at None of Stores Listed
Adult Pop.	493,000	51%	55%	9%	60%	5%
Annual Household Gross Income						
Under $10,000	26,000	26	35	4	43	22
$10,000-14,999	38,000	50	37	3	57	7
$15,000-19,999	31,000	41	53	5	58	3
$20,000-24,999	51,000	48	56	7	68	3
$25,000-34,999	98,000	36	64	12	55	4
$35,000-49,999	130,000	62	55	11	62	4
$50,000+	119,000	62	58	10	65	5

(Media General News Demographic Profile, Richmond, VA. 1989)

LEE'S TRAVELSTOP*

By James M. Kenderdine, Jack J. Kasulis, and Deborah Zizzo, Distribution Research Program, The University of Oklahoma

Background and Company History

"Our customers come to see us at least once a week. They sit quietly at our pump for 5 to 10 minutes, waiting for their gas tank to fill. We have a wonderful opportunity to offer them all kinds of merchandise. Any other retailer in the world would die for the opportunity we waste each week!" The men sitting around the lunch table in the Midland, Texas coffee shop gave tired smiles as Lee Marshall slapped his hand on the table to emphasize his final point. They had heard this speech, and its longer, more detailed version, at least once a week since Lee had joined the retail operations division of Permian Oil Company. Lee believed that the future for national oil companies lay in retailing. His vision, which he would tell to anyone who would listen, was that the future for integrated oil firms lay not in exploration and production of crude oil but rather in retailing fuel and other products to the ultimate consumer. Unfortunately for Lee, in the mid 1960s, his vision was not the vision of his firm, and he was becoming increasingly frustrated by the struggle it took to make the simplest change or get approval for the slightest modernization of operations. So in 1965, when Permian Oil decided to close several service stations they considered marginal, Lee jumped at the chance to lease them for himself, start his own company and implement his ideas. The stations Permian considered marginal were located in small communities in Texas, New Mexico, and Oklahoma. Retail gasoline prices were low in 1965, and, for a station to be profitable from an oil company's point of view, it had to sell at least 25,000 gallons of fuel per month. The stations Permian had selected for closing were all selling less than half that amount. In the summer of 1965, Lee opened his first *Lee's Speedy Stop* in Big Springs, Texas. It was a significant change from the outlet Permian had operated in the same location for 15 years. *Lee's Speedy Stop* had no mechanic and offered none of the ancillary products and services common to service stations--tires, batteries, oil changes, or mechanical work. Instead, in the space where the garage work bays had been, there was a small convenience store (modeled to some extent after 7-Eleven) offering primarily grocery items, dairy products, health and beauty aids, and packaged beer. In addition, *Lee's* sold coffee and soft drinks and offered a small selection of snack foods. Another departure from traditional service stations was the absence of "driveway employees" to fill the cars with gas. *Speedy Stop* customers pumped their own gas, and got it for 2¢ a gallon less than at the major oil companies' outlets. *Lee's Speedy Stop* was an instant hit, and by 1971 Lee operated 24 *Lee's Speedy Stops*, all in small communities in 3 states.

After the Arab Oil Embargo of 1973, some of the major, integrated oil companies began closing older outlets in large communities and major metropolitan areas, eliminating outlets where changes in highway location or urban travel patterns had significantly reduced their profitability. While the outlets to be closed were no longer competitive sites for a service station, they remained good retail locations. Located close to densely populated residential areas and in suburban and small-town commercial districts, many outlets were converted by others to retail and commercial office uses. To Lee Marshall, the station closings offered a golden opportunity--and he made the most of it, adding over 100 stores during the next twenty years.

Two factors contributed to *Lee's* growth. First, as the major oil companies closed outlets and cut operating hours after the oil embargo, it became increasingly difficult for consumers to buy gasoline after 5:00 p.m., and almost impossible to find open gas pumps in the suburbs and small towns--exactly where Lee was locating his *Speedy Stops*. Second, in 1975, there were approximately 28,500 convenience stores in the U.S., but only about 5500 sold gasoline. The fact that *Lee's Speedy Stops* sold gasoline gave them a significant competitive advantage over other convenience stores and also

---

* Used with permission of James M. Kenderdine, Jack J. Kasulis, and Deborah Zizzo. The name of the company has been changed and some data has been transformed.

contributed to their rapid growth. By 1990, *Lee's* operated 120 *Speedy Stop* locations in 6 states: Texas, New Mexico, Arizona, Nevada, Oklahoma, and Kansas, and was preparing to open its first location in California.

Background on the Convenience Store Industry

Convenience stores are generally defined as small (1200 to 3000 square feet) retail outlets that are open 24 hours per day, or at least for extended hours, and are located along heavily traveled streets and at intersections. The number of households per convenience store by state, in 1991, is listed below:

Arizona	1,210	California	2,681	Colorado	1,277	Kansas	1,291
Nevada	1,640	New Mexico	987	Oklahoma	852	Texas	833

Over the last two decades, convenience stores have had one of the best growth records in the retail sector. The industry grew from $6 billion in sales in 1975 to $55 billion in 1985. By the mid 1980s, the industry experienced a decrease in the opening of new convenience stores and an increase in the investment required for a new store. Acquisitions increased as a way to accelerate store growth, and rural locations became more attractive as the urban market became saturated. The growth in the number of stores in the rural market increased the price for attractive real estate. The substantial increases in the cost of both land and store construction reflected the competitiveness for the prime locations. Annual sales for new stores needed to exceed the averages for existing stores by a sizable amount to insure the recovery of investment.

In addition, by the mid 1980s the growth in convenience store sales had become erratic due to actions by competitive lines of trade. Many supermarkets had expanded their hours of operation and broadened their offerings of in-and-out items such as fountain beverages, salad bars, and deli or ready-made sandwiches. Oil companies had transformed existing service stations into hybrid outlets (called G-Stores) that sold gasoline, snack foods, and beverages--which became the prototype for new outlets.

The Situation in 1990

By 1990, Lee Marshall and the management of *Lee's Speedy Stop* were forecasting a limited future for their convenience store strategy. The industry, they realized, was quite different from what it had been when the first *Lee's Speedy Stop* opened. In 1990, 4 product categories accounted for 71% of all convenience store sales: gasoline (40%), tobacco products (14%), alcoholic beverages (9%), and soft drinks (8%). Groceries, which in 1975 provided about 10% of convenience store sales, accounted for just over 2% of store sales by 1990. A similar pattern had occurred in the sales of dairy products, declining from 9% of sales in 1975 to 3% in 1990, and health and beauty aids, going from 4 % of sales in 1975 to 1.4 % in 1990. Fast food sales, on the other hand, had grown from 4.6% of sales in 1975 to 5.3% in 1990, although they had been as high as 7.8% of store sales in 1988.

However, Lee Marshall and his management team noted that *Lee's* had one extremely successful store that might be used to provide direction for the future. Like their other stores, it was located on a heavily traveled road and offered the traditional convenience store concept. However, in this case, the store was located at an exit of an interstate highway. A survey of the customer mix at that store found relatively few customers who lived nearby and who stopped at the store regularly. Apparently, highway travelers were using *Lee's Speedy Stop* as a stop on their long-distance trips.

During the early 1990s, *Lee's* experimented with changing their corporate focus from local customers to long-distance travelers by opening four other stores on interstate highways. The interstate locations also sold diesel fuel for truck drivers, although truck refueling and parking was limited so that the outlets hopefully would not be viewed as "truck stops" by other travelers. Merchandise inside the stores included grill and deli items; fountain soft drinks, canned soft drinks and beer; brewed coffee; modestly priced souvenirs and gifts; ice cream bars; automotive products; travel items such as audio tapes, kids games, and puzzles; and other convenience store items. The new store concept was called *Lee's TravelStop*.

Sales and profit results from the new stores made it clear that the highway stop concept was where the company had its greatest competitive advantage. The decision was made that future stores would be *TravelStops*, and that no new *Speedy Stops* would be opened. Further, as leases on the existing outlets came up for renewal, store performance would be carefully reviewed, and not all of the leases would be renewed.

The *TravelStop 2000* Project

With that decision behind them, Lee Marshall and Bob Huber, Vice President of Operations, decided that they needed to learn more about the customers stopping at their *TravelStop* stores to successfully grow the business. "The industry has not sorted out the automobile interstate market the way truck stops have sorted out the interstate truck market," Bob Huber told members of a research firm Lee's had hired, "some of what we know about truck stops applies to automobile drivers, but there are significant differences in some areas." Lee Marshall added, "Our competition is not just truck stops and service stations--it's McDonald's, Dairy Queen, and other highway stops. We believe that we are one of the few who have figured out the broader nature of competition in this business. That's why we think we can be a market leader with long-distance auto travelers. All we need to do is fine-tune our concept--and your job is to give us the information we need to do that."

To help refine its new store concept, *Lee's* embarked on *TravelStop 2000*, a project to survey customers at its *TravelStops* to learn who they were and what they wanted in a highway stop. Over a two-week period during the summer, all customers entering a *Lee's TravelStop* were interviewed and classified as a "local customer" (those on an automobile trip of less than one hour, one way), a "long-distance traveler" (those on an automobile trip of one hour or more, one way), or a "truck driver" (those driving either a local or over-the-road commercial truck). Long-distance travelers were given an additional, longer questionnaire to complete and mail back to the research firm.

The initial interview was designed to profile the people currently stopping at *Lee's*, why they stopped at *Lee's*, how much they spent, what they purchased, and how satisfied they were with their experience. The additional questionnaire given long-distance travelers was designed to find out "who" the typical long-distance traveler was, why they were traveling, and what other highway stops they had used during the last three years. In addition, long-distance travelers were asked to "rate" the performance of Lee's and other competitors on a number of factors. The competitors listed--McDonald's, Dairy Queen, and Texaco--were selected because of the strong presence of each in the areas *Lee's* operated.

McDonald's is *TravelStops*' largest competitor on the refreshment side of the business with a 19% nationwide market share of the fast food business. Targeting families, McDonald's offers consistent food preparation and service at a reasonable price. It maintains a strong presence of prime highway locations in addition to local sites. McDonald's has a national advertising budget of over $200 million. Recently, McDonald's has been considering joint ventures with Texaco and Phillips.

Dairy Queen (DQ) operates over 5000 outlets nationwide, with a strong presence in small town America. Its menu consists of individually prepared hamburgers, soft and hard ice cream, and frozen yogurt. It has a strong lunch-time and snack following. In 1988, DQ began a four-year image improvement program of its marketing and facilities, which resulted in an 18% improvement in sales. DQ has shown an interest in the highway stop market by forming joint ventures with gasoline retailers.

Texaco is *TravelStops'* largest competitor on the gasoline side of the business, with a market share of 11% of gasoline sales. In 1991 Texaco introduced its own G-store concept called *Star Mart*. These are clean, well-lighted stores that sell snack foods, beverages, auto supplies, and gasoline. Gasoline sales alone increased 30% in the Texaco units converted to *Star*

Marts. Recently, Texaco has been considering joint ventures with fast food outlets such as McDonald's and Dunkin' Donuts.

Some results from the survey research project are presented in the Exhibits 1-12.

Questions for Discussion

1. What are the competitive strengths and weaknesses of the *Lee's TravelStop* concept?

2. Why would Bob Huber say that "restrooms are one of our most important products" when talking to groups of Lee's associates and managers?

3. Based on the survey results, do you believe Lee Marshall was correct to insist that McDonald's and Dairy Queen be included as competitors in the study?

4. If you were Bob Huber, what specific steps would you take to improve the *Lee's TravelStop* image? What would be your first step? Why?

5. What risks are involved for the company in abandoning the store concept (*Lee's Speedy Stops*) that has worked so successfully?

Exhibit 1
Interstate Travel Profile by Type of Customer

	All Customers	Long-Distance Travelers	Local Customers	Truck Drivers
(Sample Size)	[4,683]	[2,868]	[749]	[1,066]
Purpose of Trip				
Vacation	21.0%	33.7%	1.7%	0.2%
Business	44.3	27.6	30.3	98.7
Family/Personal Business	15.2	20.2	17.8	0.0
Commuting	4.4	2.8	16.3	0.4
1 or 2-Day Trip	4.1	5.3	5.5	0.0
Other	11.0	10.4	28.4	0.7
Total	100.0%	100.0%	100.0%	100.0%
Length of Trip				
Less than 1 Hour	16.0%	0.0%	100.0%	0.0%
1 to 2 Hours	1.6	2.1	0.0	1.6
2 to 3 Hours	4.7	7.4	0.0	0.7
3 to 4 Hours	6.3	9.8	0.0	1.2
4 to 5 Hours	6.8	9.8	0.0	3.7
5 Hours or More	64.6	70.9	0.0	92.8
Total	100.0%	100.0%	100.0%	100.0%
Direction Traveling				
North	25.3%	25.7%	30.0%	21.1%
South	25.0	24.0	25.5	27.3
East	23.2	23.2	23.9	22.6
West	23.4	24.7	14.3	26.3
Other/Don't Know	3.1	2.4	6.3	2.7
Total	100.0%	100.0%	100.0%	100.0%
Percent Identifying Billboards	50.1%	54.9%	26.1%	53.9%
Number of Adults in Vehicle				
One	46.3%	31.6%	60.8%	75.8%
Two	42.3	51.9	32.3	23.5
Three or More	11.4	16.5	6.9	0.7
Total	100.0%	100.0%	100.0%	100.0%
Number of Children in Vehicle				
None	78.3%	70.0%	83.0%	97.1%
One	10.3	13.6	8.7	2.6
Two	6.8	9.7	5.1	0.2
Three	4.6	6.7	3.2	0.1
Total	100.0%	100.0%	100.0%	100.0%

Notes: Long-Distance Travelers were respondents interviewed while on a trip of one hour or more (one way).
Local Customers were respondents on trips of less than one hour (one way).
Truck Drivers were respondents driving commercial over-the-road or short-haul trucks.

Exhibit 2
Reasons for Stopping at Lee's Travelstop by Type of Customer

	All Customers	Long-Distance Travelers	Local Customers	Truck Drivers
(Sample Size)	[4,683]	[2,868]	[749]	[1,066]
Reason for Stopping*				
To Buy Something to Drink	56.0%	53.1%	59.7%	61.1%
To Buy Fuel	46.7	57.0	31.1	30.0
To Use a Rest Room	44.1	50.1	13.9	49.4
To Buy a Snack	29.5	30.8	23.8	30.2
Take a Break	20.3	21.2	3.7	29.5
To Buy a Meal	17.4	13.3	16.2	29.5
To Use a Telephone	12.8	6.2	4.7	36.0
To Meet Someone	2.9	2.3	4.7	3.0
To Buy Ice Cream	1.6	1.5	1.7	1.6
For Other Reason	8.7	7.5	10.1	10.8
Primary Reason for Stopping**				
To Buy Fuel	39.4%	47.5%	27.2%	26.6%
To Get Something to Drink	13.7	10.8	29.4	10.2
To Get Something to Eat (Food or Meal)	9.8	6.3	14.1	15.9
To Use a Rest Room	8.6	11.0	3.6	5.5
To Use a Telephone	5.0	2.4	2.1	14.1
To Take a Break	5.0	4.8	1.3	8.0
To Buy a Snack	4.2	3.5	6.1	5.1
To Meet Someone	2.0	1.8	3.5	1.3
Had Car Trouble	0.8	0.8	0.4	1.1
To Buy Souvenirs or Gifts	0.5	0.8	0.1	0.0
To Buy Cigarettes	0.4	0.1	1.2	0.8
To Buy Ice Cream	0.2	0.2	0.5	0.0
For Other Reason	3.6	2.6	6.0	4.6
Could Not/Did Not Give Reason	6.8	7.4	4.5	6.8
Total	100.0%	100.0%	100.0%	100.0%

Notes: *Consumers were read a list of possible reasons for stopping at Lee's TravelStop and asked which of the reasons on the list described their reason(s) for stopping. Consumers could select as many reasons as they wished. Cell values represent the percent of all respondents who selected each reason as one of their reasons for stopping at Lee's TravelStop. Columns will not total 100% due to multiple responses.

**Consumers were asked to select the one reason (from among those on the list) which they believed best described their primary reason for stopping. Cell values represent the percent of all respondents who selected each reason as being the best description of the primary reason they stopped at Lee's TravelStop.

Exhibit 3
Customer Purchases by Type of Customer

	All Customers	Long-Distance Travelers	Local Customers	Truck Drivers
(Sample Size)	[4,683]	[2,868]	[749]	[1,066]
Amount Spent				
$.01 to $2.50	20.7%	15.0%	35.7%	25.1%
$2.51 to $5.00	18.0	14.3	22.0	25.5
$5.01 to $10.00	14.5	15.8	15.5	10.5
$10.01 to $15.00	13.0	18.0	10.0	2.0
$15.01 to $25.00	12.2	17.6	7.2	0.9
$25.01 to $100.00	8.9	10.0	2.1	10.8
More than $100.00	4.3	0.4	0.0	17.7
Nothing	4.2	3.7	4.4	5.3
Did Not Give	4.2	5.2	3.1	2.2
Total	100.0%	100.0%	100.0%	100.0%
Average Amount Spent	$18.79	$13.65	$6.43	$41.24
Items Purchased*				
Something to Drink	59.4%	56.2%	62.2%	66.0%
Gasoline	36.7	52.3	27.0	1.8
Diesel Gasoline	7.8	2.4	1.5	26.6
Snacks	27.7	29.4	21.4	27.9
Something from the Deli	21.9	18.6	19.1	32.8
Packaged Food	6.4	6.9	5.9	5.4
Tobacco	4.2	2.5	6.7	7.3
Gift Item	3.6	5.1	1.2	1.2
Automotives	1.0	1.2	1.1	0.3
Toiletries	0.8	0.9	0.5	0.9
Toys or Games	0.5	0.5	0.8	0.3
Other Items	3.1	2.8	4.0	3.2
Nothing	4.1%	3.6%	4.3%	5.3%
Percent Intending to Purchase Additional Items	7.0%	6.9%	6.1%	7.8%

*Columns will not total 100.0% due to multiple responses.

Exhibit 4
Customer's Primary Reason for Stopping at Lee's Travelstop Versus What They Purchased
Lee's Travelstops - 1991

	Customer's Primary Reason For Stopping										
	To Buy Fuel	To Get A Drink	To Use A Rest Room	To Buy A Snack	To Take A Break	To Buy A Meal	To Use Telephone	To Meet Someone	Had Car Trouble	To Buy Souvenirs	For Other Reason
Percent of Customers Purchasing:											
Fuel	91.7%	8.9%	12.7%	12.5%	15.4%	11.1%	19.1%	14.3%	0.0%	0.0%	15.4%
Drink	40.1	92.4	62.7	71.9	71.8	84.4	66.7	71.4	71.4	50.0	38.5
Snacks	22.1	20.3	41.8	62.5	30.8	26.7	19.1	42.9	14.3	33.3	11.5
Deli	10.7	16.5	8.2	37.5	18.0	86.7	9.5	19.1	28.6	33.3	3.8
Packaged Food	4.5	1.3	6.4	5.6	10.3	4.4	4.8	0.0	0.0	0.0	3.8
Gift Item	3.3	1.3	7.3	0.0	5.1	4.4	9.5	14.3	0.0	100.0	3.8
Tobacco	2.9	2.5	0.9	3.1	2.6	8.9	0.0	4.8	0.0	3.0	7.7
Diesel Fuel	4.0	0.0	0.9	0.0	2.6	0.0	0.0	9.5	0.0	3.0	3.8
Automotives	0.5	0.0	0.0	0.0	0.0	0.0	0.0	0.0	42.9	16.7	8.3
Toiletries	0.5	0.0	0.9	0.0	2.6	2.2	0.0	0.0	0.0	0.0	3.8
Toys or Games	0.0	0.0	1.8	0.0	0.0	2.2	0.0	0.0	0.0	0.0	3.8
Other Items	1.2	2.5	2.7	0.0	5.1	0.0	0.0	0.0	0.0	0.0	38.5
Purchased Nothing	0.2	1.3	12.7	0.0	10.3	0.0	9.5	9.5	28.6	0.0	11.5

Exhibit 5
Consumer Satisfaction With Lee's Travelstop by Type of Customer - 1991

	All Customers	Long-Distance Travelers	Local Customers	Truck Drivers
Level of Satisfaction with Stop				
Highly satisfied	58.1%	60.7%	60.6%	49.8%
Moderately satisfied	34.0	32.6	32.8	38.5
Neutral	6.3	5.4	5.7	9.0
Moderately dissatisfied	1.0	1.0	0.4	1.5
Highly dissatisfied	0.6	0.3	0.5	1.2
Total	100.0%	100.0%	100.0%	100.0%
Average Satisfaction Rating [possible range from 1 to 5, with 1 being 'Highly Satisfied']	2.02	1.97	1.97	2.16
Experience Compared to Other Stops				
Definitely better	38.9%	39.0%	48.0%	32.3%
Slightly better	28.6	30.0	26.5	26.0
About the same	31.1	30.0	24.0	39.1
Slightly worse	1.0	0.7	1.1	1.8
Definitely worse	0.4	0.3	0.4	0.8
Total	100.0%	100.0%	100.0%	100.0%
Average Experience Rating [possible range from 1 to 5, with 1 being 'Definitely Better']	2.45	2.43	2.19	2.52
Likelihood of Repeat Visit				
10 (Definitely stop)	53.4%	50.3%	64.7%	53.7%
9	12.0	12.8	10.4	11.1
8	11.8	12.6	8.4	11.9
7	6.1	6.6	4.0	6.2
6	2.5	2.8	1.7	2.2
5 (50-50 chance)	12.4	13.5	8.7	12.2
4-0 (Definitely not stop)	1.8	1.4	2.1	2.7
Total	100.0%	100.0%	100.0%	100.0%
Average Repeat Visit Rating [possible range from 1 to 10, with 10 being 'Definitely Stop Again']	7.6	7.52	7.93	7.56

Notes:

Satisfaction Rating - Consumers were asked to rate their level of satisfaction with Lee's TravelStop on a 1-to-5 scale (with 1 being "Highly Satisfied" and 5 being "Highly Unsatisfied"). Cell values represent the average satisfaction rating.

Experience Rating - Consumers were asked to rate their experience at Lee's TravelStop compared to their most recent experience at their "usual" highway stop on a 1-to-5 scale (with 1 being "Definitely Better Experience" and 5 being a a "Definitely Worse Experience"). Cell values represent the average experience rating.

Repeat Visit Rating - Consumers were asked to rate their likelihood of making a repeat visit to Lee's TravelStop on a 1-to-10 scale (with 1 being "Will Definitely Not Stop Again" and 10 being "Will Definitely Stop Again"). Cell values represent the average repeat visit rating.

Exhibit 6

Demographic Profile of Long-Distance Travelers- -Interstate Travelers Stopping at Lee's Travelstops (1991)

Age*	Male	Female
0 to 4	5.2%	8.9%
5 to 9	12.6	12.3
10 to 14	13.0	11.0
15 to 19	11.6	15.3
20 to 24	11.2	9.6
25 to 29	7.7	9.3
30 to 34	10.9	10.3
35 to 39	10.6	13.0
40 to 44	12.1	13.4
45 to 49	14.2	14.2
50 to 54	9.9	9.3
55 to 59	10.8	9.2
60 to 64	6.4	5.6
65 or olde	10.9	9.9

	Male	Female
Level of Education		
Some high school or less	5.3%	4.7%
High school graduate	16.7	21.9
Vocation/technical training	9.1	6.2
Some college	25.0	30.4
College graduate	17.2	16.6
Some graduate school or more	19.0	11.9
No response	7.7	8.3
Total	100.0%	100.0%
Employment Status*		
Employed full-time	62.3%	42.4%
Employed part-time	5.0	10.2
Self-employed	19.6	11.2
Unemployed	2.2	5.2
Student	4.4	7.7
Retired	16.7	11.7
Housewife/Househusband	4.9	27.8

Occupation	Male	Female
Executive/Administrative	17.7%	16.0%
Operators/Laborers	17.0	3.0
Sales	16.0	13.9
Professional	15.1	20.7
Precision Production	9.2	1.1
Technician	7.0	7.9
Service	6.4	11.1
Administrative Support	3.7	20.9
Farming	3.0	0.7
Military	3.0	0.0
Other	1.9	4.7
Total	100.0%	100.0%

*Columns will not total 100.0% due to multiple responses.

Exhibit 6 (Continued)

Demographic Profile of Long-Distance Travelers- -Interstate Travelers Stopping at Lee's Travelstops (1991)

Industry in Which Employed	Male	Female
Services	23.2%	48.6%
Transportation/Communicatio	5.7	5.7
Government	3.2	7.5
Retail Trade	9.3	14.6
Construction	8.6	1.0
Manufacturing	8.2	2.4
Finance/Insurance/Real Estate	6.3	11.0
Oil	4.0	1.0
Agriculture	3.3	1.0
Wholesale	0.8	0.5
Other	7.4	6.7
Total	00.0%	100.0%

Household Income	
Less than $5,000	1.4%
$5,000 to $9,999	2.3
$10,000 to $14,999	3.8
$15,000 to $24,999	11.2
$25,000 to $34,999	17.5
$35,000 to $49,999	22.1
$50,000 to $64,999	16.5
$65,000 or more	19.7
No response	5.5
Total	100.0%

Marital Status	
Never married	6.0
Married	81.4
Separated	1.0
Widowed	2.3
Divorced	7.7
No response	1.6
Total	100.0%
Person Completing Questionnaire	
More than one person	34.2
Female alone	34.1
Male alone	31.7
Total	100.0

Exhibit 7
Travel Profile of
Long-Distance Travelers

	Percent
Number of Vehicles Owned	
One	10.0%
Two	37.7
Three	28.7
Four	12.3
Five or more	11.2
Total	100.0%
Number of Miles Driven Per Year	
Less than 10,000	8.7%
10,000 to 19,999	15.6
20,000 to 29,999	18.0
30,000 to 39,999	15.4
40,000 to 49,999	10.6
50,000 to 99,999	17.4
100,000 or more	9.5
No response	4.8
Total	100.0%
Number of Trips Taken Per Year	
1 to 5	6.1%
6 to 9	10.4
10 to 14	10.9
15 to 24	14.2
25 to 49	14.0
50 to 99	13.9
100 to 199	8.8
200 or more	15.4
No response	6.3
Total	100.0%
Number of Stops at a Lee's TravelStop Per Year	
1 to 2	11.0
3 to 4	8.0
5 to 9	17.6
10 to 14	13.9
15 to 24	13.9
25 to 49	11.5
50 to 99	9.3
100 or more	8.9
No response	5.8
Total	100.0%

Exhibit 8
Percent of Long Distance Travelers Stopping at Selected Highway Stops During the Past Three Years

Highway Stop	Percent Stopping	Highway Stop	Percent Stopping
McDonald's	83.3%	Fina	32.3%
Texaco	62.6	Mobil	29.7
Lee's TravelStop	59.1	Amoco	28.1
Dairy Queen	58.8	Stuckey's	27.3
7-Eleven	58.8	TA (Truckstops of America)	25.5
Burger King	53.1		
KFC	52.5	Shell	25.3
Wendy's	49.5	Road Runner	23.7
Circle K	49.5	Union 76	23.1
		Kerr McGee	20.5
Denny's	48.5	Petro	16.9
Hardee's	48.3		
Phillips 66	46.4	E-Z Go	14.6
Braums	46.1	Giant	14.4
Exxon	43.2	Sunoco/DX	12.8
		Howard Johnson	12.0
Pizza Hut	41.4	Flying J	11.6
Conoco	38.1		
Kettle	36.7	Sinclair	10.9
Arby's	36.5	Pilot	7.6
Grandy's	32.7	Delta	5.0

Long-Distance Travelers were asked to indicate whether they had stopped during the past three years at any of the highway stops on a list . Cell values are the percent who had stopped at each highway stop during the past three years.

Exhibit 9
Outlets Reported as "Best Other Highway Stop"

Outlets Reported (by category)*	Percent Listing	Outlets Reported (by category)*	Percent Listing
Truck Stops		Fast Food Outlets	
Giant	6.1%	Braums	5.3%
Road Runner	4.6	Hardee's	3.6
Petro	4.2	Burger King	2.7
TA (Truckstops of America)	2.8	Wendy's	1.2
Flying J	2.7	Arby's	0.6
Union 76	2.5	KFC	0.6
Pilot	0.7	Taco Bell	0.6
Rip Griffin	0.6	Whataburger	0.6
Delta	0.4	Total Listing A Fast Food Outlet	15.2%
Total Listing A Truck Stop	24.6%		
		Convenience Stores	
Fuel Stops		7-Eleven	4.5%
Phillips 66	6.7%	Circle K	4.0
Exxon	3.1	E-Z Go	1.3
Conoco	2.5	Quick Trip	1.0
Chevron	2.1	Kwik Stop	0.6
Amoco	1.9	Git 'n Go	0.4
Shell	1.5	Total Listing A Convenience Store	11.8%
Coastal			
Fina	1.3	Restaurants	
Shamrock Diamond	1.2	Denny's	2.8%
Mobil	0.6	Kettle	1.2
Arco	0.6	Shoney's	0.9
Kerr McGee	0.4	Grandy's	0.7
Citgo	0.4	Cracker Barrel	0.4
Total Listing A Fuel Stop	23.8%	Total Listing A Restaurant	6.0%
Comprehensive Highway Stops**		All Other Travel Stops	13.5%
Stuckey's	5.1%	Total	100.0%

Notes:* Consumers were asked to list the name of the highway stop they considered the "best highway stop other than Lee's, Texaco, McDonald's, and Dairy Queen." Cell values are the percent of respondents listing each outlet as their "best other highway stop."

** A "Comprehensive Highway Stop" is a place with a complete product and service offering for travelers including fuel, food service, a convenience assortment of tobacco, groceries (including beer), picnic supplies, personal care items, automotive products, gifts, and regional/local souvenirs. Often these establishments are known for a specific product or service - for example, offering a free box of pecan candy with the purchase of 10 or more gallons of fuel.

Exhibit 10
Overal Image and Primary Image for Selected Highway Stops
Held by Long Distance Travelers

	Lee's TravelStop	Texaco	McDonald's	Dairy Queen
Consumer's Overall Image of Each Highway Stop*				
Place to use a restroom	94.2%	61.5%	74.4%	40.4%
Place to get fuel	93.6	80.6	0.0	0.0
Place to get a drink	84.3	47.5	54.6	39.0
Place to get a snack	79.6	39.2	39.1	26.8
Place to get a meal	32.1	0.0	70.5	39.9
Place to get ice cream	19.5	3.2	18.3	75.9
Consumer's Primary Image of Each Highway Stop**				
Place to get fuel	61.2%	74.7%	0.0%	0.0%
Place to use a restroom	12.4	4.8	12.5	2.1
Place to get a drink	6.4	2.5	4.9	3.2
Place to get a snack	5.5	3.3	13.2	6.1
Place to get a meal	2.3	0.0	58.1	18.1
Place to get ice cream	0.1	0.1	1.8	62.3
No response	12.1	14.6	9.5	8.2
Total	100.0%	100.0%	100.0%	100.0%

Notes: *Consumers were given a list of six possible images of a highway stop and asked to choose which of the images they felt described their view of each highway stop . Consumers could select as many of the six images as they wished. Cell values represent the percent of all respondents who selected each image for each highway stop. Columns will not total 100.0% due to multiple responses.

**For each highway stop, consumers were asked to select the one image (of the six possible) they believed best described the highway stop. Values represent the percent of all respondents who selected each image as being the best description of each highway stop.

Exhibit 11
Performance Ratings of Selected Highway Stops

	Attribute Importance Rating*	Highway Stop Performance Ratings**				
		Lee's TravelStop	Texaco	McDonald's	Dairy Queen	Other Travel Stop
Restrooms						
Clean restrooms	9.56	7.63	6.75	7.96	6.29	7.36
Restrooms in working order	9.56	7.78	6.81	8.08	6.43	7.38
Adequate supplies in restrooms	9.50	7.74	6.68	7.75	6.28	7.33
Disposable hand towels	9.06	7.63	6.36	5.97	5.69	6.75
Adequate size of restrooms	9.01	7.66	6.14	7.37	5.70	6.81
Average Restroom Rating	9.34	7.69	6.55	7.43	6.08	7.13
Facilities						
Clean and appealing facilities	9.44	7.87	7.10	8.30	6.43	7.77
Well-lighted facilities	8.74	8.45	7.99	8.42	6.60	8.16
Average Facilities Rating	9.09	8.16	7.55	8.36	6.52	7.97
Gasoline						
Reasonably priced gasoline	8.92	7.33	6.40	--	--	6.38
Employees						
Friendly and courteous employees	8.83	7.94	7.27	7.68	6.82	7.73
Helpful employees	8.73	7.66	7.04	7.31	6.55	7.42
Average Employees Rating	8.78	7.80	7.16	7.50	6.69	7.58

*Consumers were asked to rate the importance to them of a list of attributes of the highway stop experience on a 0-to-10 scale (with 0 being "Unimportant" and 10 being "Important"). Cell values are the average importance ratings for all respondents for each attribute.

**Consumers were asked to rate the performance of Lee's TravelStop, Texaco, McDonald's, Dairy Queen, and a highway stop of their choosing on a 0-to-10 scale (with 0 being "Poor Performance" and 10 being "Excellent Performance"). Cell values are the average performance ratings for all respondents for each highway stop. Numbers are averages, with'0' being 'not important' and '10' being 'very important' or 'excellent'.

Exhibit 11 (Continued)
Performance Ratings of Selected Highway Stops

	Attribute Importance Rating*	Highway Stop Performance Ratings**				
		Lee's TravelStop	Texaco	McDonald's	Dairy Queen	Other Travel Stop
Quickness						
Easy access to and from highway	9.14	8.38	7.88	7.78	6.15	7.90
Speedy service	8.53	7.75	7.40	7.77	6.39	7.65
Quick and easy to pay	8.09	7.88	7.63	7.79	7.07	7.86
Adequate number of pumps	7.83	8.16	7.13	--	--	6.56
Average Quickness Rating	8.40	8.04	7.51	7.78	6.54	7.49
Reputation						
Reputation of the stop	7.32	7.39	7.62	8.11	6.50	7.62
Drinks						
Selection of things to drink	7.55	8.20	7.34	7.21	6.95	7.66
Freshly brewed coffee	6.50	7.41	6.07	7.01	5.95	7.00
Average Drinks Rating	7.03	7.81	6.71	7.11	6.45	7.33
Food						
Reasonably priced things to eat	7.25	6.99	4.63	7.63	6.69	6.34
Good quality things to eat	7.19	7.08	4.47	7.42	6.87	6.63
Selection of things to eat	6.52	7.15	4.49	7.60	6.81	6.64
Average Food Rating	6.99	7.07	4.53	7.55	6.79	6.54
Extras						
Selection of ice cream products	4.27	5.88	4.25	4.87	7.80	5.36
Selection of personal care products	3.99	7.02	5.42	--	--	5.59
Selection of souvenirs	2.90	6.73	4.64	2.44	--	4.90
Average Extras Rating	3.72	6.54	4.77	3.66	7.80	5.28
Overall Evaluation	--	7.62	6.68	7.35	6.18	7.46

Exhibit 12
Future Stopping Intentions of Long-distance Travelers for Selected Highway Stops

Likelihood a Long-distance Traveler Will Stop at the Selected Highway Stop in the Future:	Percent of Long-distance Travelers for Each Highway Stop				
	Lee's TravelStop	Texaco	McDonald's	Dairy Queen	Other Highway Stop
75 to 100 Points	2.4%	0.0%	2.4%	0.1%	4.6%
50 to 74 Points	5.2%	2.3%	10.4%	2.4%	7.4%
25 to 49 Points	37.5%	32.5%	26.4%	13.7%	34.2%
1 to 24 Points	37.3%	42.9%	48.9%	63.1%	48.3%
0 Points	17.6%	22.3%	11.9%	20.7%	5.5%
Total	100.0%	100.0%	100.0%	100.0%	100.0%
Average Likelihood of Stopping in Future:	23.9%	18.8%	24.4%	14.5%	27.3%

Notes: Consumers were asked to assign 100 points among the 5 highway stops (the 4 they were asked to rate plus the one they had listed as the "best other highway stop") in proportion to their likelihood of patronizing each highway stop again. For example: if they had an equal likelihood of stopping at all 5 in the future, then they would assign 20 points to each outlet; alternatively, if they did not intend to stop at a particular highway stop again, they would assign 0 points to that outlet. Cell values represent the percent of the respondents who assigned that number of points to that outlet.

HENRI'S: COMPETING WITH OFFICE DEPOT AND STAPLES

By Robert F. Lusch, University of Oklahoma

Henri Schultz leaned back in his chair and looked once again at the financial data he had just reviewed on Office Depot and Staples. He couldn't believe what he was seeing. Office Depot and Staples separately, but in the same year, started the office supply superstore industry. In May of 1986 Staples opened its first office supply superstore in Massachusetts and in October of the same year Office Depot opened its first store in Florida. Office supply superstores are 20,000 to 25,000 square foot stores that merchandise office supplies, office furniture, office machines, and computers. A typical store has annual sales of $4 million to $5 million and carries 5500 SKUs. Both Office Depot and Staples have experienced explosive growth over the last eight years. By year end 1993, Office Depot had 351 stores and Staples had 230 stores. Office Depot ended 1993 with sales of $2.6 billion and Staples ended 1993 with sales of $1.1 billion. Within the last year, each of these chains acquired stationery supply wholesalers in an attempt to develop a supply channel to serve the needs of large businesses that typically do not purchase through a retail outlet.

As Henri reviewed the financial performance of these two superstore chains (see Exhibit 1) he was shocked at their relatively average financial performance. He had assumed that because of their size and rapid growth that they were extremely profitable companies. As an early investor in Wal*Mart in the mid 1970s, Henri was familiar with how this chain regularly earned 30% to 35% return on equity after taxes, and even in the 1990s was earning over 20% return on equity after taxes. He was therefore surprised to learn that Office Depot earned 11.4% return on equity (after taxes) in 1993 and Staples earned a modest 9%.

Background

Henri's was founded in 1967 by Henri Schultz when he opened a 7900 square foot store in Los Angeles. Henri had worked for several years after graduating from the University of Southern California for an office supply wholesaler. Henri was a salesperson who called on office supply stores in the Los Angeles area. One day, Mr. John Ryans, a 52 year old businessman that was one of the accounts he called on, mentioned he wanted to get out of the office supply business. His wife, Iris, was taking retirement from a local government agency and John felt he had accumulated sufficient savings that they would both retire while they could enjoy life. John had a very successful store that he had operated since 1953. Henri was getting a little frustrated with his career potential as a salesperson in wholesale distribution and thought to himself this might be just the opportunity for him. After several meetings, Henri agreed to purchase the store for $20,000 in goodwill and to pay the book value for the inventory, fixtures, and equipment on hand. Henri arranged for a $75,000 loan from his grandfather to assist in this venture. He also agreed to take over the remaining 4 years on a 10 year lease. Eighteen months after taking over the store and after the clientele of the store became comfortable with Henri, he changed the name of the store to Henri's.

Henri threw himself totally into the business and became a very talented retail merchant. Each year from 1967 until 1974 sales grew at double digit percentage rates. In 1975, Henri opened a second store six miles north of his present store. This store was 9500 square feet. Within one year it was profitable. A third store of 9100 square feet was opened in 1981 four miles north of the second store, and a fourth in 1987 was opened five miles east of the original store. Beginning in 1990, the local economy began to soften and Henri refrained from opening additional stores. Nonetheless, he was pleased with his small four-unit chain, which had achieved sales of $6.4 million in 1993.

Henri's specialty was office machines and repairs, which represented 38% of sales. Other merchandise lines included desks and chairs 21%; paper 14%; general office supplies 13%; computers (both hardware and software) 10%; and office cleaning supplies 4%. A total of 1850 SKUs were regularly stocked and thousand of other items could be special ordered. Henri purchased 80% of his merchandise from wholesale-distributors in Los Angeles and the other 20% direct from manufacturers. This was typically office furniture and selected lines of office equipment.

Henri's Financial Performance and Strategic Redirection?

Exhibit 2 provides some financial data on Henri's. Henri was especially pleased about the firm's 3.3% net profit margin (after taxes). In fact, when he learned that Office Depot and Staples had net profit margins in the 2.3 to 2.5% range, he was even more satisfied. Nonetheless, he was a bit uneasy. Both Office Depot and Staples had entered the Los Angeles market and all four of Henri's stores were within two miles of either an Office Depot or Staples. He attributed his firm's stagnant level of sales to this increased competition and also to the overall softness of the Los Angeles economy. Sales had been virtually flat since 1991. Office supply retailers in other cities that Henri had become acquainted with told him he was fortunate. Their experience had been that when an office supply superstore opened within a couple miles of their store, sales would drop from 5% to 20% within a year.

Henri began to wonder just how severely his profitability would be impacted if his firm's sales declined. Office Depot had recently begun to offer free delivery service on any order over $50. Henri became more disturbed at the aggressive prices that Office Depot and Staples would have on high velocity or high turnover items such as file folders, copying paper, and computer discs. It might not be long before his sales also began to falter. The fact that Henri's sales weren't growing clearly indicated that Office Depot and Staples were having an impact on Henri's. Henri worried that if their penetration of the market would increase, his sales might begin to decline.

Henri thought he had two options. First, he could try to better contain operating costs. His fixed costs of $630,076 were primarily for occupancy ($440,000) and salaries. Included in the salaries was a $65,000 salary for himself. Consequently he didn't see a way that he could cut these costs. The variable costs that ran 15% of sales were primarily for the variable component of employee costs (about 11% of sales) and advertising, which he budgeted at 3% of sales. The variable cost of compensation was due to paying his salespeople on commission and also due to the fact that he felt that he could either add or cut employees based on the overall level of sales activity.

A second option would be to develop a revenue enhancement strategy. In this regard, Henri wasn't sure what he could pursue that he wasn't already pursuing. One possibility was expanded store hours, which would involve staying open evenings and on Saturdays and possibly Sundays. Current hours are 9:00 a.m. to 5:30 p.m., Monday through Friday. Another possibility was increased advertising; but he wasn't sure if spending more on advertising would be worthwhile. Most of the current advertising was direct mail and some advertising in local business-oriented magazines. Virtually all of his customers were small to medium size businesses and he especially served the needs of legal and doctor offices/clinics. He had decided to focus on this market 15 years ago and had been quite successful. Henri's had a strong emphasis on customer services such as credit, delivery (both regular and emergency), no-questions-asked return policy, and knowledgeable sales personnel. The sales personnel are not only available in the store, but also regularly make phone calls and personal visits to persons responsible for purchasing office supplies and equipment. In the case of small businesses, this is often the owner/manager of the firm. Terms of payment were 2% for cash or check, or 1% if paid within 10 days and net 30. Major credit cards were also accepted, comprising about 40% of purchases.. Approximately 40% of customers used Henri's own charge plan and paid within 30 days. However, there were always some late payers and about 1.65% of credit sales were never collected.

Market Research

Henri decided to conduct some market research to determine the views of small to medium size businesses about Office Depot and Staples. He wanted to determine what they felt was important in the purchase of office supplies and how Office Depot and Staples were rated on these attributes. At the same time, he wanted to gain knowledge of the information sources that are used by businesses in deciding where to purchase office supplies. Henri met with a professor of marketing at one of the local colleges and together they designed a questionnaire. The questionnaire was mailed to 1320 businesses and 585 were returned. The sample was randomly selected, however, it was weighted toward sampling legal and doctor offices/clinics.

Henri was surprised to learn that over 90% of the respondents had heard of Office Depot and Staples and that approximately 87% had shopped at either or both of these stores. The typical firm shopping at an Office Depot or Staples was 6.8 miles or 12.8 minutes away from the store. 96.9% of those that shopped at these office supply superstores purchased office supplies and 78.7% purchased paper/stationery; 34% purchased office machines, 30.2% purchased computer software, 28.6% purchased office furniture, and 21.9% purchased computer hardware.

Additional findings are reported in Exhibits 3 to 5. Exhibit 3 reports on the sources of information used in purchasing office supplies. Exhibit 4 reports on how important 22 factors are in the purchase of office supplies and how the office supply superstores scored in terms of performance on these 22 factors. Finally Exhibit 5 presents data on which items the respondents would not be willing to give up for a 10% price reduction.

Concluding Comment

In reviewing the data, Henri was beginning to think that perhaps he didn't need any change in his strategy. He was earning a higher return on equity than the office supply superstores and he noted that their performance ratings in the market research survey just completed were not noteworthy. Perhaps he should just continue to conduct business as usual.

Questions for Discussion

1. Estimate what would happen to Henri's profitability if sales were to decline 5%? What if they declined 15%?

2. What changes do you recommend for Henri's?

Exhibit 1
Financial Performance of Office Depot and Staples
Fiscal Year 1993

	Office Depot Inc.	Staples, Inc.
Total Sales	100.0%	100.0%
Cost of Goods	76.8	76.2
Gross Profit	23.2%	23.8%
Operating Expenses	18.8	20.2
Operating Profit	4.4%	3.6%
Other (expenses) Income	(.2)	0.0
Net Income	4.2%	3.6%
Taxes	1.7	1.3
Net Income (after tax)	2.5%	2.3%
Asset Turnover (Sales/Total Assets)	1.8x	1.9x
Return on Assets	4.3%	4.4%
Financial Leverage (Total Assets/Equity)	2.6x	2.1x
Return on Equity	11.4%	9.0%

Exhibit 2
Henri's
Financial Performance (1993)

Financial Data	Dollars
Total Sales	$6,364,400
Cost of Goods	4,442,351
Gross Profit	1,922,049
Fixed Operating Expenses	630,076
Variable Operating Expenses	954,660
Operating Profit	337,313
Income Taxes	128,179
Net Profit (after Taxes)	209,134
Total Assets*	2,371,074
Equity	1,408,788

*Some of the major assets are: Inventory ($1,209,980), Accounts Receivable ($412,343), Cash ($298,887).

Exhibit 3a
Sources of Information Used in Purchasing Office Supplies (Percent of Mentions)

Information Source	Always	Frequently	Seldom	Never
Catalogs	8.7	41.7	40.6	8.9
Word of Mouth	5.0	43.6	37.5	13.9
Local Business Club	3.3	15.4	29.6	51.8
Visit from Salesperson	2.7	14.3	46.9	36.1
Trade Magazine	1.4	19.9	43.2	35.5
TV/Radio/ Newspapers	1.3	15.7	41.3	41.7
Direct Mail	1.0	17.3	54.2	27.6
Phone Call from Salesperson	1.0	6.0	37.9	55.2
Trade Shows	.8	10.6	30.9	57.7

Exhibit 3b
Trustworthiness of Information Sources Used in Purchasing Office Supplies (Percent of Mentions)

Information Source	Always	Frequently	Seldom	Never
Catalogs	14.6	73.2	10.7	1.4
Word of Mouth	11.2	72.5	14.3	2.0
Local Business Club	9.5	70.0	16.4	4.1
Visit from Salesperson	4.4	46.9	40.4	8.3
Trade Magazine	5.7	73.4	17.2	3.8
TV/Radio/ Newspapers	4.4	57.0	34.0	4.6
Direct Mail	2.6	59.6	32.7	5.1
Phone Call from Salesperson	2.1	23.6	48.6	25.7
Trade Shows	3.1	64.1	24.9	7.9

Exhibit 4
Factors Influencing Patronage Decisions

Factor	Importance Rating*	Performance of Office Supply Superstores**
Trustworthiness of Supplier	8.2	7.1
Merchandise in Stock	8.0	6.6
No Hassle Returns	8.0	7.1
Easy to Ask Questions	7.7	6.0
Lowest Prices	7.6	6.3
High Quality Products	7.5	6.2
Good Prices on Small Orders	7.5	6.6
Easy to Place Orders	7.4	6.7
Hard-to-Find Items	7.1	5.4
Accurate Deliveries	6.9	5.8
Dependable Deliveries	6.8	6.3
Sales Reps Friendly	6.7	6.7
One Source Supplies All My Needs	6.6	6.5
Accessible After Hours	6.3	7.5
Sales Reps' Technical Knowledge	6.3	5.9
Flexible on Last-Minute Order Changes	6.1	6.1
Regular Deliveries	5.4	6.0
Emergency Deliveries	5.0	4.8
Credit Terms With Adequate Time to Pay	5.0	5.4
Credit Terms Reasonable	4.6	5.5
Sales Reps Keep Me Informed	3.8	5.4
Sales Reps Call Regularly	2.8	3.5

* Importance Ratings range from (1) low importance to (9) high importance.
** Performance Ratings range from (1) low performance to (9) high performance.

Exhibit 5
Items Businesses are Not Willing to Give Up for a 10% Reduction in Price of Office Supplies and Products
(Percent of Mentions)

Factor	#1 Item	#2 Item	#3 Item
Merchandise in Stock	14.5	12.7	11.2
Trustworthiness of Supplier	16.9	5.0	12.0
One Source Supplies All My Needs	19.5	3.8	4.1
Easy to Ask Questions	9.9	9.2	5.5
High Quality Products	6.6	7.8	6.9
No Hassle Returns	3.6	6.8	7.5
Accurate Deliveries	3.2	6.6	6.9
Lowest Prices	7.6	5.2	3.4
Hard-to-Find Items	4.0	5.8	5.1
Dependable Deliveries	1.4	7.0	6.5
Good Prices on Small Orders	2.4	5.6	5.7
Accessible After Hours	1.8	4.2	4.7
Easy to Place Orders	0.8	5.0	4.3
Sales Reps Have Technical Knowledge	1.6	2.6	3.2
Sales Reps are Friendly	1.0	2.2	4.1
Regular Deliveries	2.2	2.8	1.8
Emergency Deliveries	0.6	1.4	2.6
Credit Terms With Adequate Time to Pay	1.0	2.0	.8
Credit Terms Reasonable	0.6	1.0	1.6
Flexible on Last-Minute Order Changes	0.2	1.4	1.4
Sales Reps Call Regularly	0.4	0.6	0.6
Sales Reps Keep Me Informed	0.0	1.0	0.2

WAL*MART: SELLING BELOW COST - AND CONWAY, ARKANSAS[*]
By Robert Kahn

Unlike *The New York Times*, *The Wall Street Journal*, and other publications which have given you bits and pieces with disjointed comments, *Retailing Today* brings you all of the facts about the suit of American Drug, Inc., et al. vs. Wal*Mart Stores, Inc., which was tried in Conway, Arkansas. The suit alleged that Wal*Mart violated Arkansas law by selling pharmaceutical and health and beauty products below cost.

Read the entire decision of Chancery Judge David L. Reynolds. Note that the decision is divided into two parts: "Findings of Fact" and "Conclusions of Law." The "Conclusions of Law" should be supported by the "Findings of Fact."

IN THE CHANCERY COURT
FAULKNER COUNTY, ARKANSAS

FIRST DIVISION

AMERICAN DRUGS, INC., et al.		PLAINTIFFS
VS.	NO.E-92-1158	
WAL*MART STORES, INC.		DEFENDANT

Findings of Fact

1. Plaintiffs, American Drugs, Inc. ("American Drugs"), Tim Benton d/b/a Mayflower Family Pharmacy ("Family Drug") and Jim Hendrickson d/b/a Baker Drug ("Baker Drug") (collectively the "Plaintiffs"), own and operate drug stores in Faulkner County, Arkansas.

2. Plaintiffs' drug stores offer for sale a full line of pharmaceutical items and health and beauty aids. Plaintiffs are multiple-line marketers relying on local sales of pharmaceuticals for the majority of their retail sales and income.

3. Defendant Wal*Mart, Inc., ("Wal*Mart") the world's largest retailer, owns and operates a discount store at Conway, Faulkner County, Arkansas ("Conway Wal*Mart"), which offers a variety of products, including pharmaceuticals and health and beauty aids, but does not rely on pharmaceuticals for a substantial amount of its retail sales. For the purpose of determining competitive impact in this litigation, the relevant market is the pharmaceutical and health and beauty aids product-lines ("relevant product lines") in Faulkner County, Arkansas, where Conway Wal*Mart and Plaintiffs are competitors.

4. Faulkner County has experienced strong population and commercial growth during the past 20 years. The sale of pharmaceutical and health and beauty aids has expanded correspondingly. Retail sales in the relevant product-lines increased from $5,184,000 in 1988 to $9,897,000 in 1990. The number of pharmacies located in Faulkner County has increased from 5 in 1967 to 12 in 1981 and 14 in 1992. Conway Wal*Mart began selling prescription

---

[*] Robert Kahn, *Retailing Today* (November 1993), used with permission. Permission applies to material following the sub-heading **Problems in Understanding the Decision.**

drugs in 1987. Other competitors of Plaintiffs and Defendant in the relevant product lines are other drug stores and large volume chain discount stores in Faulkner County, including Kroger, Harvest Foods, and Fred's.

5. Healthy competition in a market tends to result in lower retail prices; and a competitive marketplace is beneficial to consumers. Prices for the relevant product lines in Conway Wal*Mart tend to be the same or slightly higher than in the Clinton, Arkansas, or Flippin, Arkansas, Wal*Mart stores (areas of less competition).

6. Wal*Mart determines the "everyday" price for its products at its headquarters in Bentonville, Arkansas. Local store owners [managers] cannot raise their store's prices above the price determined at its headquarters. It is Wal*Mart policy that its store managers monitor the retail prices charged by competitors in their respective market area and lower prices for highly competitive merchandise without regard to the cost of individual items. This price is frequently below Wal*Mart cost of acquiring some of these products in highly competitive markets.

7. After monitoring prices charged by other competitors, the manager of Conway Wal*Mart has reduced the retail prices of some items in its relevant product lines below Wal*Mart's invoice or acquisition cost. Conway Wal*Mart has advertised for sale, in the local market, pharmaceutical items at prices below Wal*Mart's acquisition cost. Conway Wal*Mart occasionally has displayed a pricing "scorecard" near the front of the store comparing Conway Wal*Mart's prices on certain merchandise with prices charged by other local retailers, including Plaintiffs.

8. The stated purpose of Wal*Mart's pricing policy is to "meet or beat" the retail prices contemporaneously charged by competitors for highly competitive, price-sensitive merchandise; to maintain "low-price leadership" in the local marketplace; and to "attract a disproportionate number of customers into a store to increase traffic." The stated purpose of below cost sales is to generate traffic that will purchase other items offsetting any loss on a particular item sold below cost.

9. Although Conway Wal*Mart has sold, at prices below its cost, items in the relevant product lines, Conway Wal*Mart sells the whole product line above cost. Conway Wal*Mart and its pharmacy are profitable even in the short run.

10. There is no direct evidence that the purpose of Wal*Mart's pricing policy or Conway Wal*Mart's implementation of the policy is to injure competitors or to destroy competition. However, such purposes may be inferred from the stated policy, the effects of the stated policy, and other circumstantial evidence.

11. Plaintiffs have lost prescription and related sales and customers to Conway Wal*Mart as a result of Wal*Mart's advertising and sale of the relevant product lines below Wal*Mart's acquisition costs. The growth in sales and profits experienced by Plaintiffs substantially decreased primarily as a result of Wal*Mart's below-cost advertising and pricing in spite of the dramatic increase in sales in the local market.

12. Plaintiffs have been injured by Conway Wal*Mart's aggressive and unfair pricing practices. American Drugs has been damaged in the amount of $42,407. Baker Drug has been damaged in the amount of $33,767. Family Drug has been damaged in the amount of $20,295.

Conclusions of Law

1. Act 253 of 1937, "The Unfair Trade Practices Act," Ark. Code Ann.§ 4-75-201 through 4-75-211, ("the Act") specifically sets out the legislative intent of "the Act":

   The General Assembly declares that the purpose of this subsection is to ...foster and encourage competition by prohibiting unfair and discriminatory prices by which fair and honest competition is destroyed or prevented.

2. The Arkansas Supreme Court recognized "the Act's" purpose in Beam Brothers v. Monsanto, 259 Ark. 253,532 S.W.2d 175 (1976):

   This subsection (of the Act) is intended for the primary benefit of the public by protecting dealers, especially small dealers, from unfair competition by large dealers.

3. The purpose of "the Act" is not to protect small business from large business, downtown from malls, or to guarantee any business a share of the market, but to encourage "fair and honest competition." The protection afforded by the "Act" is from "unfair competition."

4. "The Act" states that "...it shall be literally construed so that its beneficial purposes may be subserved." "The Act" is penal in nature and imposes liabilities unknown at common law, therefore it must be strictly construed in favor of those upon whom the burden is sought to be imposed, and that which is not expressed will not be taken as intended. Davis v. Fowler, 230 Ark. 39, 320 S.W.2d 938(1959).

5. "The Act" makes it unlawful for a business to sell, or advertise for sale "any article or product" at less than the "cost thereof." "Cost" in this instance is defined as the "invoice or replacement cost of the article to the distributor or vendor plus the cost of doing business." "Cost of doing business" is defined as:

   ...all costs of doing business incurred in the conduct of the business and must include without limitation the following items of expense: labor, which includes salaries of the executives and officers, rent, interest on borrowed capital, depreciation, selling cost, maintenance of equipment, delivery cost, credit losses, all types of licenses, taxes, insurance, and advertising. Ark. Code Ann. § 4-75-209 (2) (b) (2).

6. The prohibition against sales below costs does not apply to the sale below cost of seasonal, damaged, deteriorated and perishable items; good faith closing business sales; and court ordered sales.

7. Wal*Mart contends that the Court should look at "market-basket" cost rather than single product or article cost. While the Court can find no Arkansas judicial decision construing this issue, the Court finds that Ark. Code Ann. § 4-75-209 is clear — "the Act" applies to "any article or product" and not "market-basket" or "overall product line" cost.

8. The burden of proof is on Plaintiffs to establish three essential elements: that Conway Wal*Mart sold, offered to sell or advertised to sell products (1) at less than the cost to Conway Wal*Mart, (2) for the purpose of injuring competitors, and (3) for the purpose of destroying competition. Ark. Code Ann. § 4-75-209 (a) (1).

9. The evidence is clear that Conway Wal*Mart advertised and sold pharmaceutical and health and beauty products below invoice or acquired costs (without taking into consideration the "cost of doing business") on a regular basis. These below cost sales do not fall within the exemptions set out in "the Act."

10. The Court finds that purpose to injure competitors and destroy competition cannot be inferred from below cost advertising and sales alone. There must be other proof of intent or purpose. A person's purpose or intent, being a state of mind, ordinarily cannot be proven by direct evidence, but may be inferred from other circumstances. Alford v. State 34 Ark. App 113, 806 S.W.2d 29(1991).

11. The Court finds from the following circumstances that Conway Wal*Mart advertised and sold pharmaceutical and health and beauty products below cost for the purpose of injuring competitors and destroying competition:

    1. The number and frequency of below cost sales.
    2. The extent of below costs sales.
    3. Wal*Mart's stated pricing policy - "meet or beat the competition without regard to cost."
    4. Wal*Mart's stated purpose of below cost sales–to attract a disproportionate number of customers to Wal*Mart.
    5. The in-store price comparison of products sold by competitors, including Plaintiffs.
    6. The disparity in prices between Faulkner County prices of the relevant product lines and other markets with more and less competition.

Relief and Damages

Plaintiffs' request to enjoin Conway Wal*Mart from selling below cost as defined by the "Unfair Trade Practices Act" is GRANTED.

Plaintiffs' request for damages is GRANTED and the Court awards damages as follows:

American Drugs	$42,407
Baker Drug	33,767
Family Drug	20,295

Plaintiffs' request for treble damages and costs is GRANTED.
Plaintiffs' request for attorney's fees is DENIED due to the lack of statutory authority for such allowance.

IT IS SO ORDERED THIS 11TH DAY OF OCTOBER, 1993.

DAVID L. REYNOLDS
CHANCERY JUDGE ON EXCHANGE

Problems in Understanding the Decision

The text of Paragraph 6 in the "Findings of Fact" states: "It is Wal*Mart's policy that its store managers monitor the retail prices charged by competitors in their respective market area and lower prices for highly competitive merchandise without regard to the cost of individual items." This statement is enclosed in quotation marks but is not attributed. In addition, the decision fails to indicate whether or not the store *will meet but not go below those prices which are already at or below cost,* thus selling at below cost only in those cases when matching a competitor who is already below Wal*Mart's cost. No illuminating examples were quoted in the decision. From their public statements and advertising (i.e., Joe Antonini, CEO of Kmart, stating on TV, "We will not be undersold"), I believe both Kmart and Target have similar policies.

The text of Paragraph 8 in the "Findings of Fact" includes the phraseology "...'meet or beat' the retail prices...by competitors; 'attract a disproportionate number of customers into a store to increase traffic.'" The decision contained these statements within quotation marks but, again, does not indicate whether the words are those of the Plaintiffs, Wal*Mart, or of the judge himself.

Continuing with Paragraph 8, there is no indication of the source of the statement: "The stated purpose of below cost sales is to generate traffic that will purchase other items offsetting any loss on a particular item sold below cost." Was the "Stated" by the Plaintiffs? the defendant? or was it a conclusion by the court? The purpose of all advertising, at above or below cost, is to "attract a disproportionate number of customers"; if it does not, the expenditure has been wasted.

Paragraph 8 in the "Conclusions of Law" recites that the Plaintiffs must submit proof that the acts of Wal*Mart were "...(2) for the purpose of injuring competitors, and (3) for the purpose of destroying competition." Yet, nothing in the decision identifies any such proof.

Observations

The "Conclusions of Law" in Paragraph 1 cite Act 253 of 1937, "The Unfair Trade Practices Act", Ark. Code Ann. § 4–75-201 through 4-75-211 [this is the first suit in 56 years], but at no time in either part of the decision does the judge cite the key provision of the law:

> **§4-75-209 (a) (1). It shall be unlawful for any person, partnership, firm, corporation, joint-stock company, or other association engaged in business within this state to sell, offer for sale, or advertise for sale any article or product, or service or output of a service trade, at less than the cost hereof to the vendor, or to give, offer to give, or advertise the intent to give away any article or product, or service or output of a service trade, *for the purpose of injuring competitors and destroying competition.*** [Emphasis added.]

The law seems clear. To be guilty under the law, selling below cost must have taken place for the purpose of both:

1. **"injuring competitors and**
2. **destroying competition."**

Paragraph 10 in the "Findings of Fact" states:

> **There is no direct evidence that the purpose of Wal*Mart's pricing policy or Conway Wal*Mart's implementation of the policy is to injure competitors or to destroy competition.** [Emphasis added.]

<u>RThought</u>: The "Conclusions of Law" in Paragraph 8 states: "The burden of proof is on Plaintiffs to establish [these two] essential elements..." One would think such a finding of "no direct evidence" would have determined the case. But it did not.

It was Wal*Mart which located the direct evidence that the Plaintiffs had actually benefited during the period for which they claimed damage. How could the Plaintiffs have greatly increased profits/compensation and, at the same time, be damaged?

During the period from 1987 (when Wal*Mart opened a pharmacy in Conway, Arkansas) until the trial date, it would appear that the three Plaintiffs, American Drugs, Family Drug, and Baker Drug, had there been injury, ought to have been able to assemble evidence which showed:

1. **as competitors, they were injured; or, at least,**
2. **competition was destroyed.**

Under discovery procedures, it was Wal*Mart which obtained the tax returns of the Plaintiffs and submitted the following information at the trial, showing that the Plaintiffs actually benefited.

NET INCOME
AND OFFICERS' COMPENSATION ($000)

Company	1993*	1992	1991	1990	1989	1988	1987
American Drugs	$41.5	$11.7	$32.8	$30.0	$13.8	$20.6	$40.9
Family Drug	63.3	71.5	91.8	50.3	9.7	1.3	4.9
Baker Drug	64.5	46.2	61.7	43.4	57.1	39.6	40.5
Total	$169.3	$129.4	$186.3	$123.7	$ 80.6	$ 61.5	$ 86.3
NET SALES ($000)							
American Drugs	$1,204	$1,199	$1,187	$1,199	$1,162	$1,113	$1061
Family Drug	606	538	605	627	519	459	439
Baker Drug	1,236	1,231	1,216	1,094	1,067	1,041	1,042
Total	$3,046	$2,968	$3,008	$2,920	$2,748	$2,613	$2,542

*Annualized sales, profits, and salary based on actual figures through May 1993.

Observation: *The Plaintiffs' combined net income and officers' compensation from 1987 to 1991 increased by 116%. That figure dropped in 1992 but is projected to increase again in 1993, reaching 96% above the base year.*

If one reviews the sales, the increase from 1987 to 1991 was 18%; the projection for 1987 to 1993 is an increase of 20%. The greater gain in profit/earnings came from an improvement in gross margin.

Do these figures reflect the type of injury to a competitor that Arkansas law was designed to prevent? I think not.

Not only did the Plaintiffs remain in business from 1987 to 1993, *with a substantial increase in profits*, but the "Findings of Fact" (Paragraph 4) point to an increase in the number of pharmacies in Conway. This evidence indicates that competition, far from being destroyed, was actually stimulated.

The "Findings of Fact" (Paragraph 4) mention a Fred's discount store. Fred's opened during the period covered by the complaint. Wal*Mart introduced evidence that *Fred's often undersold Wal*Mart*, but this appears not to have been considered in rendering the decision.

RThought: Despite finding "no intent" on the part of Wal*Mart to "injure competitors" and/or to "destroy competition" (Paragraph 10, "Findings of Fact"), despite the healthy survival of the Plaintiffs during the period of alleged destruction of competition, and despite the reported increase in the number of pharmacies in Conway during the period of complaint, Judge Reynolds found "intent" based upon the following factors set forth in Paragraph 11, "Conclusions of Law":

1. **The number and frequency of below cost sales.**

2. **The extent of below cost sales.**

3. **Wal*Mart's stated pricing policy – "meet or beat the competition without regard to cost."**

4. **Wal*Mart's stated purpose of below cost sales – to attract a disproportionate number of customers to Wal*Mart.**

5. **The in-store price comparison of products sold by competitors, including Plaintiffs.**

6. **The disparity in prices between Faulkner County prices of the relevant product lines and other markets with more and less competition.**

RThought: One looks to the courts for guidance in the proper conduct of business so as to comply with the law. Judge Reynolds' decision fails to provide guidance regarding any of his six "proofs" of intent. Worse, the decision raises more questions than it answers.

1. Judge Reynolds' decision does not instruct us as to how many and how frequently sales can be made below cost without creating the presumption of an intention to "injure competitors" and "destroy competition".

2. Judge Reynolds' decision does not clearly set forth the extent of below cost sales which are permitted without creating the presumption of an intention to "injure competitors" and/or "destroy competition."

3. Judge Reynolds' decision recites the good brought about by competition (Paragraph 5, "Findings of Fact"), but certainly, a retailer should have a right to meet any other price in the market, even if that price is below his or her cost.

4. Judge Reynolds' decision now renders illegal the use of price to draw into a store a "disproportionate number of customers." But, what is a "disproportionate number?" Who determines that a number is "disproportionate?" If a store approaches that number, must it then refuse to serve additional customers in order to avoid being charged with

intent to "injure competitors" and "destroy competition?" Must Judge Reynolds' decision be posted in the store so that a customer of average intelligence knows why a product cannot be sold?

5. Judge Reynolds' decision now precludes in-store comparison of prices with those of competitors (but the First Amendment of the United States Constitution permits such a comparison in newspapers, on TV, in throwaways, etc.). As an example, the Kroger store in Conway can no longer lawfully show a basket of foodstuff next to another shopping cart filled with identical goods purchased at a competing store, coupled with a cash register tape showing the higher price at which the items were bought.

6. Judge Reynolds' decision now appears to exclude from Faulkner County every major chain which sells at a higher price in a smaller community, where sales per square foot are lower and costs per square food are higher, or at a lower price in larger communities, where sales per square foot are higher and costs are lower as a percentage of sales and where competition is greater. [The tribute to competition in Paragraph 5 of the "Findings of Fact" must have been made with tongue in cheek, because, certainly, it could not have been sincere.]

RThought: In light of Judge Reynolds' decision, any firm on the edge of bankruptcy running a "50%-off" sale, in an attempt to raise cash and survive, will now be subject to charges of "injuring competitors and damaging competition" under the provisions of Paragraph 11, "Conclusions of Law." If the price is not low enough to avoid bankruptcy, the firm will bankrupt itself; if the price is low enough to stave off bankruptcy, the business will become subject to the cost of triple damages under Judge Reynolds' interpretation of the law, and the result will be the same forced bankruptcy.

RThought: Many *RT* readers know a great deal about Wal*Mart. They must be surprised at the "intent" which Judge Reynolds ascribed to Wal*Mart and that despite "intent" by the largest retailer in the world the net result was that three small Plaintiffs increased both their sales and their profit/earnings. They will wonder, could Wal*Mart have been so ineffective in carrying out its alleged "intent" that it helped rather than hurt its competitors?

RThought: The award, too, was inconsistent with the intent alleged by Judge Reynolds. The amount of damages, in relation to 1987-1933 compensation/profit for each Plaintiff, was:

	Net Income/Compensation ($000)	Award	Percentage
American Drugs	$ 191.3	$ 42.4	22.2%
Family Drugs	292.8	33.8	11.5
Baker Drug	353.0	20.3	5.8

By what evidence was American Drugs hurt four times as much as Baker Drug and twice as much as Family Drug? It does appear that American Drugs is not as good a merchant as the other two. Why should punitive damages award compensation for a difference in merchandising skills?

One wonders with which store it was that Judge Reynolds was not familiar. One trusts t
patronizes nor fraternizes with any of the three Plaintiffs (out of 15 available pharmacies) in Conv
(1990 census).

Some court renderings don't make sense. Judge Reynolds' opinion is one of them. An example such
states have a Supreme Court to review the decisions of their lower courts.

The Business Climate in 1937

I have pointed out that the law under which the suit was filed is called "Unfair Trade Practices Act" and was pass
Now, 56 years later, the first suit has been tried under it.

We might well look at the "anti-chain store" feelings during the 1930s. The theory pushed by independents was tha
would come into a town and sell merchandise at below cost. The fear was that such practices would drive o
independents. The stores selling below cost would be supported by the profit from their other stores. When
independents were gone, the chains would then raise prices to monopolistic levels.

Amongst the states, two approaches were taken to stop this attack on independent stores. One approach was a progressive
tax based on the number of stores in a chain. The other was to ban sales below cost. Arkansas chose the latter.

Between 1923 and 1957, 1297 bills based upon taxation of the number of stores were introduced in state legislatures, but only 62 were passed. A few were still on the books in 1957, as well as a few of the laws passed by some 70 cities.

But small businesses were more interested in obtaining a higher price if the brands they carried could be protected against price cutting. It was the chains in 1931, led by Charles R. Walgreen, which come out for legalized price maintenance. Starting at that time, states began passing fair trade laws. California came up with the "nonsigner" version: if any single retailer in California signed a price maintenance agreement with a manufacturer, that price would be binding on all other retailers in California.

Even when there were such laws in 45 states, not all manufacturers availed themselves and, as time passed, some withdrew. The early forms of off-price selling were already developing in the 1930s, although not in the form of discount stores as we know them today.

In 1937, Congress passed the Miller-Tydings Act which exempted such "nonsigner" form. In 1951, the United States Supreme Court overturned the application of Miller-Tydings to California's "nonsigner" law. Eventually, fair trade laws completely disappeared.

I am told that Judge Reynolds is a relatively young man; anyone who is younger than the law would be unfamiliar with this history. Only an old codger such as I is likely to have records of this background.

There is no indication, when Judge Reynolds had a problem with interpreting "intent" that, for assistance, he referred to the 1937 hearings which took place in the Arkansas Legislature. In 1940, Arkansas had only 1,900,000 people. Arkansas was so small that perhaps the committees of the legislature did not record their hearings.

that if each legislator who voted for "The Unfair Trade Practices Act" were questioned today as to whether he had his vote to apply as interpreted by Judge Reynolds, most would say no; most would likely express surprise that the ll on the books, especially since no case has sought protection under the act in 56 years. There is merit to sunset ns perhaps, if there is no application of the law for 20 years, the sun should set on their law.

ons for Discussion

Do you believe the courts and legal system in the U.S. should allow sales below cost on specific items as long as store traffic is increased and other items are purchased that offset any loss on a particular item sold below cost?

2. As the Arkansas Unfair Trade Practices Act has been defined and interpreted by the court, what are some of the problems in determining "costs"?

3. Do you agree with Judge Reynolds' opinion in this case? Why or why not?

COLLEGE SUBS*

By Patrick Dunne, Texas Tech University and George Kirk, Texas Tech University

Janet Cooper made it a point to be early for the monthly meeting of the Caprock Restaurant Association. She hoped to catch Bill Black and Jenny Mettler, the owners of the local McDonald's and Burger King franchises, during the premeeting mixer. After all, Janet needed their advice on what was to be the most important decision of her retailing career.

The History of College Subs

After graduating with an accounting degree from State U. in 1978, Janet Cooper went to work for a major accounting firm. Ms. Cooper soon grew tired of the long hours and constant shifting from client to client. So in 1981, with her sister's help, she opened a sandwich shop across the street from the largest dorm on the State U. campus and called it "College Subs." She would have preferred to use the name "University Subs," but another restaurant was already operating with that name in the state, although in a different city. College Subs was an immediate hit and by the end of the first year it was making a profit.

In 1987 College Subs #2 was opened at the other end of the campus and in 1990 College Subs #3 was opened across town at the intersection of the highway loop that circled the city and the interstate. While both of these newer restaurants were profitable, neither approached the success of the first one. [See Exhibit 1 for each store's income statements, as well as the combined statement for all three stores.] Janet assumed that the second store, while producing a satisfactory profit, would never match the first store's margins because many students now lived off campus and in the opposite direction from the #2 location. What worried her was the failure of the third store to do much more than breakeven.

Several reasons were advanced to explain store #3's shortcomings:

1. The management was not as good as in the other stores. However, Janet dismissed this idea since she herself had taken over the management of the store six months ago, and performance had not improved.
2. The location was wrong. Granted, the exit ramp near #3 wasn't one of the loop's busiest, but it still had more than 10,000 cars passing by each day--which was more than the number passing most successful fast food chain operations.
3. If it wasn't the first two reasons, Janet feared it was the name. The name College Subs was either not appealing to the non-college crowd passing by each day or, worse yet, it wasn't recognized. This would be especially true for those people passing by on the interstate.

If it was the third reason, what could Janet do? After a great deal of thought, Janet decided that franchising was the answer. She could convert the #3 store, or, if needed, all three stores into franchise operations. Janet believed that the name recognition of a major franchisor would make #3 a winner. In addition, both Subway and Blimpie, the nation's two leading submarine sandwich franchisors, hadn't yet entered the city. She believed they both would welcome the opportunity to add her three successful stores.

Concerns About Franchising

Despite the obvious benefit of gaining instant recognition by becoming a franchisee of either one of the two major franchise systems, Janet had some concerns. As she saw it, by joining either system, she would lose her independence. No

---

* This case was prepared as a basis for class discussion. All names - persons, locations, universities, and stores - have been changed to ensure the confidentially of retailer(s) involved.

longer would she have complete control over her stores. Every element of the retailing mix would be managed and controlled by someone else. Even the store's layout and design would have to be changed to meet franchisor specifications.

However, the thing that really bothered her the most was some of the articles she had read over the years in *Restaurant News* about how some franchisees had complained about franchisors. That is why she wanted to meet with Bill Black and Jenny Mettler.

Bill had been a McDonald's franchisee for over two decades and Jenny had been with Burger King for nearly 15 years. She had known them both as members of the Caprock Restaurant Association since she joined in 1983. In fact, Janet had served on committees with both of them, so she felt they would be honest with her.

Janet was particularly interested in talking to Jenny, since no franchisor has gotten as much bad press in recent years as Burger King. Over the years, BK franchisees have been growing increasingly unhappy with their advertising campaign. In fact, four times in the last five years BK has responded to franchisee discontent by putting the domestic advertising account up for review in hopes of getting a new agency to come up with a campaign to match its earlier success. That was when BBDO came up with its "Have it your way" in the early 1970s. Since then, franchisees have complained that nothing has enabled the chain to differentiate itself from archrival McDonald's. Probably the worse campaign was J. Walter Thompson's "Herb the Nerd" campaign of the mid-1980s. However, the most recent "Sometimes You've Gotta Break the Rules" campaign from D'Arcy Masius Benton & Bowles and Saatchi & Saatchi has left even their core market confused as to the message they are trying to send. No wonder Burger King's market share has been declining in recent years.

Janet would be forced by her franchise agreement to pay another 3 percent for the franchisor's advertising campaign, in addition to her regular royalty payments on all sales. Therefore, she didn't want to see her money wasted on an ineffective campaign.

This is especially true since Janet was highly successful at her #1 store by spending only 2.5 percent of sales on flyers passed out in dorms, ads in the campus paper and radio station, and an occasional ad on the city's leading radio station on weekends. Nonetheless, any type of recognition would be great for #3.

Janet was also concerned about the recent trend among fast-food franchisors to get involved in price wars with so-called "value meal" packages. She didn't feel that this was a major problem for her market, but that she would have no choice but to reduce prices if that was what the franchisor required.

Some other concerns that Janet had included the fact that the franchisor, or its representatives, could arbitrarily force her to make changes in her stores--covering such items as background music, floor tile, and number of parking places. Janet also didn't want to be forced to serve as a test market site for a franchisor's new products attempts. In addition, several articles in the *Wall Street Journal* had discussed how some franchisees had questioned the value of some of the services that the franchisors provide for the franchisees. In particular, site selection was questioned, which would be a concern for Ms. Cooper if she wanted to expand.

Ms. Cooper was also worried about the fact that the slow economy of the mid-1990s had seen some franchisors reverse course in order to make ends meet. An article in *Supermarket News* pointed out that some fast-food franchisors had signed agreements with supermarket chains to open up outlets in their stores, despite the fact that they would compete with nearby franchisees. A "homemade" ice cream franchisor had recently been sued by several franchisees when it decided to sell factory-made ice cream through other retail outlets. What would happen if the franchisor she decided to join forces with experienced some sort of financial trouble?

Finally, she was particularly concerned with the fact that Subway, the nation's largest and fastest growing franchise system, was the subject of an FTC inquiry into its marketing practices. Subway was accused of making unrealizable financial projections in their sales pitches and placing units so close together that they cannibalized each other. In addition, Ms. Cooper was concerned about a report claiming that over 40 percent of all Subway shops opened 5 years ago had changed ownership.

Advantages of Joining a Franchise System

While Ms. Cooper felt that the number one reason for joining a franchise system was the recognition and resulting increase in sales it would bring her #3 store, she was also aware of other advantages joining would offer. She knew that she would get two types of services in exchange for her royalties: initial and continuous. However, she wasn't quite sure of the benefits of these services, since she already had a successful operation.

Initial services include market survey and site selection, facility design and layout, advice on negotiating leases, operating manuals, management training programs, and employee training programs.

Continuous services include field supervision, lower prices on materials and product as a part of a group buying plan, quality inspection, national name recognition achieved by national advertising, auditing and record keeping, and a group insurance plan.

Requirements for Entering the Franchise Systems

Subway requires a $10,000 licensing fee in addition to an initial capital investment which Cooper has since she is an on-going operation,with an 8 percent royalty on sales, and a 2.5 percent advertising fee on sales. Blimpie, while requiring an $18,000 licensing fee, only charges a 6 percent royalty and a 3 percent advertising fee.

The Arrival of Black and Mettler

Just as Janet was getting her thoughts together, Bill Black and Jenny Mettler came in together. After a few pleasantries, Janet explained her dilemma.

Bill was the first to respond by saying, "I really don't know what to say. I hadn't had any experience in the restaurant business before hand, so I really needed all the McDonald's training and handholding. Besides, I haven't really felt pressured by the way they perform their continuous services. However, since you already know the business, you might find their services to be a pain."

"I agree with Bill," Jenny was quick to add. "I had worked in a Burger King as an assistant manager while I was in college and I thought I knew the business, but I really didn't. Besides, if anyone should be against the franchise system, it should be BK franchisees. However, after all that fighting between the franchisor and the franchisees, I would say that we are finally working together now."

Soon everybody was heading for their seats and Janet Cooper knew she had to make up her mind soon.

Questions for Discussion

1. Given her current financial performance, should Janet Cooper continue to explore the possibility of making her #3 store part of an existing franchise system?

2. If an existing system will only let her join if she brings all three stores into the system, would that change your answer?

3. Besides joining an existing franchise system, what other alternatives does Janet Cooper have?

4. What do you see as the major advantage(s) and disadvantage(s) for Ms. Cooper joining an existing system?

5. What would be the impact on Janet Cooper's breakeven point if she joins either of the systems with her #3 store?

Exhibit 1
College Subs
Income Statement Summary for All Stores

	Store 1	Store 2	Store 3	Combined
Sales	$150,000	$135,000	$50,000	$335,000
Less Return and Allowances	1,825	1,460	1,095	4,380
Net Sales	148,175	133,540	48,905	330,620
Less Cost of Goods Sold				
Beginning Inventory	1,230	1,410	610	3,250
Purchases	55,000	45,400	16,700	117,100
Cost of Goods Available				
For Sale	56,230	46,810	17,310	120,350
Ending Inventory	1,180	1,300	580	3,060
Cost of Goods Sold	55,050	45,510	16,730	117,290
Gross Margin	93,125	88,030	32,175	213,330
Less Operating Expenses				
Salaries & Wages	28,000	30,000	15,000	73,000
Advertising	4,704	4,339	2,223	11,266
Delivery	9,500	9,750	4,000	23,250
Rent	7,900	8,490	6,000	22,390
Utilities	1,950	2,900	1,900	6,750
Total Operating Expenses	52,054	55,479	29,123	136,656
Operating Profit	$41,071	$32,551	$3,052	$76,674

MULESHOE DRUG STORE*

By Patrick Dunne, Texas Tech University, and Jan P. Owens, University of Wisconsin - Madison

It was a hot June afternoon in 1995 on the Texas Panhandle, but Mike Rowley didn't seem to notice the 114 degree heat as he left the real estate office. He was coming back home. Earlier that day, Mike and his wife Kay had purchased the Muleshoe Drug Store in Muleshoe, Texas (see Figure 1) from Robert Piekos. Fifteen years earlier, Mike had worked in that drug store while in high school. However, after graduating from Creighton University's School of Pharmacy, Mike decided to remain in the Midwest and work for a large drug chain--Walgreen's. Now in their thirties with two young children, Mike and Kay wanted to come back to small town America to raise their family.

Robert Piekos's father, Thaddeus Piekos, started the drug store during the darkest days of the Depression in 1933 and it had provided a comfortable living for the family ever since. However, recent changes in the structure of the marketing channel for prescription drugs caused Robert Piekos to want to get out of the business.

Thaddeus Piekos was the first member of his family to attend college. Robert's grandfather, Nicholas Piekos, immigrated from Poland in 1902 and found a job laying railroad track in the Southwestern part of the U.S. for the various spur lines seeking to connect with the Santa Fe Pacific Railroad. After meeting and marrying Julia Botaskis in 1908, Nicholas Piekos settled down in Muleshoe and found a job as a station clerk at the local railroad station.

While in high school, Thaddeus worked at Bailey County's only pharmacy for Mr. Sam Jenkins. At the time Thaddeus was working for Mr. Jenkins, medicinal dispensers were known as either druggists or chemists because they compounded the medications they dispensed according to a doctor's direction. At the time druggists had their own "special" formulations and prepared prescriptions. It was only later, when manufacturers started to mass produce prescription drugs, that the term pharmacist became popular. In addition, during this time period, the drugstore, along with the general store, served as sort of a city hall for small town America and the druggist was one of the most respected persons in the town.

After graduating from high school in 1928, Thaddeus Piekos wanted to be like Mr. Jenkins. He enrolled at Southwestern Oklahoma College (SWOC) in Weatherford, Oklahoma, the nearest school offering a degree in pharmacy. While at SWOC, Thaddeus met his future wife, Teresa Irza.

During Thaddeus Piekos's third year of college, Mr. Jenkins was killed in an automobile accident leaving the town of 1400 without a registered pharmacist. As a result of this accident, Thaddeus Piekos decided that he would return to Muleshoe when he graduated. This inspired some of the citizens of Muleshoe to contribute to Thaddeus Piekos's educational fund for his final two years of schooling. To help him get started when he returned to town, these same citizens provided him with Jenkins' old 8000 sq. ft. store, "rent free." As a result, Thaddeus Piekos was able to use his family's rather limited resources toward the purchase of fixtures, equipment, and merchandise. Banks, during the Depression years, weren't too interested in making loans to unproven businessmen.

Muleshoe Drug Store (1933-1972)

Thaddeus Piekos opened his new store on July 4, 1933, and the town celebrated with him. He called it the Muleshoe Drug Store, in honor of the citizens of Muleshoe who provided him so much financial support during those trying times.

Like most drugstores in the middle of the 20th century, Muleshoe Drug was a multi-line retail outlet. It carried a variety of products including cosmetics, toiletries, and vet supplies, as well as patent medicines. Sometimes called over-the-

---

* This case was prepared as a basis for class discussion. All names - persons, locations, universities, and stores - have been changed to ensure the confidentially of retailer(s) involved.

counter (OTC) medicines[1], these often contained a high percentage of alcohol, and could only be purchased from licensed pharmacy retailers. Many of the cosmetics were franchised products and were subjected to "fair trade" or resale price maintenance laws, which made them highly profitable even for small retailers. Stores such as Muleshoe Drug stocked large quantities of these specialty items in order to capture heavy customer traffic. [Remember, it would be years before the supermarket would impact small town America.] In addition, drugstores during this period also carried gifts and wrapping supplies, and had boxed candy counters, tobacco counters, soda fountains and grills, and usually had the town's most complete magazine stand. Of course, the focal point of all drugstores was the pharmacy, or prescription-case.

Throughout the 1960s, drugstores in small towns like Muleshoe, with its population of 3890, remained open 12 to 15 hours a day in order to serve the various needs of the community. Workers depended on these stores to be open during the times they were off work. In addition, many pharmacists were asked to recommend an OTC product for families too poor to see a doctor or for a patient not quite sick enough to see one.

The major change impacting the operation of a small town drugstore during Thaddeus Piekos's ownership of Muleshoe Drug was the post-WWII availability of manufactured prescription medications. These would replace the medicinal ingredients that druggists had to mix, compound, and package. Consequently, the pharmacist became a "counter" and a "pourer" instead of a chemist. Pharmacists began to follow the manufacturer's marketing plans and put away their scales, weights and measures, mortars, and graduated cylinders. Drugstores became dispensers of pre-manufactured pills and liquids into pre-manufactured containers.

Still, the business was profitable for Thaddeus Piekos. In 1952, he moved to a new 11,500 sq. ft. building on the city's square. By 1961, the drugstore would record its fifteenth consecutive year of record earnings.

Over the years, Thaddeus Piekos and his wife had three children. Sarah was born in 1934 and had married a local cotton farmer in 1957. Robert Piekos was born in 1935, and like his father, graduated from SWOC and entered the business in 1958. Theo, the youngest, was away at Texas A&M University in 1961, majoring in petroleum engineering.

A review of the store's records for 1961 showed that it did a steady $5000 a week in business, except for the Christmas season when it averaged $10,000, for annual sales of $280,000. The store's gross margin was 29 percent and operating expenses were 21 percent. Profit for 1960 was $22,678 or 8 percent of sales. Exhibit 1 provides a summary of that year's results.

Beginning in 1962, Thaddeus Piekos started to spend more time away from the store and began to leave Robert in charge of operations. However, other events were occurring in 1962 that would impact Muleshoe Drug in future years.

The most immediate impact came from the decision by United Supermarkets, headquartered in nearby Lubbock, to enter the Muleshoe market with a 22,000 sq. ft. supermarket. United had two advantages over Muleshoe Drug. First, with its 53 supermarkets in West Texas, it had enormous buying power with its suppliers. Second, it was managed by trained retailers, not by pharmacists seeking to expand into other retail lines. United was able to use these advantages to underprice Muleshoe on both OTC items and its general merchandise lines, especially its health and beauty aids.

1962 also saw the first discount drug stores enter the Lubbock and Amarillo markets, both a little over an hour away by car.

However, the event that would have the greatest impact on Muleshoe Drug was the advent of general merchandise discount stores with their tremendous buying advantages. During 1962, the first four of these chains began operations. In April, S.S. Kresge, the large variety store chain, opened its first Kmart in Garden City, Michigan; in June, Herb Gibson opened his first three discount stores in Amarillo, Lubbock, and Abilene, Texas; later that month, F.W. Woolworth opened its first Woolco; and finally, on July 2, 1962, Sam Walton opened his first Wal*Mart in Rogers, Arkansas. Within a decade these discounters, each with a pharmacy, would cover America.

---

[1] Prior to 1951, when new federal legislation took effect, all medicines were OTC.

Drugstores, such as the one in Muleshoe, tried to prepare for the onslaught by holding on to both their loyal clientele and their profit margins. However, both dwindled as soon as these new competitors entered the trading area. Established drugstores had to devise new and better ways to combat their losses, and in doing so had to adopt many of the methods their competition used against them. For example, many pharmacists had to cut profit margins and expenses, i.e. services. They had to advertise loss leader merchandise and turn to volume sales as keys to their survival. Many of their specialty departments had to be downsized or eliminated. For example, cosmetic counters were no longer profitable as drugstores lost the customer franchise to department stores and discount store merchandisers. They were no longer the exclusive carriers of selected products, and many eliminated marginal or unprofitable wares, even if these centers drew loyal trade and some business.

The soda fountain, one of the most fascinating and profitable drugstore departments, almost became extinct. These centers became expensive to operate, and at best, small-ticket-no-profit hassles to store owners. The fountain was especially satisfying to the Piekos family since they had so many pleasant memories of conversations with customers, many of whom were close, personal friends. For Robert, it was especially satisfying and full of memories. When he was still in high school, he would often wait on the late music legend, Lubbock native Buddy Holly. Holly often would stop in the drugstore on his way to Norman Petty's recording studio in Clovis. With his friend Waylon Jennings, Buddy would order vanilla cokes at the fountain. Still, Muleshoe's fountain was a money-loser.

Finally, in late 1972, Thaddeus sold the business to Robert. He moved to Houston so that Teresa would be near M.D. Anderson Medical Complex, where she could get the best treatment possible for the malignant brain tumor found earlier that year.

Muleshoe Drug Store (1973-1990)

Throughout the rest of the 1970s, Muleshoe Drug was spared from having to do battle with these new forms of competition. Still, Robert began to prepare for its inevitable arrival by studying what others were doing. Increased competition from discounters and supermarkets forced small druggists to focus on managing their retailing mix and catering to the whims of every possible customer segment. As a result, many drugstores began to copy their competition. As the discounters expanded their product assortment to include drug items, nearby drugstores felt the squeeze. To fight back, these drugstores added general merchandise and food items. By the mid 1980s, drugstores were more like convenience stores--a place to purchase snack items and everything else under the sun. Sixty percent of their revenues came from non-drug items. They felt forced to use advertisements and coupons to make prescription drugs their "loss leaders" in an effort to regain local market share and their pharmacy image.

From 1973 to 1984, Robert Piekos was able to weather the storm. However, 1985 saw Revco Drug and Wal*Mart both enter the Clovis, New Mexico market. Clovis was only 20 minutes away and many Muleshoe residents either worked in Clovis or traveled there weekly to do their grocery shopping at one of the three large supermarkets. Despite a two to three percent annual sales increase over the past decade, profits had been holding steady or slightly declining each year. Robert felt he was prepared for this new development since he had spent the last decade trying to secure customer loyalty.

At worst, he expected a 5 to 10 percent decline in general merchandise sales, which had his lowest gross margins, and a two to four percent decrease in his prescription business. Overall, Robert felt that his profit margin would decrease from 7 to 5 percent of his annual net sales of $600,000. Still things could have been worse. Several of his classmates had similarly prepared but were forced out of business when a Revco, Kmart, or Wal*Mart entered their markets.

While able to withstand Revco's and Wal*Mart's arrival, the late 1980s saw further changes in the pharmaceutical drug channel. These changes were to jeopardize the very existence of small town druggists like Robert Piekos.

New Pricing Policies by Manufacturers

With their rapid growth, discounters began to seek even larger quantity discounts from the drug manufacturers so that they could offer their customers the lowest prices and still maintain their profit margins.

Aggressive pricing policies have always been the pharmaceutical manufacturers' best method of attracting business. However, these policies often differ from retailer to retailer. Despite the Robinson-Patman Act, manufacturers effectively offer special prices to their largest 5 percent of customers who account for nearly 60 percent of their volume. By limiting their menus to a single brand of every drug, these large drug providers can guarantee drug makers a high market share. As a result, they can negotiate substantial price reductions from manufacturers by playing one against another, especially for maintenance drugs. Maintenance drugs are those that patients take on a regular, predictable schedule. These drugs include those taken for high blood pressure, arthritis, diabetes, and other chronic ailments. For example, retailers who buy maintenance drugs in bottles of 1000 (which come 6 to a case) receive an additional 20 percent discount over the retailer purchasing the drug in the standard 100 tablet bottles (48 to a case). These savings can be passed on to the ultimate consumer or used to improve profit margins. Unfortunately, small retailers like Muleshoe cannot take advantage of the large quantity discount because the carrying cost of such large inventory is prohibitive.

Cost Reduction Plans by Insurance Providers

In the past, insurance providers such as Blue Cross/Blue Shield would pay member druggists a fixed fee, usually $2.75 to $3, plus the average wholesale price (AWP) for filling a prescription. Recently, in an attempt to reduce costs, this fee has been lowered to approximately $2. In addition, many insurance plans pay druggists AWP less 10 to 12 percent, reflecting the discounts offered by manufacturers to the largest drug retailers. This has put the small independent druggist at a disadvantage when competing for this business.

The Emergence of Mail-Order Fulfillment Centers

Mail-order prescription service had been around for several decades before Robert Piekos first started to worry about it in 1990. That was before Martin Wygod's impact on the industry. While he didn't invent the mail-order drug business, Wygod perfected it. In 1983, he bought the fledgling National Pharmacies, which later became Medco, the largest mail-order prescription drug company in the world. In 1993, Medco was in turn acquired by Merck, one of the largest pharmaceutical manufacturing companies in the world. At the time Wygod acquired Medco, the dominant mail-order retailer was a division of Walgreen. However, Wygod calculated that Walgreen would shy away from expanding its mail-order service since this might jeopardize its drugstore traffic and margins.

Wygod was the first to see that drug benefit plans would be a major growth area, yet less than five percent of Americans were currently covered by such a program. Mail-order drugs were the means to both capitalize on and revolutionize a stagnant industry. He sold his idea to big corporations and labor unions that already had drug benefit packages in place. For these institutions, the cost of drugs as an employment benefit was growing at three to four times the rate of inflation, and the potential for meaningful savings was evident. In addition, he sought out new companies and unions to provide pharmaceutical benefits for their employees.

Wygod's plan was simple. The local druggist would fill the prescriptions for drugs that patients needed immediately but his managed-care firm would fill the 75 percent of prescriptions that are for "maintenance" drugs which Medco can dispense to employees from one of its 11 regional pharmacies. By specializing in maintenance drugs and encouraging customers to use generics, Medco claims it can save its customers 20 percent or more over what a local druggist charges.

Because of its large volume purchases, Medco was able to obtain lower prices from some pharmaceutical manufacturers. In an attempt to maintain the cost advantages of its program over local druggists, Medco has tried to influence which drug doctors prescribe. This is something a local druggist, especially one in a small town, would find difficult to do.

For example, when a doctor prescribes a medicine that doesn't provide a special volume discount to Medco, one of the Medco pharmacists goes into action. After checking the patient's medical history that was filed when the patient joined the program, the Medco pharmacist telephones the doctor and suggests a less expensive, but equally effective, therapeutic alternative. The choice of drugs is still left with the doctor, but the doctor will switch to the lower cost product in the majority of cases.

The close of 1990 saw Robert Piekos in his mid fifties and getting tired of seeing every day as a struggle for survival. His father, now in his eighties and living alone in Houston, called him to say that he had heard of a job opening for a manager with one of the nation's large mail-order fulfillment centers in Houston. Did Robert want to forget about the day-to-day pressures of running a small town drugstore and move to Houston?

After thinking about his father's offer for a couple of weeks, Robert decided that being a small town druggist wasn't so bad a life. After all, the changes that were causing so much trouble in the industry weren't really bothering him. The discounters had stayed out of Muleshoe and Revco had even left Clovis. Fine-tuning his retailing mix had resulted in a large retention of his customer base, especially the senior citizens who had the highest needs.

Robert had recently joined a group of smaller chain and independent pharmacists to create a company to compete for prescription drug programs offered by corporate health care plans. The purpose of starting the organization was to enable the "mom and pop" drugstores, like Muleshoe Drug, to become more competitive by achieving the buying scale efficiencies of the larger chains. This way, he was even able to profitably serve, albeit at a lower margin, the Medicaid and insurance provider plans. "As long as those damn mail-order plans stay out of Muleshoe," Robert said as he headed home one night after making his decision, "I can survive."

Muleshoe Drug Store (1991-1995)

The competitive situation stayed largely the same through the early part of the 1990s for Muleshoe Drug. Sales held steady but the profit margin in 1993, as shown in Exhibit 2, fell to 3.6 percent on sales of $784,108. Still $28,224 was a nice profit to add to the salary Robert paid himself. And besides, Muleshoe was a low cost place to live and his house was paid for.

Piekos didn't even seem to mind that nearly 60 percent of American workers covered by health insurance had a managed-care drug benefit plan, or the recent moves by drug manufacturers to acquire managed-care providers. In 1993, Merck acquired Medco. In 1994 Eli Lilly and SmithKline Beechham acquired PCS Health Systems, a unit of McKesson, and Diversified Pharmaceutical Services, the number two and three players in the field, respectively. The major purpose of these moves was to provide preferential access to large buying groups for the manufacturers' drugs. Such acquisitions would also enable the manufacturers to learn more about the usefulness and cost advantages of their products by tapping the enormous electronic records database of patient and physician behavior that these plans had accumulated over the years. By both tying up large groups of drug purchasers and fostering a price-competitive environment, this industry re-alignment would further damage the profitability of small town operators like Piekos.

Still believing that such damage was still years away as he prepared for the 1994 Christmas season, Robert Piekos was at peace with the world. Then it happened!

Late one Tuesday night in early November, Billy Bob Burke called Robert to tip him off to an unsettling school board decision. Billy Bob, one of Robert's golfing buddies, had been on the Muleshoe Independent School District (MISD) Board for 20 years and for the first time he felt that his vote was going to hurt the community. He told Robert that in order to make up for shortfalls in the state's funding of local school districts, the board was forced to cut the budget by five percent. One of the things they voted on that night was to change insurance carriers. As part of the new package, school employees would only have their prescriptions covered if they used a mail-order firm. Under the new plan scheduled to begin in September 1995, school employees using the mail-order firm would get generic drugs for $2 and brand-name pharmaceuticals would cost $10 for a 90-day supply. All prescriptions purchased at Muleshoe Drug would be subject to the employee's $500 deductible. Burke told Robert that he was sorry about voting to hurt a local business, especially one that had been such a strong supporter of the school, but he had a duty to the district's students and employees.

For Robert the news meant the end of the world. MISD was the county's largest employer covering 114 families, nearly all of whom had used Robert's store in the past. The next morning he called both his trade association and the local realtor and listed his business. Still he wasn't very confident that he would find a buyer in the near future, especially when word got out about what the school board had done.

Muleshoe Drug Store (1995)

For Mike Rowley, the news about Muleshoe Drug couldn't have come at a better time. For the past two years, the Lubbock native had wanted to return to West Texas and get out of the Midwestern winters. Besides, Kay, who had graduated with a marketing degree from Drake University and had spent seven years with Procter & Gamble, had family in Clovis. Together they thought they could make good with the drugstore. Unlike Robert Piekos, Mike actually believed that mail-order would not capture over 50 percent of the prescription drug business, but would taper off and remain between 15 and 20 percent. Having once worked in the area, Mike believed that mail-order was too inconvenient for the customer and that only a small percentage of customers expressed satisfaction with the service.

That night Mike and Kay wrote down what they considered to be the keys to success for Muleshoe Drug.

Here is what Mike and Kay plan to do with Muleshoe Drug:

1. Provide SUPERIOR SERVICE (and try to convince the local citizens this service is worth any slightly higher prices). The entire pharmacy industry is slowly moving toward compensation for cognitive services such general advice on how to take combinations of drugs, evaluating alternative drugs, and providing information on how to spot and prevent adverse reactions from prescription drugs. Even insurance plans are starting to compensate for these services, since they save money in the long-run.

2. Work with local physicians to develop a list of "quality" generic drugs that could be less costly to the patient, while providing a significantly larger gross margin for the drug store.

3. Diversify the store's services to include Home Health Care, I.V. maintenance, and Nursing Home Fulfillment and Consulting.

4. Introduce a program for overnight mail of prescription drugs to neighboring towns, using standard U.S. postage. After all, we are still the only drugstore in the county and 1 of only 14 in the 480 sq. mile triangle between Amarillo, Lubbock, and Clovis.

5. Join every health care plan available. The increase in volume will more than offset the decrease in profit margin per prescription.

6. Directly address the MISD's insurance carrier decision. Work with other Muleshoe merchants to convince the school board that they should support the community if they want continued support from local businesses. In addition to providing local service, Mike would match the mail-order firm's prices.

7. Streamline the store's inventory. Mike, after looking at Robert Piekos's current inventory, believed that he could lower average inventory from $125,000 to $90,000 by limiting the selection, not only in general merchandise lines but in pharmaceutical lines as well. After all, why should the store carry 27 different SKUs in toothpaste. Mike believed that reducing this to 11 would still enable him to cover all the major brands and sizes. Furthermore, Mike believed that since he would have a close working relationship with the customers he could sometimes get by not being able to completely fill every prescription at once. For example, for some seldom-used drugs he could give the customer a couple of days' supply and order the rest from wholesalers in Lubbock or Amarillo. He would then deliver the rest to the customer's home and reinforce his service image.

8. Develop a closer working relationship with the local nursing home. By law, these establishments must have a registered pharmacist review each patient's prescription records every month. In the past, Muleshoe Drug provided the prescriptions for these patients. However, the nursing home used the services of a health care provider to review each patient's records. Mike felt it was important for him to provide this service, even at the lowest cost allowed by law ($2 per patient per month) in order to prevent others from making in-roads into his market. Besides, Mike didn't want a discounter from Clovis to capture this otherwise profitable segment.

9. Finally, Mike and Kay would attempt to become active members of as many civic and community organizations as possible. After all, this was still the best way to develop relationships with the customer.

Kay and Mike both agreed that in the future, the surviving drugstores will be similar in price and that it will be the services offered that provide the differential advantage. The profitable pharmacies will be the ones that have a marketing program that generates repeat business. Pharmacies in the future will be reimbursed for cognitive services and the mail-order business, such as provided by Medco, will become a jungle as more firms keep trying to enter the field.

Questions for Discussion

1. Do you believe that Mike and Kay are right about mail-order fulfillment tapering off, or was Robert Piekos right? Explain your reasoning.

2. If Mike and Kay were your relatives, would you lend them money to purchase Muleshoe Drug? Can they make a success of this venture?

3. How has the changing environment (consumer, technological, competition, legal) altered the structure of the drug distribution channel?

4. What other environmental changes do you foresee in the future and how will these impact the channel for prescription drugs?

Figure 1

County Population	
Bailey	8,168
Lamb	18,669
Castro	10,556
Parmer	11,033

City Populations	
Muleshoe	4,851
Amarillo	151,252
Lubbock	189,374
Clovis	31,053

Exhibit 1
1960 Gross Margin Contribution
by Product Line

Product Line	Sales	Percentage of Total Sales	Gross Margin Percentage	Gross Dollars
Pharmacy	$112,013	40%	37%	$41,445
Cosmetics/toiletries	69,984	25%	30%	20,995
Fountain	22,453	8%	N/A	(573)
Tobacco	19,602	7%	25%	4,900
OTC	19,541	7%	31%	6,058
Gifts - Candy	16,848	6%	20%	3,370
Vet supplies	11,153	4%	28%	3,123
Magazine	8,427	3%	22%	1,886
	$280,021	100%	29%	$81,204
		Total Operating Expenses		**$58,526**
		Net Profit		**$22,678**

Exhibit 2
1993 Gross Margin Contribution
by Product Line

Product Line	Sales	Percentage of Total Sales	Gross Margin Percentage	Gross Dollars
Pharmacy	$431,273	55%	30%	$128,051
OTC	86,209	11%	19%	16,651
Cosmetics/toiletries	118,691	15%	30%	35,208
Greeting cards/gifts/ candy	39,205	5%	40%	15,682
Video rentals	38,980	5%	9%	3,508
Magazine/other front end	37,720	5%	38%	14,501
Fountain	32,030	4%	N/A	(1,907)
	$784,108	100%	27%	$211,694
		Total Operating Expenses		**$183,470**
		Net Profit		**$28,224**

A.B.KING'S
By Robert F. Lusch, University of Oklahoma

In mid 1994, Vance Womack, menswear buyer at A. B. King's, requested permission from the general merchandise manager to change the present pricing policy on men's suits. Womack felt that a change in pricing was necessary due to increased local competition in this merchandise category.

Background

A. B. King's is a locally owned and operated full-line department store in a midwestern city of approximately 250,000 inhabitants. The store was founded by Alfred Bailey King in 1902. The store remains in its original downtown location and is still primarily owned and operated by the King family. Tom King, the grandson of A. B. King, is the current president and chief executive officer. In 1993, annual sales approached $15 million. The company has consistently shown a profit every year since 1902 except 1932, 1933,1957, and 1990.

Since 1978, competition has intensified in King's trading area, which happens to be its entire MSA. Sears remodeled its downtown store and opened another store in a regional shopping mall on the outskirts of the city. In addition, Kmart has built three new stores since 1980. Specialty store competition has also intensified, especially in women's apparel and menswear. A. B. King's has always been one of the most fashionable places for upper-middle and upper-class residents to purchase their clothing. Several generations of families have purchased their clothing at King's.

In the area of menswear, one competitor that has grown to be a dominant market leader is Franklin's. Franklin's is a locally owned company founded in 1969. The store sells only menswear and women's apparel in about a 65/35 mix. Franklin's first store was located downtown, directly across the street from A. B. King's. In 1980, its sales were $1.8 million. Today Franklin's has a total of five stores, and in 1993 its sales were $9.7 million. Franklin's sells moderate-to-good quality clothing at a relatively low markup. It is very promotion and price-oriented and concentrates on high inventory turnover. Recently, Franklin's introduced a line of high-grade men's suits priced at $279, which most local retailers (including A. B. King's) sell in the $325 to $425 price range. This line has been heavily promoted in the local newspaper.

Current Situation

Vance Womack is concerned about the sales performance of the men's suit lines at A. B. King's. In 1989, King's sold 1445 suits, but in 1991 that number dropped to 1208, and in 1993 suit sales were only 940. 1994 results look even less promising.

On July 24, 1994, Vance wrote a memo to John Stern, the general merchandise manager, about this slackening of demand.

Memorandum

TO: John Stern, General Merchandise Manager
FROM: Vance Womack, Buyer, Menswear

It is time we came up with a strategy to combat our declining sales of men's suits. The inroads that Franklin's and other specialty stores are making into our market share is increasingly becoming a problem. We continue to hold on to our loyal patrons, but the transient, bargain-seeking shopper is being intercepted by competition. The problem is not one of poor buying. We have as good a selection and assortment of suits as anyone in town. Our sales assistance and alteration department are superior. In short, I believe we are simply not price-competitive. Given the level of competition, our present prices are simply too high.

Stern immediately phoned Womack and told him that he concurred with his observation. He instructed Womack to put together relevant merchandising statistics for men's suits for the first six months of 1994 and also to develop hypothetical merchandising statistics based on his proposed price changes. These statistics are provided in Exhibits 1 and 2.

After Womack started to compile these statistics, he realized that A. B. King's did not have the selection he had initially thought it had, especially in the moderate to lower-price range. In fact, it currently had no suits priced under $189. As a result, two lower-price lines were added--one at $139 and another at $109, and the $189 line was reduced to $169. Neither of these lines was expected to be a best-seller, but Womack thought they might help to generate more traffic in the menswear department.

Womack also suggested an increased level of advertising. Currently, advertising of men's suits had been averaging 1.9 percent of net sales. Womack proposed this be increased to 3.8 percent of net sales. Most of the advertising would be directed at the $298 and $398 lines and the $109 and $139 lines. Some consideration was given to putting the $109 line in a new "bargain basement" department of the store, but Womack felt this would defeat the purpose of generating more traffic in the upstairs menswear department.

Questions for Discussion

1. Why did A. B. King's wait so long to respond to its declining sales volume in men's suits?

2. Will the price cuts be profitable?

3. How will competition react to the price cuts?

4. What are the pros and cons of advertising both high and low-priced men's suits?

5. What are the pros and cons of starting a "bargain basement" department?

Exhibit 1
Merchandising Statistics for
Men's Suits (1/1/94 - 6/30/94)

Price Unit	Cost Range (billed cost)	Average Markup*	Average Unit Stock	Unit Sales	Workroom Cost Per Unit	Cash Discounts (as % of billed costs)	Retail Reductions (as % of original retail)#
$419	$200 - 240	$213	60	50	$21	2%	8.1%
329	160 - 199	155	90	108	18	2	9.8
259	125 - 159	118	120	154	13	2	18.1
189	90 - 124	80	70	47	12	2	19.4

*Average markup represents original markup over original billed cost.
#Retail reductions include markdowns, employee discounts, and shortages as a percent of original retail.

Exhibit 2
Projected Annual Performance on Men's Suits

Price Line	Cost Range (billed cost)	Average Markup*	Planned Unit Stock	Planned Unit Sales	Planned Workroom Cost per Unit	Cash Discounts (as % of billed cost)	Planned Reductions (as % of original retail)#
$398	$200 - 240	$184	78	140	$20	2%	3.1%
298	160 - 199	124	96	312	16	2	6.2
219	125 - 159	78	128	420	12	2	10.4
169	90 - 124	60	96	164	11	2	9.8
139	84 - 99	49	96	140	9	2	6.1
109	64 - 83	37	78	116	9	2	5.1

*Average markup represents original markup over original billed cost.
#Retail reductions include markdowns, employee discounts, and shortages as a percent of original retail.

OAKLAND DEPARTMENT STORE
By Robert F. Lusch, University of Oklahoma

Rodney Hayes is the merchandise manager of the shoe department for Oakland Department Store, which is located in a large metropolitan city of more than 750,000 people in the southwestern U.S. Oakland has 250,000 total square feet of floor space, and 80 percent is selling space. In 1994, the store had $49 million in sales, and 3.8 percent of this total was attributed to the shoe department. The shoe department occupies 6500 square feet of selling floor space. The 1994 income statement for Oakland Department Store is presented in Exhibit 1.

Hayes is currently in the process of preparing a merchandise budget for the 1995 fall/winter selling season. The fall/winter season consists of the months of August through January; the spring/summer season consists of the months of February through July. The distribution of sales for the fall/winter season for the last three years is presented in Exhibit 2.

Toni McClain, the store controller, has informed all department managers that overall store sales in 1995 should be 5 to 6 percent above 1994. This forecast is based on an assumption of continued moderate inflation and increased competition. Oakland Department Store has been especially hard hit by a growing number of price- and promotion-oriented retailers such as Mervyn's and factory outlet malls. Also, a growing number of specialty shoe stores, such as Thom McAn, Athlete's Foot, and Open Country have had a detrimental impact on the performance of the shoe department at Oakland. Over the last 10 years, the shoe department has generally experienced a rate of annual growth in sales lower than the overall growth in store sales (see Exhibit 3).

Since 1990, the shoe department has used a 55 percent planned initial markup for preparing its seasonal merchandise budget. However, Hayes is considering raising this to 60 percent because of the increased level of markdowns over the last several years, the result of increasing competition. When Hayes mentioned to McClain his desire to raise the initial markup to 60 percent, she suggested that a better solution may be to cut the initial markup to 50 percent. She argued that lower everyday prices should reduce the need for markdowns and might also result in higher sales. Actual reductions from the initial markup for the 1994 fall/winter season are presented in Exhibit 4.

In prior years, the seasonal merchandise budget for the shoe department was prepared using the beginning-of-the-month stock/sales ratios as shown in Exhibit 5. This year, Hayes is contemplating using the basic stock method to develop the seasonal merchandise plan because this method allows him to plan for a target stockturn. Hayes is especially concerned about achieving a planned stockturn of 2.5 times per year because this is one of the standards by which senior management will evaluate his performance. Management has also established a 40 percent target gross margin for the shoe department. Hayes was told to plan to have beginning-of-the-month retail stock of $400,000 for February 1995.

Hayes is somewhat concerned about his ability to achieve a 40 percent gross margin and retail stockturn of 2.5, since he has no control over advertising expenditures. In 1994, his department was allocated $29,000 for advertising for the fall/winter season. Hayes believes that if he could double his advertising, sales would grow by at least 20 percent.

It was five days before his merchandise budget was due to McClain when Hayes realized that his long-term future at Oakland was to be largely determined by his ability to reverse the declining performance of the shoe department. He wanted to develop a no-nonsense merchandise budget to convince McClain that his department required special resources and attention.

Questions for Discussion

1. Prepare two seasonal merchandise budgets for the Oakland shoe department, using the BOM stock method and the basic stock method. Which budget should Hayes submit to McClain?

2. How can Hayes convince McClain of the need to double the advertising budget for the shoe department?

3. What should the planned initial markup be?

Exhibit 1
Oakland Department Store
1994 Income Statement

Gross Sales	$50,210,000
Less: Return and Allowances	1,210,000
Net Sales	49,000,000
Less: Cost of Goods Sold	32,095,000
Gross Profit	16,905,000
Less: Operating Expenses	13,720,000
Net Profit (before taxes)	$ 3,185,000

Exhibit 2
Oakland Department Store Shoe Department
Distribution of Annual Sales by Month

Year	Aug	Sept	Oct	Nov	Dec	Jan
1992	10.1 %	9.2 %	6.3 %	8.4 %	8.0 %	5.9 %
1993	10.1	9.1	6.5	8.2	8.1	6.0
1994	9.9	9.4	6.4	8.3	8.2	5.8

Exhibit 3
Oakland Department Store
Sales Growth (1985- 1994)

Year	Total Store	Shoe Department
1985	6.4%	5.2%
1986	11.8	10.3
1987	12.1	11.4
1988	10.3	10.1
1989	4.9	5.0
1990	6.2	5.7
1991	7.9	6.3
1992	11.2	9.8
1993	10.1	6.9
1994	7.3	5.4

Exhibit 4
Oakland Department Store Shoe Department
Reductions from Initial Markup (1994)

Reductions	Aug	Sept	Oct	Nov	Dec	Jan
Markdowns	12.1 %	12.4 %	18.2 %	11.5 %	11.0 %	17.5 %
Discounts	5.0	4.0	4.5	5.0	5.0	3.0
Shortages	1.0	.9	1.0	1.0	1.0	.9

Exhibit 5
Oakland Department Store Shoe Department
BOM Stock/Sales Ratios

Month	BOM Ratio
August	5.34
September	5.01
October	4.45
November	5.95
December	5.84
January	4.10

SELFHELP CRAFTS OF THE WORLD*

By Shelley M. Rinehart, E. Stephen Grant, University of New Brunswick

In March 1990, Sue Daley, manager of SELFHELP Crafts of the World, Saint John, New Brunswick, hung up the telephone and breathed a sigh of relief. She had just been speaking with a faculty member from the local university and had agreed to allow a group of marketing students to develop a comprehensive marketing strategy for the store. This was welcome news to Sue because she had to address the Board of Directors in four weeks and they were expecting a document that would outline Sue's proposed marketing strategy for the upcoming year. The Board expected this document to include recommendations on alternative locations to meet increased space requirements as well as strategy adjustments resulting from these recommendations.

Background

SELFHELP Crafts was a job creation program founded by the Mennonite Central Committee, the relief and service organization of Mennonite and Brethren in Christ Churches. It was established in 1946. The purpose of the SELFHELP organization was to provide "fair paying employment"[1] for those in less-developed countries to help them exert control over their lives and meet their basic physical needs. SELFHELP Crafts saw themselves as working toward long-term stability rather than as a "short-term fix."

SELFHELP Crafts was a nonprofit organization with outlets and representatives throughout Canada and the U.S. Most people involved in the organization, including clerks in the retail outlets, came from a variety of backgrounds and religious denominations, and worked as volunteers.

SELFHELP Crafts was involved with over 65 producer groups in a number of countries. Therefore, a wide variety of products, ranging from children's toys to hand made tablecloths, were available. SELFHELP encouraged groups to use traditional skills in goods production so that their material culture would be maintained rather than changed. The groups represented were diverse and changed continually. Once members of a producer group had gained enough skills to function effectively on their own, SELFHELP withdrew their support and sought another group in need of assistance.

The Saint John Retail Outlet

The Saint John, New Brunswick, Canada outlet began operations in October 1988. It was only the second outlet to be established east of Ontario. The other outlet was located in Petitcodiac, just outside of Moncton, New Brunswick, approximately 130 kilometers from Saint John. The Saint John outlet operated under the direction of a 12-member Board. It had a directory of 140 volunteers, 60 of whom were active. The city of Saint John, with an approximate population of 77,000 people, provided a large base from which to attract volunteers. SELFHELP also drew volunteers from areas outside the city limits such as Rothesay, Hampton and Quispamsis.

SELFHELP Crafts of the World, Saint John, had recently celebrated its first year in business. First year sales had surpassed all expectations. However, Sue realized that if the store was to enjoy continued success, there were a number of problems that needed to be dealt with immediately. Sue believed that by combining her knowledge of the store's operations with the students' business skills, she could successfully address these problems. A problem common to most nonprofit organizations and many private enterprises is that there never seems to be enough money--certainly not enough to hire professional business consultants to develop strategic plans. SELFHELP Crafts of the World was no exception. Sue could not help but wonder if the outlet would have had higher sales if they had hired experts in marketing and retail management

---

[1] Fair Paying Employment: to pay individuals fair market value for their labor as defined by the individuals' domestic economy.

prior to beginning operations. She believed that both she and the volunteers who worked in the store would have benefited from this type of outside consultation.

Sue decided it was useless to dwell on the past, and began to develop a list of issues to be addressed in the store's strategic plan. She realized that if the store were to exceed or even maintain its current sales volume, a new, larger, location would have to be identified and an organized promotional campaign put in place. Compared to other outlets, the Saint John store had performed extremely well. However, as with most businesses, growth was a definite goal. Sue was also concerned about the store's current method of inventory control.

Board of Directors

The Board of Directors for SELFHELP Crafts of the World, Saint John, was made up of individuals from the business community and other members who were familiar with the characteristics of developing countries. Brian Elliot was the Maritime Representative, Mennonite Central Committee, and he and Sue served as exofficio Board members.

The Board had multi-denominational representation in keeping with the organization's bylaws, which stipulated that at any one time representation from at least five denominations was necessary. Only one board member was of the Mennonite faith, which made the Saint John outlet unique when compared to its counterparts.

The Board consisted of a president, vice president, secretary, and treasurer. Board members who missed more than three meetings without a valid reason were asked to resign their positions. Members met on a monthly basis and operated as a working Board. Board members not only worked in the store, but were also expected to help clean and count inventory.

Volunteers

SELFHELP Crafts was constantly seeking volunteers, especially those with some retail expertise or experience. Volunteers were expected to educate themselves on the background of the producer groups and the products sold in the store. Pamphlets and information cards describing producer groups and product origin and care were available to consumers who purchased the items. There was also a master text that volunteers were expected to be familiar with that acted as a reference for volunteers to help them answer customers' questions regarding products, producers, and host countries. The tasks of the volunteers were quite similar to those of any employee in the retailing industry.

Products

SELFHELP Crafts of the World offered a wide, dynamic selection of products. The product line included hand-crafted jewelry and baskets, hand-woven mats, lace tablecloths, clothing, items carved from rare woods such as teak and ebony, ceremonial masks, and greeting cards. There were even some foodstuffs such as packaged wild rice. The assortment of products changed as producers were dropped and new ones added. At times the products available were so unique that not even the staff were quite sure of the product's purpose. For example, one year at Christmas, banana leaves formed into circular shapes were received. The staff, believing they were wreaths, decorated them with ribbon and Christmas decorations. The "wreaths" sold quickly. The staff later learned that these circular forms were in fact meant to be used as trivets to keep hot pots from burning the table surface.

All products sold in the outlets were expected to meet national safety standards. This was occasionally a problem for SELFHELP until the organization could convince producer groups to raise the quality, change the design, or use different raw materials to produce their goods. For example, some children's toys received by the Saint John outlet were removed from the shelves because they were too small and therefore deemed dangerous for young children by Canadian standards. In such cases it was SELFHELP Crafts Canada who absorbed the loss. Another product restriction originated from the organization itself. In keeping with the Christian faith, SELFHELP outlets would not carry any violent products such as toy guns for children.

Distribution

All SELFHELP Crafts retail outlets purchased their products from the national office of SELFHELP Crafts Canada in New Hamburg, Ontario. The national office provided a central warehouse for all goods shipped into Canada. It also handled all purchasing from producers. Each retail outlet could place its orders based on items available and quantities available for each item. Each outlet was given equal access to the various items, but was encouraged to carry a minimum number of the products available. This policy was meant to ensure that each outlet would carry a variety of products and that no one outlet had the advantage of carrying only "good sellers." Once products were ordered, it was the responsibility of each outlet to arrange delivery. Any loss or damage of goods during transportation was the responsibility of the individual store.

Location

SELFHELP Crafts, Saint John, was located at 114 Prince William Street in a protected area of the downtown core of Saint John called Trinity Royal (see Exhibit 1). Since it was one of the preservation areas in Saint John, a number of restrictions were placed on businesses operating there. The original design of fronts of historic buildings had to be maintained as much as possible, signs had to meet certain requirements, and hours had to be consistent.

Various offices, restaurants, and specialty shops were located in the Trinity Royal area. These specialty shops included office supply stores, retail outlets carrying hand crafts and decorative items, antique shops, and clothing boutiques. Three of the city's major employers were located within walking distance of that area, along with numerous smaller employers, three high schools, and two of the city's major shopping complexes. Consumer traffic was heavy in the downtown area, especially during lunch hours and on Saturdays (see Exhibit 2).

The outlet itself was very small, consisting of only 640 square feet, a portion of which was taken up by the restroom, office, and storage area (see Exhibit 3). Sue Daley saw this as one of the greatest problems she faced in the operation of the store. Because there was too little storage space, Sue had to store some products at her home and transport them back to the outlet on an "as needed" basis. Sue would often make a special trip to her home to get a particular item requested by a customer, only to find that the customer had changed his/her mind. This was not only inconvenient, it made accurate inventory control difficult or impossible.

The store was currently using a manual inventory control system. This system had proven inefficient for a number of reasons. The description given on the packing slips was often insufficient to accurately identify the packaged items. Once inventory was confirmed as received, it was placed either in storage or into stock. Stock was reordered on the basis of visual inspections of the store. Items were reordered if the visual inspection suggested a low inventory, or if they were "fast sellers." This made it difficult to determine what portion of absent items had been sold, as opposed to broken or stolen. This system depended heavily on Sue Daley's ability to remember whether the item had been sold, was still in the store, or was at home.

Most of the outlet's furnishings were obtained as "gifts-in-kind." For example, Mark's Work Warehouse, a local outlet of a national clothing retailer, donated a number of shelving units when they moved to a new location. The main cash counter was an old lab desk donated by the local community college, and the curtains were made by a volunteer using imperfect material and remnants from a local fabric store. Shelf coverings and window displays were made from donated scraps of fabric. Despite the use of donated and used items, the products were quite attractively displayed, although somewhat crowded. Almost every available inch of floor and wall space was in use. Additional shelving space and display areas were obtained by using items that were for sale such as wicker bookshelves. This caused problems because when the furnishings were sold, the volunteers had to find another way to display or store the products.

Sue had been looking for a larger location or a storage facility that was near the outlet. She believed that it was important for the store to remain in the same general area. This would minimize confusion for customers who were just becoming familiar with SELFHELP Crafts. Past searches for a new location had been futile: either the rental fees were too high, the spaces were too small, or the traffic volume was much lower than in the current location. Property rental fees were extremely high in the downtown area and lease requirements were restrictive. In many locations, business hours were determined by building owners or retail associations. Rents in the downtown area ranged from $500 per month to $30 per square foot of retail space per month. Exhibit 4 provides information on selected rental spaces that were available as of March 1, 1990.

The hours of operation in the current location had to be consistent with those of other businesses operating in the Trinity Royal area. The hours changed seasonally and during some special occasions the store was open on Sunday. Typically the store was open Monday to Thursday 10:00 a.m. to 5:00 p.m., Friday 10:00 a.m. to 8:00 p.m., and Saturday 12:00 p.m. to 4:00.p.m. Volunteers were asked to work four-hour shifts. Scheduling problems arose, especially during the summer months due to vacations, etc. Since only 60 volunteers were active, and since these individuals were volunteering their time, schedules had to be both convenient and flexible. Board members were expected to work in the store and when there were no available volunteers, Sue had to be available. Volunteers were not expected to work alone in the store; normally there were two or three people working at a time.

Pricing

The national office of SELFHELP Crafts Canada was responsible for pricing all products distributed in Canada. All products were therefore priced consistently throughout the Canadian outlets, and were priced before being delivered to the individual outlets. This price was calculated by adding 25 percent to the cost of the goods to the retail outlet. This 25 percent markup was meant to provide the outlet with enough resources to meet its expenses, including shipping, export duties, overhead, and taxes. SELFHELP Crafts, Saint John, also sold a few items that did not come from the producer groups. These were complementary items such as candles for candle holders available in the store. These items were priced competitively with other stores selling the same or similar products in the area.

Finances

SELFHELP Crafts, Saint John, began operations in October 1988 with approximately $9000 to cover startup costs. This money was obtained through personal loans from third-party donors. These loans were to be paid back within two to three years at zero percent interest (see Exhibit 5).

The store, although one of the smallest, had sales that made it one of the top four outlets in Canada in 1988/89. This was surprising since it was the first year of operation and an extremely small percentage of the Saint John population was of the Mennonite faith. Sales appeared to follow a cyclical pattern typical of the retail industry in general where sales were low from January through April, rose during the summer months and peaked during the Christmas season.

More money was needed to realize the promotional, educational, and sales objectives of SELFHELP Crafts. The organization had two primary objectives. Education was one objective in that it sought to educate society about the purpose of SELFHELP Craft's activities. Its other objective was to increase awareness and stimulate sales for the retail outlets. This, in turn, would benefit the producer groups and move them closer to self sufficiency.

Because there was only a 25 percent margin to work with, the budgeting process took on particular importance for SELFHELP, Saint John. Sue Daley was also concerned with the limited amount of capital (see Exhibit 5). She feared that this lack of capital would restrict her ability to accomplish the objectives of the organization. She also feared that a change of location could result in increased overhead expenses, and make even greater demands on the available capital. Sue recognized that a change of location would require additional promotional expenditures to ensure that existing customers were aware of the store's new location, as well as to encourage new consumers to make their first visit.

Promotion

Because education, increased awareness, and sales were such important promotional objectives for SELFHELP, Sue and Lieth Box, education chairperson for SELFHELP Crafts Saint John, were active public speakers to various groups in the greater Saint John area. These groups included church groups, senior citizen's clubs, university and community college classes, and service clubs. A typical presentation would include an explanation of the SELFHELP Crafts concept, its purpose, organization, and history. These presentations also included a display of various products and descriptions of the producer groups. A slide presentation was occasionally given, time permitting. Sue and Lieth gave approximately 60 presentations during the first year of operation in Saint John.

SELFHELP Crafts relied heavily on publicity. When the store celebrated its grand opening, it received a great deal of publicity in the local newspapers as well as on the local television channels. The Saint John outlet had a number of press releases, and an article that promoted the outlet as a good place to purchase Christmas gifts was published in the December 1989 issue of the *Atlantic Advocate*, a regional publication (see Appendix A).

Sue had appeared a number of times on a local noon-hour talk show to discuss the SELFHELP concept, the outlet's activities, new producer groups, new products, or upcoming events associated with SELFHELP Crafts. She expected to make another appearance soon. The local cable community channel frequently aired a 45-minute, documentary style piece about the store, and Maritime Independent Television had often provided news coverage on the store. The store had bought a few newspaper advertisements, but due to cost and budget restrictions these advertisements were kept to a minimum.

SELFHELP Crafts also used a variety of pamphlets as promotional and educational tools. Pamphlets were provided with every purchase to ensure that the consumer received information on the origin and care of the products purchased. These pamphlets were product specific. A variety of other pamphlets were available that described the SELFHELP concept and its purpose. All promotional pamphlets were produced by a printing company that was sympathetic to the organization's cause and were distributed, free of charge, through the national office of SELFHELP. SELFHELP, Saint John, also used locally produced inserts in area church bulletins to promote the outlet and its products.

Since SELFHELP Crafts was located in Trinity Royal, the Association of Trinity Royal businesses afforded SELFHELP a number of promotional opportunities. During Trinity Royal Days all shops in the area remained open on Sunday. While consumers could not make purchases, due to Day of Rest restrictions, they could browse and obtain information from the clerks on duty in the store. The event was well promoted in the newspapers and on radio, with costs shared among all participating businesses.

A Look to the Future

Sue Daley's dream was to find a new location with at least 2000 square feet. In the new store, she wanted to have adequate storage facilities coupled with a more progressive system of inventory control. She also wanted to see room for a repair shop that would permit damaged goods to be repaired on the premises rather than taken home. In the retail portion of the new premises, Sue wanted enough room to display the available products in a more complimentary manner. She wanted to be able to set up educational and promotional displays in the store to give customers more information on the concept, as well as on the individual producer groups and their products.

Sue hoped that community awareness of SELFHELP Crafts would increase in the future, and that increased awareness would translate into more business for the store. Sue realized that well planned promotion was necessary for the success of any business, nonprofit or private. She also realized that if the store relocated, promotional activities would become even more important. However, the limited cash flow of SELFHELP imposed significant restrictions on promotional activities. Another complication was that Sue was not really sure who her customers were or how to reach them. Given the low number of Mennonites in the area, SELFHELP Crafts, Saint John, had to push their products and the concept much more aggressively than outlets in other centers.

Questions for Discussion

1. How do the operations of SELFHELP, Saint John, differ from the operations of a comparable for-profit organization?

2. What factors must be considered when searching for a new retail location? What impact will each of these factors have on sales performance? Why? What can SELFHELP do to lessen the impact of a change in store location?

3. How can consumer awareness of the SELFHELP concept be increased in general, and specifically, the Saint John retail outlet? What promotional activities do you believe are the most appropriate? Why?

4. Are the financial resources of the organization currently being allocated to their best potential? Why or why not?

Exhibit 1
SELFHELP Crafts
Map of Saint John Uptown Core

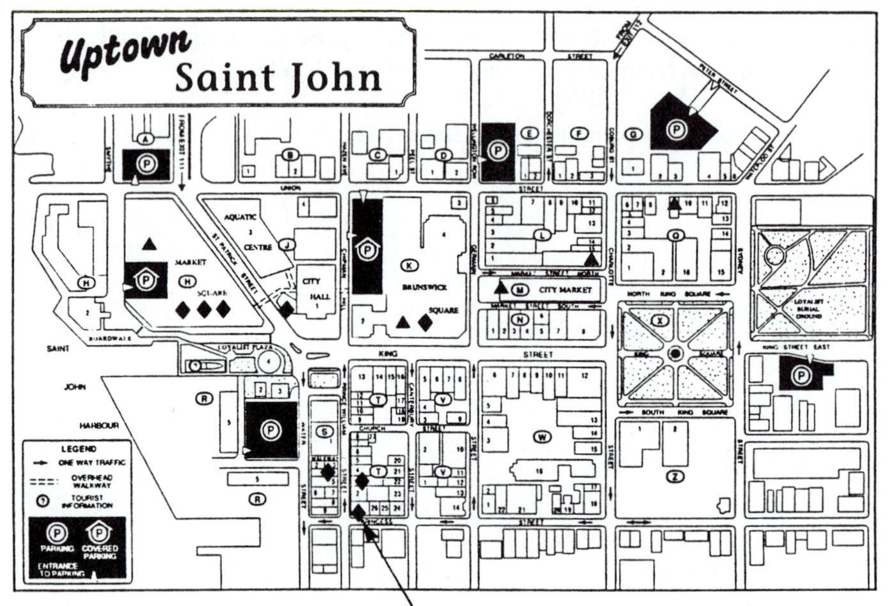

Gifts and cards Δ		**Handcrafts** ♦	
Guy Watts	Q9	Country Ceramics	K1
Holder's Cards & Gifts	H1	Country Treasures	S4
Holder's Cards & Gifts	K1	Croft House	H1
Linja Gift Shop	M	Magic Lantern	H1
Your Candle Shop	L16	**SELFHELP**	**T1**
		The Rocking Chair	T3
		The Waterside Shoppe	J2
		The Whale	H1

NOTE: Blocks T, V and W are the Trinity Royal preservation area.

Exhibit 2
SELFHELP Crafts
Excerpts from the Traffic Volume Report
(Vehicular Traffic)

Street	Traffic count (per 24 hrs)	Year of Count
Cantebury St. (Princess)	4,310	1987
Charlotte St. (Union)	5,060	1989
Duke St. (Prince William)	9,300	1989
Germain St. (Union)	6,500	1989
Germain (Princess)	3,990	1988
King St. (Market Square)	14,930	1987
King St. (Germain)	22,870	1988
King St. (Charlotte)	10,900	1989
Prince William St. (Princess)	12,980	1988
Union St. (Germain)	34,100	1989

Source: 1989 Traffic Volume Report (12th ed.). Traffic Engineering Section, City of Saint John, Engineering Department, Municipal Operations

Exhibit 3
SELFHELP Crafts
Store Layout

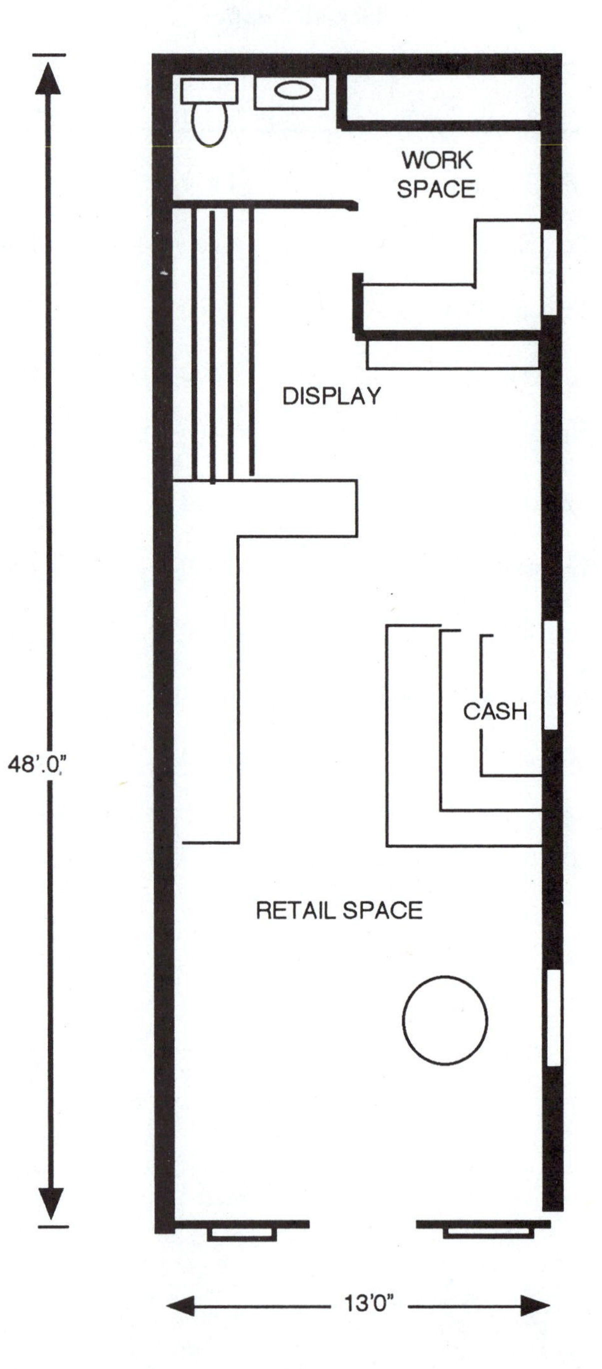

Exhibit 4
SELFHELP Crafts
Available Retail Space

LOCATION	SIZE(ft^2)	COST/ MONTH	ATTRIBUTES
Prince William St. (Between Princess Church) (T2)	2200	$1500	Tenant pays heat, site is next door to present location, has large display windows, heating costs identified as a problem by former tenants, meter parking
Canterbury St. (Between Princess and Church) (T23)	1000	$675	Heat included, attractive area, large display windows, meter parking
King St. (Between Prince William and Canterbury) (T13)	1100	$15/$ft^2$	Tenant pays heat, site is close to Prince William St. intersection and therefore near present location
Charlotte St. (Between Union and King) (L13)	1100	$900	Heat included, private office located in rear, site is in business core, meter parking
Union St. (Between Charlotte and Germain) (L10)	1000	$800	Tenant pays heat, site is from central business core and shopping district, unattractive location, meter parking
Major Downtown Shopping Centre (Facing King between Chipman Hill and Germain) (K)	5%	gross	Location determined by the mall, can be forced to move if a for profit wants to rent the space, variety of stores draw more potential consumers, meter and garage parking available
Princess St. (S9)	128	$102	Storage space only, approximately one block from current location

Exhibit 5 - SELFHELP Crafts
Financial Statements
Balance Sheet at January 31, 1990

Assets		
Current Assets		
Cash	18,277	
Inventory	41,282	
Total Current Assets		59,559
Fixed Assets		
Furniture and Equipment		2,500
Deferred Assets		
Leasehold Improvements		850
Total Assets		$62,909
Liabilities and Equities		
Liabilities		
Short-term Liabilities	10,696	
Long-term Liabilities	2,000	
Total Liabilities		12,696
Equity		
Surplus/Deficit 1988-1989	25,036	
Surplus/Deficit 1989-1990	25,177	
Total Equity		50,213
Total Liabilities and Equity		$62,909

Exhibit 5
SELFHELP Crafts (Continued)
Financial Statements
Income Statement for the Period March 1 - January 31, 1990

Revenue		
Store Sales	$184,249	
Cash Short/Over	-86	
Donations	282	
Sales Tax Commission	138	
Interest	908	
Challenge '89 Grant[1]	1,472	
Total Revenue		$186,963
Cost of Goods Sold		137,479
Gross Margin		$49,484
Operating Expenses		
Rent	5,190	
Electricity	293	
Telephone	747	
Maintenance/Supplies	2,102	
Advertising/Promotion	1,864	
Wage Related Expenses	6,681	
Travel	1,815	
Items for Resale	52	
Insurance	300	
Extraordinary Expenses	3,500	
Losses	1,763	
Total Expenses		$24,307
Net Income and Surplus		$25,177

[1] Government sponsored work program for students
(Source: Company records)

APPENDIX A
SELFHELP CRAFTS

CHRISTMAS GIFTS
From the Third World

By Carolyn Van Buskirk

In the waterfront section of Saint John, New Brunswick, a gift shop window reflects far beyond the harbor to the harsh realities of the Third World.

Cozy and unpretentious, the store's interior is a bustling maze of exotic handicrafts. Mingled with wooden elephants from India and exquisite West Bank manger scenes, are Thailand's exquisite linens, rich woolen rugs from Vietnam, plant hangers of Bangladesh jute, beaded work from the natives of Labrador, and a wealth of brass, wicker, lacquerware and basketry.

Since opening its Prince William Street doors one year ago, SELFHELP Crafts of the World has met an overwhelming demand for useful and decorative items from struggling producers in areas of extreme poverty, refugee camps and rehabilitation clinics.

Only the second shop of its kind east of Toronto (with a parent operation also located in New Brunswick at Petitcodiac), SELFHELP Crafts benefits both producer and consumer by paying a fair wage and charging a fair price. Retail markup covers shipping costs, export duty, taxes, and overhead expenses but not profit. Managed and staffed by more than 60 volunteers, it took Saint John's downtown store just 6 months to establish itself as one of the most active in Canada, ranking second in sales nationwide.

Such support and enthusiasm shocked no one more than the nucleus of organizers who, buoyed by a series of SELFHELP Craft fairs in local schools and churches, grew committed to the cause. "What began as a dream of helping the world's underprivileged to help themselves quickly became a responsibility," says manager Sue Daley, "then an obligation, and finally an obsession."

After conducting a feasibility study, the tiny group took a long, hard look at its resources and clearly came up short. Needing about $50,000 in seed money, a high-traffic location with lower overhead, display fixtures, decorating supplies, and an army of man-power--it had, in fact, nothing.

Although SELFHELP Crafts is a program of the Mennonite Central Committee, Saint John formed an inter-denominational Board of Directors with a bylaw requiring that a minimum of five denominations be represented at all times. Meanwhile, education chairman Leith Box lined up talks and slide presentations for any group willing to listen, taking along a sampling of the handiwork to be offered by the prospective store. "The key to SELFHELP," she believes, "is educating our society; making us more aware of millions of people around the world, including some parts of Canada, who do not have enough to eat, cannot afford decent housing, and have no savings to help them cope in a disaster because they don't have a job."

While sending food and money is a stop-gap measure, she says, helping through job creation and teaching self-sufficiency is the long-term solution to hunger and poverty.

As SELFHELP's speaking engagements escalated and the word spread, more and more workers enlisted. MCC's Maritime Representative Brian Elliot, of the Petitcodiac store, helped the fledgling enterprise by contributing proceeds of special sales and offering expertise. Small grants and loans from interested individuals trickled in, "but," says Mrs. Daley, "never fast enough to get on with the job at hand."

Standing at intersections, the organizers counted cars and studied traffic patterns. Finally, they agreed to search out a flat, wheelchair-accessible retail space in historic Trinity Royal.

When the City of Saint John called with a 640 sq. ft. storefront on a sunny corner, it sounded like just the thing. "Rushing to inspect the premises," she recounts, "we recoiled at the sight of silverfish, fleas, and rodents. The ceiling dropped from three different altitudes, walls were caving in, and the decor was an unbelievable blend of electric blue, yellow, and psychedelic orange."

Deflated but not defeated, they negotiated a $1500 facelift. But as one calamity led to another, the city wound up spending 10 times that amount.

Rolling up sleeves and donning coveralls, the SELFHELP troops moved in with gallons of paint supplied at cost, discarded shelving from a clothing warehouse, and light fixtures from their own family rooms. Unpacking dozens of cartons of stock ordered from the Canadian SELFHELP headquarters in New Hamburg, Ontario, they had little but imagination for conjuring creative displays. Volunteer staff attended orientation sessions focusing on theft-prevention, the backgrounds of various craft items, and cash register training.

"From opening day, however, until a cash register was generously donated to the store," muses Mrs. Daley, "we worked out of a cardboard box."

Within weeks of the store's official opening in mid October 1988, it was virtually sold out to the bare walls. Declaring a "Third World Christmas," many shoppers brought long gift lists and filled them on the spot. Others, amazed to find such unique and individually crafted items so reasonably priced, returned day after day, week after week. Desperately awaiting its next scheduled shipment, SELFHELP Crafts borrowed truckloads of stock from Petitcodiac.

"People feel good knowing their gift is giving more than once," says Pauline Steinmann, treasurer of Saint John's SELFHELP. "And they seem to really appreciate the enclosure slips available with most of the crafts--describing the area of origin, the culture of the people, and the conditions they must work under."

By avoiding sweat shops and dealing directly with co-operatives and cottage industries, SELFHELP Crafts of the World eliminates excessive middleman profits and encourages independence. As soon as new markets for a craft can be found, she explains, SELFHELP withdraws support in favor of another deserving group.

Action Bag Handicrafts, a producer group in Bangladesh, for example, requires its women crafters to put a specified portion of their wage into a savings plan. With the accumulated money, they are expected to invest in a profitable enterprise. One woman, having the imagination and foresight to buy a photocopier with her savings, is gainfully employed today in the marketplace at Saidpur.

Another woman, severely disfigured and deformed by leprosy, spends her days splashing paint onto small greeting cards at the McKean Rehabilitation Clinic in Thailand. After 30 years of exclusion from her village and "doing nothing," SELFHELP has given her "a reason to get up in the morning."

Besides being effective therapy, Miss Steinmann says, the work at such clinics restores self esteem by allowing the patient to be productive and self-supporting again.

Sixty-five producer groups are now involved in SELFHELP, including young families in the slums of Calcutta, Manila and Nairobi; displaced farmers in Central America; Palestinian refugees from West Bank; and hill-tribe peoples of Taiwan. All are required to use products only from their native country, she stresses, and must also contribute to such social and economic improvements as hygiene, nutrition, family planning, well-baby clinics, and better technology to help raise living standards.

Due to a U.S. trade embargo, $250,000 annually in Vietnamese ceramics, linens, lace, rugs, and baskets are available only in Canadian stores. And, as a subtle reminder that Third World poverty exists in Canada too, the Saint John shop carries handiwork from the Eskimos of Labrador and wild rice grown and processed by the Ojibwa Indians of Wabigoon, Ontario.

Started in 1946 as an outlet for the needlework of Puerto Rican women, SELFHELP Crafts of the World now operates 120 stores in

Canada and the U.S., supporting one family for a year with each $1000 worth sold.

"One thing our volunteers and customers share is an appreciation for living in a country where, generally speaking, we have much more than we need. It's this privilege," says Sue Daley, "that makes us painfully aware of the hardships of others and we want to give some back."

(Source: The Atlantic Advocate, December 1989)
(Reprinted with Permission)

CITY DRUGSTORES, INC.*
By Michael W. Little, and Heiko B. Wijnholds,
Virginia Commonwealth University

Background

Michael James is vice president of City Drugstores, a privately owned pharmacy chain headquartered in Fairfax, Virginia. Recently, Michael commissioned a feasibility study for a new site location. He has mixed feelings about the location, however, believing there are better opportunities elsewhere. There is some difference of opinion between Michael and his father, Morton James, who is president.

Until now, little market research has been used for store locations. In the past, Michael's father would locate a store near a major supermarket chain or in a university town. Michael strongly believes market analysis must replace this outdated type of location analysis. Michael and his father have agreed to conduct research before a decision is made on the proposed site.

Over the years, City Drugstores has grown from a single store in Fairfax to a profitable corporation with 62 stores located in central cities throughout Virginia. This expansion was due to a combination of acquisitions, mergers, and new store construction.

City Drugstores enjoys a good reputation because of its convenient locations, competitive prices, and branded product lines. Like many drugstore chains, City Drugstores has four core departments. The most profitable is prescription drugs, followed by over-the-counter drugs (OTC), cosmetics, and toiletries. Requests for prescription drugs must be presented to a registered pharmacist with a doctor's written order; whereas OTC drugs, such as pain relievers and vitamins, can be sold without such restrictions. Cosmetics and toiletries are referred to as health and beauty aids and add to a drugstore's product mix. A medium-sized store must register approximately $750,000 in sales annually to break even. A profitable store will produce $150 in annual sales per square foot of selling space, with prescription drugs as the product line most instrumental in generating volume.

The Proposed Location

Michael's father has asked him to consider a site near the local university, a state-supported institution with 15,000 students located in Fairfax. Morton James graduated from the Pharmacy School there in 1949. Recently, a fellow graduate, who is owner of Paramount Pharmacy and who wishes to retire, offered to sell James his drugstore.

Paramount Pharmacy is within one block of the university's three student residence halls and is located on the corner of a busy one-way street heading to the downtown business district. If this site were purchased, Paramount Pharmacy would be razed and a modern City Drug unit built in its place. Estimated construction costs are $950,000 and other capital needs (assets) would amount to $475,000. Annual fixed costs for operating a new drugstore are $160,000, with cost of goods expected to be 67 percent of sales and other variable costs estimated at 5 percent of sales.

Paramount Drugstore attracts a small but loyal group of low to middle-income customers and some university students and faculty. It has not been very profitable or competitive in recent years, however, despite being the only drugstore within the immediate area. For example, Paramount has not taken advantage of university health service contracts for prescription drugs, which are based on bidding. Often these contracts include prescriptions for several hundred students during the academic year.

---

* Used with permission of Michael W. Little and Heiko B. Wijnholds

Upon Michael James' urging, marketing faculty at the university were contracted for the study he and his father agreed to undertake. They decided to conduct a telephone survey of a representative sample of 200 residents living within census tracts surrounding the present Paramount Drugstore and university fringe. In addition, a survey was mailed to 250 college students living in the nearby dorms. An estimate was to be made of the traffic flow past the planned store and the proportion of customers it could attract from this traffic. A guesstimate was also to be provided on walk-in traffic from other students, faculty, and staff. With this information, annual sales potential for the proposed site could be estimated.

The Jameses must decide within 30 days whether or not to buy Paramount Drugs and build one of their own drugstores. Michael has reviewed the data that the researchers collected and needs to make a recommendation to his father.

Research Findings

A summary of responses to some key questions in the resident survey are presented in Exhibit 1. The data in Exhibit 1 are responses from households represented by randomly selected adults (18 years and older). The expenditure data represent individual purchases and have to be converted to household expenditures by multiplying by the average number of adult spenders, that is, 1.18. The average overall household size amounts to 2.27. (Hint for estimating expenditures, try to substitute average dollar amounts for the tabulated ranges.)

According to the latest U.S. Census data, the number of people living in the target area is 2949. Unfortunately, these data are four years old. The City's Planning Department has estimated that this mostly low-income population has been declining at an approximate rate of 1 percent per annum. According to the survey, the average household makes approximately 65 percent of all its drugstore purchases at one store (average purchase ratio).

In the student survey, on-campus dormitory students, as a whole, appear to have little store preference when buying prescription drugs. Approximately 28 percent of the respondents didn't purchase prescription drugs. When buying health and beauty aids, however, a significant number of respondents shop near campus. More than half the students surveyed buy something at a drugstore at least twice a week. More than one-third buy at least once a month. This indicates a sizable number of students who are frequent purchasers of drugstore products. In fact, on their last visit to a drugstore, these students spent approximately $5 on the average.

When asked if they would shop at a modern drugstore at the Paramount site, half the dormitory student respondents were not sure--implying price, product offerings, and distance as factors in their decision to shop. If the drugstore were City Drug, almost two-thirds would shop there, with about one-third undecided.

Based on the survey data, the dormitory students' total monthly per capita expenditure in drugstores is estimated at $21.80 during the regular academic year. (Academic year is 7.5 months due to Christmas and other holidays.) The average purchase ratio was found to be 60 percent while 62 percent of the students indicated they would shop at the new drugstore.

According to university records, the fall and spring dormitory population is 2232 (all singles). During the three summer months, approximately 20 percent of this number attend school and stay in the dorms. Summer students spend approximately the same (per capita) monthly amount in drugstores as regular students. Some decline in student population, including dormitories, is expected during the next 10 years.

Traffic flow past the new store is estimated at 5000 per day for approximately 300 days per year (allowing for Sundays, holidays, and bad weather). This figure includes an estimated 20 percent duplication of the student population discussed previously. It is estimated that 5 percent of this traffic results in actual store visits and purchases averaging $5 per trip.

Based on a very limited survey and some rough estimates; walk-ins, representing faculty, staff, and other students, are expected to spend roughly $30,000 per annum at drugstores in the vicinity of the intended new store.

Questions for Discussion

1. Estimate the market potential for all drugstore sales in the area and, using this figure as a base, estimate the sales potential for the new City Drugstore.

2. Determine the expected profitability of the proposed store.

3. What are the main arguments for and against locating a City Drug unit on the intended site?

4. Based on your answers to the previous questions, what should Michael James do? Why?

Exhibit 1
Summary of Responses to
Resident Survey

1. Do you buy Prescription Drugs? (n=201)

	N	%
Yes	134	67
No	67	33

2. Where Do You Buy Prescription Drugs? (n=174)

	N	%
People's Drug	46	34
City Drug	37	28
Paramount	19	14
Revco	19	14
Other	53	40

(Scores do not add up to 200% due to multiple responses.)

3. Buying Frequency and Expenditures on Drugstore Items (n=179)

	Expenditures				
Frequency	**Under $3**	**$3 - $5**	**$5 - $15**	**> $15***	**Total**
Daily	2	1	1	2	6
Twice per week	3	3	2	3	11
Once per week	9	8	19	2	38
Twice per month	7	10	14	9	40
Once per month	12	9	17	19	57
Other**	5	11	6	5	27
Total	38	42	59	40	179

* Assume none over $25
** Assume once per six months on the average

4. Would You Shop at Modern Drugstores?

	N	%
Yes	107	55
No	52	27
Don't Know	37	18

5. Would You Shop at City Drugstores?

	N	%
Yes	166	84
No	15	8
Don't Know	15	8

6. Why Would You Shop at City Drugstores?

	N	%
Close and Convenient	142	71
Cheaper Prices	52	26
Products	21	11
Already Loyal to City Drug	28	14
Loyal to Paramount	8	4
Other	29	10

(Scores do not add up to 100% due to multiple responses).

FIRST FEDERAL BANK AND TRUST: PART B*
By Robert F. Lusch, University of Oklahoma

Introduction

"I have made the decision to begin our new marketing campaign in 30 days. Later today I will be meeting with the Thompson advertising agency so we can begin to develop our advertising program. Jay, I feel this is our best approach. To grow by acquiring other financial institutions at a high premium over book value is simply too expensive." As Fred paused, Jay Sterling seized the opportunity to comment. "Fred, you know I trust your judgment, so lets get on with this program. Keep me updated on your major decisions; and, as always, if you want to run some ideas by me please don't hesitate to call."

That afternoon Fred Wade met with Susan Federico of the Thompson Agency. The meeting was more of a "get acquainted" meeting, but at the conclusion Susan told Fred that she wanted to meet with him on Friday morning. She asked if he could be prepared with a list of advertising objectives so that they could proceed on developing an advertising theme, campaign, and media plan.

Development of the Advertising Campaign

When Fred and Susan met on Friday, Fred had developed a pair of advertising objectives. The previous day he had met with Larry Peeler, who was his sales manager, and they had decided that one of their first objectives should be to increase their account base by 20% the next year. Since they already had 37,000 accounts, that implied 7400 new accounts needed to be opened. A second objective was to develop an increased awareness of First Federal Bank and Trust's 8:00 a.m. to 8:00 p.m. hours. Since more households were pressed for time, both Fred and Larry thought increased awareness of First's long hours would translate into more account openings.

Susan really liked the objectives because they were measurable. Immediately, she suggested they begin to think of an advertising theme. Several banks already had themes they were promoting. Community Bank promoted itself as "your friendly bank," Bank III promoted itself as "a bank for all people," and Liberty Bell promoted itself as "a bank for your family." Susan thought that all these themes were too institutional. She was more concerned with helping Fred build a theme that would create action and help him meet his objective of opening 20% more new accounts over the next year. Susan had nothing against institutional advertising that helped to build the image of the bank. However, she knew the pressure Fred was under from Jay Sterling to make this bold strategy work. Fred had been frank with Susan and said that his future rested on the marketing strategy he developed. As Susan so well knew, it was no easy feat to convince a company to spend money on such an intangible as advertising. She was impressed that Fred could convince Jay to spend over $1 million on a marketing campaign rather than purchasing other banks. In brief, she wanted to see Fred win on this one.

Susan suggested the theme of "Test Us." Susan felt that with the 8:00 a.m. to 8:00 p.m. hours and the friendly corporate culture that Fred was creating, households would need only test First Federal Bank and Trust, then they would open an account. Fred liked the theme because it was simple and was clearly action oriented.

Although Fred had $1.5 million to spend on promotion over the next 18 months, Susan suggested that the first 6 months be more proportionately heavy in promotion spending. Consequently, she suggested the following schedule for the first 6 months:

---

* This case is based on actual data and information, however, names and data have been disguised for proprietary reasons. The case is intended not to indicate the right or wrong way to handle certain problems, but rather as a means of instruction.

Month	Expenditure
1	$150,000
2	$125,000
3	$110,000
4	$100,000
5	$100,000
6	$100,000

If the advertising was to be successful, Susan also felt that First Federal Bank and Trust had to use newspaper, radio, television, and billboard ads and focus on dominating at least one of these media. Without a doubt, it was too expensive to dominate with television ads. The high cost of television advertising, especially during the evenings, would require at least $1 million be spent on television. The problem with newspaper ads was that people were spending less time reading the newspaper. Susan mentioned that approximately 20% to 25% of the population do not regularly read a newspaper. Susan was a big supporter of the radio ads. Realistically, however, she knew that with seven FM and six AM stations available, each with different formats and programming, the radio listening audience was too fragmented. To dominate on radio, at least four FM and three AM stations would need to be a part of the media plan. What was left was billboard ads. Billboards create exposure among all income and social class groups. A billboard ad on a high traffic road is almost impossible to ignore.

Fred had never used billboard advertising and was quite interested in learning more. He was surprised at the data Susan had shown him on the billboard exposure ratings and the attention score they received. Furthermore, he was impressed that a six-month billboard was priced at $9375, if at least five were leased. Susan recommended that 12 billboards be used over the next 6 months. This would allow the bank to virtually dominate the billboard advertising market of financial institutions in the community. Susan recommended four boards on the west and east sides of town and two each on the south and north sides of the community.

In summary, Susan recommended the following dollar allocation.

Television	$280,000
Radio	$115,000
Newspaper	$177,500
Billboard	$112,500

The Early Results

As Fred greeted Susan for lunch, he exclaimed, "Susan, you simply won't believe what is happening; last week we opened 400 new accounts and the campaign has only been running for 2 weeks." Predictably, Susan was pleased. "I guess the public is willing to 'test us'."

Fred had quite a few things to discuss with Susan over lunch. He was already beginning to wonder if the advertising budget needed to be adjusted. He asked if Susan had any feel for which of the four media was influencing customers to open new accounts. Susan emphasized the interactive effect of the media on the public's behavior and encouraged Fred to be patient, "Lets allow the advertising to run for 60 days and then think about how to assess its effect more precisely and talk about reallocation to different media."

When Fred returned from lunch he had several phone messages. Jay Sterling had called and Fred thought he should get back with him quickly. He was excited about telling him about the 400 new account openings last week. When he visited with Jay about the early results, Jay was quite pleased. However, Jay did have some concerns. "Fred, I was thinking the other day that with the large amount we are spending on advertising it would be wise to spend a little money on some research to help us assess the public's changing attitudes and opinions toward First Federal Bank and Trust." Fred mentioned to Jay that he had just talked about that very thing with Susan Frederico and she had urged him to wait until the campaign had run 60 days. Jay thought that was reasonable, but, nonetheless, he felt they should identify a firm to help them conduct some research. Fred mentioned the good job that Anne Morgan had done previously and that he would get with her next week and ask her to put together a proposal to help assess the advertising effectiveness.

Advertising Effectiveness

When Anne Morgan met with Fred she agreed that the campaign should run 60 days before they enter the market to test the results. She suggested that 500 households be interviewed at random using a short questionnaire. Five or six main questions should be able to determine how the advertising is doing. Anne estimated that the entire project could be done for $7500 and that it could start on March 1, which would be precisely 60 days after the launch of the campaign. She promised to deliver a management report by late March.

The Management Report

Fred reviewed the report Anne had dropped by his office late that afternoon. Exhibits 1-5 were especially informative. Tomorrow morning he would meet with his management committee. "Shelby, please take Dr. Morgan's report and make five copies and give one to each of the members on our marketing task force. I want them to review the report this evening in preparation for our meeting at 7:00 a.m. tomorrow.

Questions for Discussion

1. Based on the research findings, should First Federal Bank and Trust make any changes in their advertising program?

2. Are there other potential changes that the bank should consider based on the research results?

3. Fred needs to decide soon on at least two more additional branches. Should he consider going to more branches in supermarkets or discount department stores vs. using more traditional locations?

Exhibit 1
Awareness and Attention Ratings for First Federal Bank and Trust Advertising: Customers

Advertising Media	Percent Aware Last Two Months	Attention Rating
Newspaper	39.5%	4.2*
Radio	37.7%	5.1
Television	39.5%	5.0
Billboards	77.5%	6.1

*The attention level represents the attention paid to advertisements if the respondent responded yes to the awareness question. Attention is rated from 0 to 10 with 0 representing no attention and 10 indicating high attention; intermediate numbers are used for rankings in between these extremes.

Exhibit 2
Awareness and Attention Ratings for First Federal Bank and Trust Advertising: Non-Customers

Advertising Media	Percent Aware Last Two Months	Attention Rating
Newspaper	23.6%	3.3*
Radio	21.6%	4.5
Television	29.3%	3.7
Billboards	35.5%	4.9

*The attention level represents the attention paid to advertisements if the respondent responded yes to the awareness question. Attention is rated from 0 to 10 with 0 representing no attention and 10 indicating high attention; intermediate numbers are used for rankings in between these extremes.

Exhibit 3
Identification of Advertising Themes
by Primary Banking Relationship
(% Identifying Correct Theme)

Advertising Theme*	First Federal Bank and Trust	Other Financial Institution
"Test Us" (First Federal Bank and Trust)	55.1%	13.1%
"Your Friendly Bank" (Community Bank)	2.2%	1.5%
"A Bank for Your Family" (Liberty Bell Bank)	4.0%	3.1%
"A Bank for All People" (Bank III)	14.5%	9.7%

*correct theme is in parentheses

Exhibit 4
Bank Image of Respondents Who Had
First Federal Bank and Trust as Primary Relationship
(Which Financial Institution is Best Known for its___)

	Friendly/ Personal Service	Early and Late Hours	Money to Loan	Convenient Locations
Bank III	3.6%	.7%	3.6%	14.1%
Community Bank	2.5%	1.1%	15.6%	14.5%
Liberty Bell Bank	.7%	0.0%.	2.5%	3.3%
First Federal Bank and Trust	52.5%	85.5%	15.2%	30.4%
Teachers Credit Union	0.0%	0.0%	0.0%	0.0%
Other	.3%	1.1%	4.0%	2.5%
Don't Know	36.4%	11.6%	59.1%	35.2%

Exhibit 5
Bank Image of Respondents Who Did Not Have First Federal Bank and Trust as Primary Relationship (Which Financial Institution is Best Known for its___)

	Friendly/Personal Service	Early and Late Hours	Money to Loan	Convenient Locations
Bank III	9.3%	5.0%	4.2%	22.4%
Community Bank	11.2%	4.6%	14.7%	20.5%
Liberty Bell Bank	4.2%	3.1%	3.1%	5.0%
First Federal Bank and Trust	9.7%	27.0%	2.7%	5.0%
Teachers Credit Union	0.8%	.4%	1.2%	0.8%
Other	16.2%	5.4%	8.8%	10.0%
Don't Know	48.6%	54.5%	65.3%	36.3%

QUALITY MARKETS*
By Richard M. Petreycik

As a customer was leaving the new Quality Market in Lakewood, NY, Randy Sweeney noticed the shopper had left a package of cold cuts in her shopping cart. Sweeney grabbed the cold cuts and ran outside after the woman.

"Ma'am, I think you forgot this," Sweeney called after the customer.

"Why thank you very much," said the woman.

When Sweeney came back inside he said to a visitor, laughing, "See how friendly we are? I don't even know whether she paid for them."

Such displays of customer service are not unusual at Quality Market. "We're interested in our customers more than we're interested in the supermarket," says Sweeney, who is vice president of sales for 24-store Quality Markets, based in Jamestown, NY. "We want to show our customers that we're interested in the things that are important to them."

Since opening less than six months ago, the store has done just that by becoming involved in three community events: a radio marathon fund raiser for the American Heart Association, free transportation and food for a local Winter Special Olympics group and a hefty donation to the American Red Cross.

The store has also made an impression with aggressive promotional activities. For example, a two-day Italian sausage campaign pushed out 6500 pounds of sausage at 99 cents a pound. During a "Lobster Main-ia" promotion, 800 lobsters sold for $3.99 a pound.

Other promotions included a giveaway featuring a refrigerator filled with dairy products, a trip to Disney World, a baby derby, a pizza party complete with party favors, a "Taste of Jamestown" food sampling promotion, appearances by members of the Buffalo Bills, and a home and garden show.

In addition, two company employees participate in a popular cooking show featured on a nearby Jamestown cable television station. "These girls can't even go into a store without people constantly huddling around them," says Sweeney. "It's good to get the exposure. When customers come to a new location, they expect more."

And, that's just what they've gotten. The 42,000 square-foot Quality Market features a floral shop, fresh seafood, bakery, deli, cheese island, salad and soup bar, and takeout pizza and sub shop.

Although this particular store is new to Lakewood, Quality Markets is not. The new unit is located across the street from the company's 20-year-old store, which was closed when the new Quality Market opened.

Sweeney says the old 22,000 square-foot store just wasn't large enough. The Lakewood area was growing quickly as a result of the heavy tourist trade from the nearby Chautauqua Lake community. "A developer came to us and said, 'We're building a strip center across the street. Are you interested?' We said yes," says Sweeney.

The store's extra space has allowed the company to expand departments as well as add new sections such as seafood and pizza. Linear footage in most departments was doubled in the new store.

"Everything in the older store was on a much smaller scale," he says. "For example, our dairy and frozen food departments were easily doubled. They were both a problem in the older store, especially the dairy department. We couldn't fit everything into the departments."

Space is not the only thing there's more of in the new store. Sales have nearly doubled since the move across the street. *Progressive Grocer* estimates the new store's weekly volume is averaging about $350,000. This figure is particularly strong, considering that two Bells stores and a Super Duper are located within a three-mile radius.

---

*Source: Richard M. Petreycik, "Nice Guys Can Finish First," Store of the Month *Progressive Grocer* (February 1991): 95-99. Used by permission.

Sweeney attributes the new store's success to more than just its increased size and emphasis on customer service and community relations. Quality, variety, and freshness are also important, he says. The strong decor package is another factor.

A boutique-like atmosphere greets shoppers as they enter the low-ceilinged "Market Square" area. This section extends along the right side of the store and includes florals, produce, deli, seafood, and bakery.

Each Market Square department features a different layout and decor. For example, seafood sports a blue and white tiled prep area. A blue fishnet is hung loosely from the ceiling above the refrigerated cases.

The produce department features a very different decor. The walls are made of oak, which is milled locally. Red brick-colored chalkboards containing product and pricing information are mounted above the low-profile product cases.

Although the perishables departments were changed considerably, the section in the new store that experienced the greatest growth is GM/HBA. The department consists of 444 linear feet, or approximately 26 percent of the store's grocery shelving.

"We added photo albums, picture frames, cosmetics, automotive accessories, telephone jacks, speaker wire, home repair supplies, and other items," says Smith. "We did it to try to capture the drugstore and mass merchandise categories. We have three drugstore chains in the area, but we really didn't expand our GM/HBA section to take anything away from anyone. We just wanted a better position. We wanted a better share."

Despite the increased size of the new store, management was determined not to lose sight of its number one priority--to service all its customers in the best way possible.

Maintaining the store's level of service meant making some adjustments in store operations following the move. One change involved the parcel pickup service. The old Quality Market provided this service, which was especially popular with senior citizens, who comprise almost 28% of the area's population. However, because many departments were expanded in the new store, there was no room for parcel pickup. To make up for that, employees now carry out customers' groceries.

Senior citizens are only one of the many groups that make up the area's diverse population. Quality Market's customers represent many backgrounds and income levels. To appeal to this diverse base, the company has kept its advertising and promotional strategies general, rather than targeting just one or two groups.

Advertised products are carefully selected to appeal to everyone. "For example, during the summer months we'll merchandise basics like soft drinks, hot dogs, snack items, ground beef, and rolls," says Sweeney.

Smith adds that "We target our advertising toward the season, not toward types of people like blue-collar groups or upscale groups. We want all our customers' business, not just one group."

The area's population includes an upscale tourist trade. The store is located near the Chautauqua Institution, a 750-acre national historic landmark. The Institution is a well known cultural and educational center offering activities for all ages.

"It's a town in itself," says Store Manager Steve Lombardo. "We get 5000 summer residents in 2 weeks. The institution brings a lot of talented people into the area, making it more upscale during the summer."

Quality Markets is a division of Penn Traffic, based in Johnstown, PA, which owns and operates more than 500 supermarkets including P&C, Big Bear, Riverside, and Grand Union.

However, Randy Sweeney, Quality Markets' vice president of sales, says the company maintains a high degree of autonomy. "We're able to do what we see best," he says. "Whatever decisions Penn Traffic makes center around financial matters involving the entire corporation. But as far as day-to-day business decisions are concerned, they're done by Quality Markets."

What this means, says Steve Smith, Quality Markets' vice president of store operations, is that Quality still has to set certain goals, which Penn Traffic must approve. If approved, Quality is free to pursue those goals in whatever fashion it sees fit, as long as the goals are met. "The goals revolve around sales projections, payroll, and other capital expenditures," says Smith. "Penn Traffic acts as overseer of the entire operation."

Exhibit 1a shows the layout of the Lakewood Village Quality Market. Exhibit 1b explains the 11 store areas. Exhibit 2 is a detailed breakdown of the Lakewood Village Center Quality Market.

Questions for Discussion

1. Randy Sweeney needs to design the upcoming in-store promotions for the October - December period and it is now July 1st. Design promotions for Columbus Day, Veterans Day, Halloween, Thanksgiving and Christmas.

2. How do you propose that the promotions you designed be evaluated for their effectiveness?

Exhibit 1a
Layout of Lakewood Quality Market

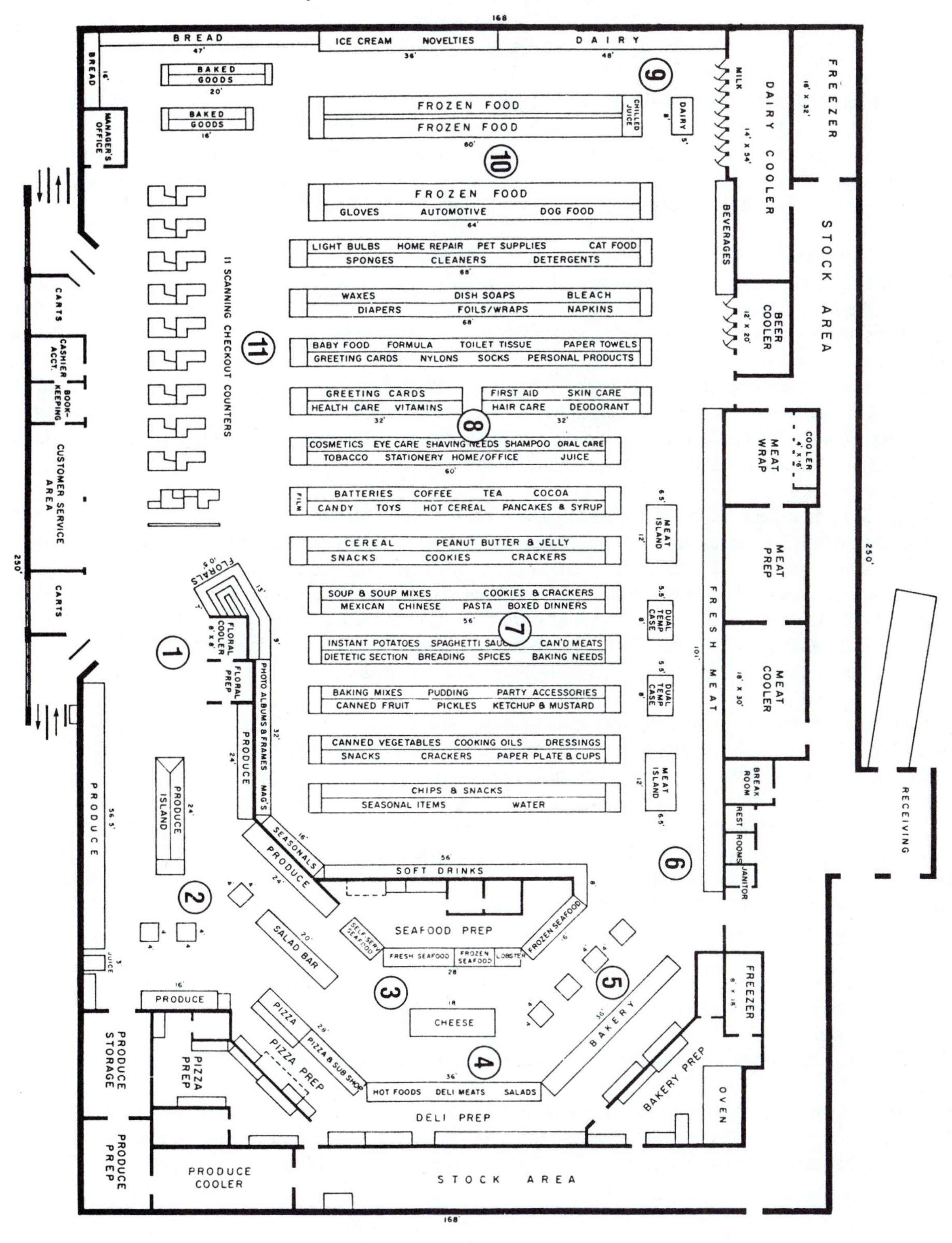

Exhibit 1b
Eleven Areas Explained

1. Florals: Florals, which is part of the produce department, is the first section customers see when they enter Quality Market's "Market Square." The focal point is an oak-paneled display section that houses a variety of plants. Popular items include azaleas and mums. Produce Specialist Dave Holmberg says 60% of floral sales are in fresh bouquets and arrangements. "Green plants and potting plants make up 35% of the business, and potting soil makes up the additional 5%," he says. Low oak-paneled display cases are used for seasonal displays.

2. Produce: The produce department features about 180 items and comprises 7.1% of sales. The department is highlighted by oak-paneled walls and low-profile cases. Holmberg says customers' interest in health and nutrition has benefited the store's salad bar. The salad bar features more than 60 items including taco meat with salsa, marinated vegetable salad, German cole slaw, and bacon-broccoli-cauliflower salad. One of the more popular salad bar items is a "Fruit Pizza," which consists of a pie crust covered with peaches, strawberries, kiwi, grapes, vanilla pudding, and whipped cream. "We brought the idea back from a share group meeting with our parent company, Penn Traffic," says Steve Smith, vice president of store operations. "The idea originated with one of our sister companies, Big Bear in Columbus, Ohio." The produce department also features many locally grown vegetables, especially during the summer months. Some of these items include tomatoes, corn, and yellow squash.

3. Seafood: Seafood accounts for 1.5% of sales. The biggest seller is shrimp, which constitutes 20% of department sales. Seafood Specialist Joe Jessey says orange roughy and North Atlantic whitefish are next in popularity, followed by salmon fillets. Product and pricing information are written in bright colors on blackboards, which are hung on the department's tiled wall. In addition to fresh seafood, the department includes an 8-foot service case with frozen items such as breaded scallops at $7.99 a pound and stuffed flounder at $4.29 a pound. The department also contains a 16-foot case for frozen packaged fish. "This case helps support the overall department," says Smith. "It shows our customers that they can buy all the seafood items they want in one place."

4. Deli: The deli department contains a pizza and sub section (called "The Hot Spot"), hot foods, cold cuts, and salads. According to Joanne Nalbone, manager of the pizza and sub section, pizza can be made to order and so far, customers have been responding well. "Lunch and dinner are the busiest periods, and customers like the fact that they can buy pizza whole or by the slice," she says. A hot-food menu featuring daily lunch and supper specials is published each week. Selections include stuffed peppers, vegetable lasagna, and breaded pork chops. Deli Manager Sharon Foti says health-conscious shoppers like "the healthy deli," which features low-sodium and low-cholesterol products such as ham, Lorraine cheese, and Jarlsberg cheese. These items are identified with pink signs. A cheese case features prepackaged domestic and international cheeses. Popular international cheeses include Brie and blue nego, which is a Brie combined with blue cheese. The deli department accounts for 4.8% of total store sales.

5. Bakery: The bakery, also known as the "Pastry Shop," is a frozen bake-off operation. Cookies, pastries and doughnuts are piled on yellow trays in European-style cases. Popular items include cream puffs priced at two for $1.29, cream cannoli at 69 cents each and brownies featured at three for $1. Wooden racks display rolls, bagels, and crusty breads, which Foti says are growing in popularity. The bakery department accounts for 2.2% of sales.

6. Meat: Meat Cutter Ron Johnson says the trend in meat these days is toward poultry or lean beef. "People are on this diet kick," he says. "Turkey is selling better than ever, especially products like turkey sausage." Johnson also notes that a lot of his customers want smaller packages and convenience-oriented meat items such as strip steaks, tenderloins,

cube steaks, and top and bottom rounds. "Ninety percent of our customers know exactly what they want," he says. "If a recipe book calls for 12 ounces of beef, that's what they want. They want to just put it in the oven and eat it." The new store features more than 100 feet of multi-deck cases, compared with single-deck cases in the old store. The department also features four dual-temperature coffin cases for frozen or refrigerated meat products. Meat comprises 14.7% of sales.

7. Grocery: "A lot of effort goes into facings and appearance in the grocery department," says Smith. Shelves are constantly replenished and squared down to give a full appearance. "It's an image that says we're ready for business," says Smith. Shelved endcaps reinforce the store's full appearance by giving more depth to product arrangements. Grocery accounts for 48.3% of sales.

8. GM/HBA: The non-foods department underwent a large expansion in the new store. In addition to adding items, Smith says the magazine section was expanded to include hard cover books. "We brought in clay-colored Formica book displays and put in 20 feet of magazine racks," says Smith. "We also expanded our greeting card offerings." The low-profile greeting card fixture features a lighted canopy. The GM/HBA section accounts for 5.6% of sales.

9. Dairy: The dairy department accounts for 8.1% of sales, 70% of which comes from low-fat milk. "Milk is promoted very heavily in New York state," says Randy Sweeney, vice president of sales. "And 1% milk is becoming a very strong item because people are more health conscious." The department's milk section is loaded from the rear and is housed beneath a yellow canopy that says "The Milk House." Other strong movers include low-salt cheeses, juices, gelatin and pudding products, and yogurt.

10. Frozens: Suspended signs identifying frozen poultry, meat, dinners, and vegetables make it easy for customers to find items behind the department's 54 doors. Sweeney says shoppers continue to look for quick entrees that are low in sodium and cholesterol. In addition, frozen yogurt is doing well. "It takes time for people to try it, but once they do, they find out they like it," says Sweeney. The frozens department accounts for 7.7% of sales.

11. Front end: The front end features 11 checkout counters equipped with side-scanning registers. Craig Howard, director of store systems, says the registers are designed so that if the main office controller goes down, each scanner has the capability of operating on its own. The front end also features an EFT system that honors Visa, MasterCard, and Discover cards.

Exhibit 2
Detailed Breakdown of Lakewood Village Quality Market
Lakewood Village Center

Date opened	Septmeber 30,1990
Type of location	Strip plaza
Overall area	42,000 square feet
Selling area	29,000 square feet
Hours of operation	24 hours, 7 days a week
Parking capacity	418 spaces
Architect	Reinhart & Schwartz
Design	In-house
Cost of store (incl. equipment and fixtures)	$3.4 million
Grocery/nonfood shelving	1683 linear feet
Display cases (linear feet)	
Produce	168
Florals	48
Salad bar	20
Deli	100
Bakery	36
Meat	182
Frozens	220
Dairy	110
Estimated weekly volume	$350,000
Number of employees	183
Wholesaler	Penn Traffic
Store manager	Steve Lombardo

Exhibit 2 (Continued)
Detailed Breakdown of Lakewood Village Quality Market
Lakewood Village Center

Trade Area Statistics	
Median age	33.2 years
Average household size	2.6 people
Average household income	$28,221
Median education	12.4 years
Percentage owner-occupied housing	60.2%
Percentage working women	42.0%
Percentage blue collar	51.4%
Percentage single-family dwelling units	63.3%

Percent Sales by Department

	Quality Market	Industry Average
Grocery	48.3%	40.1%
Meat	14.7	17.0
Dairy	8.1	7.8
Frozens	7.7	6.0
Produce	7.1#	9.8##
GM/HBA	5.6	8.2
Deli	4.8	2.7
Bakery	2.2	1.6
Seafood	1.5	N/A

Including florals and salad bar
Including florals only

CIRCLE K CORPORATION*

By Deborah Zizzo, University of Oklahoma

Introduction

The rise and fall of Circle K is a story of a quiet regional company that grew to be called the largest publicly owned convenience store chain in the U.S.--before collapsing into bankruptcy. In 1983, Circle K operated 1221 stores in 12 states with sales just over $750 million. A crucial change in leadership that year sparked the company's voracious appetite and it began devouring other convenience stores, from profitable operations to what one seller termed "a bunch of crap." By 1989, the company boasted 4685 convenience stores in 32 states and sales were over $3 billion. To finance this growth, Circle K gorged on the money readily available through the junk bond market, until it became bloated with debt. In its consuming quest for growth, the company apparently ignored the competitive environment and, worse, neglected operations of its own stores. Yet almost until the very end, the investment community applauded and rewarded Circle K's flashy growth. Apparently, no one suspected that this series of management lapses would lead Circle K to the brink of demise.

The Convenience Store Industry

The convenience store concept originated in 1927 in Dallas, Texas, when "Uncle Johnny" Jefferson Green began stocking bread, milk, and eggs at the Southland Ice Dock he operated. This dock was open 16 hours a day, 7 days a week, and Green had realized that customers often needed these and other staples after local grocery stores had closed. This type of store and others of similar format increased modestly in number for many years. They were more successful in warmer climates, partly because of their open storefronts.

The number of convenience stores began to grow more rapidly after World War II. As the increased ownership of automobiles helped spur the growth of the suburbs, downtown supermarkets became less accessible to consumers. New supermarkets were much larger than before and often could no longer provide the customer with quick service. Convenience stores stepped in to fill this gap. Stores were small, usually containing between 1600 and 2400 square feet, were built in residential areas, and offered fast service and extended hours of operation. Products sold usually included dairy products, bakery items, snack foods, beverages, tobacco, health and beauty aids, and candy. As the larger supermarkets also began to drive "mom and pop" corner groceries out of business, convenience stores again filled in. By 1960, there were 2500 convenience stores in operation, which accounted for less than 1 percent of total U.S. grocery sales.

The 1960s were growth years for the convenience store industry (see Exhibit 1). The increasing mobility of the population as well as the growing number of working women led to time-pressured, dual-income families. Convenience stores rushed to build stores in suburban neighborhoods, where they saw consumers, especially commuters, with more discretionary income and less time. During the mid 1960s, convenience stores introduced coffee, slush drinks, 24-hour operations, and, most importantly, self-service gasoline. At first, the retail industry attributed little significance to the installation of self-service gasoline at convenience stores, especially since it seemed to invite so many problems. Several states banned self-service as a fire hazard and often town ordinances were restrictive. Pumping facilities were not especially inviting or attractive, and equipment was unreliable. Convenience stores did not offer gasoline at discount prices, and few customers elected to pump their own when gasoline was only 30 cents per gallon. Still, since equipment was relatively inexpensive, many companies installed it. By 1970, there were 13,250 convenience stores, which accounted for nearly 3 percent of grocery sales. The number of these stores selling gasoline was not even noted at the time.

The 1970s were the big boom years for the convenience store industry, due in large part to this almost reluctant addition of gasoline to the product mix. When the Arab Oil Embargo of 1973 tripled the price of gasoline, consumers

---

* Used with permission of Deborah Zizzo

suddenly became willing to pump their own in order to save money. Convenience stores could and did underprice their competitors on gasoline to lure customers into the store to purchase more profitable items. Oil companies keenly felt this loss of gasoline sales at a time when their traditional gas service stations were most vulnerable. Service stations had historically obtained most of their profits from car repairs and sales of tires, batteries, and other accessories. Yet during this time, specialty stores and the national chains, including Midas Muffler and Sears, had taken much of that business. As a result, the major oil companies were forced to close many of their neighborhood service stations, most of which were located on corner sites. The glut of these sites on the market forced prices to drop, in many cases by as much as one-half between 1972 and 1975, and convenience stores quickly bought these locations.

For convenience stores, gasoline had become an important element of the product mix and an even more important customer draw. From 1975 to 1980, gasoline as a percentage of total sales rose from 7 percent to 28 percent. Industry estimates indicated that between 30 and 40 percent of customers purchasing gasoline also bought at least one more item inside the store. By the end of the decade, traffic counts had replaced household density counts as the primary determinant of site selection for convenience stores. Many said that convenience stores located on streets in suburban, residential areas were "doomed" and that primary locations, that is, corner sites on high-traffic intersections, would become prerequisites for survival.

History of Circle K

In 1951, Fred Hervey purchased three neighborhood stores in El Paso, Texas, operating under the name "Kays Drive-In Grocery." In keeping with the regional flavor, he created a brand-type logo for his stores by encircling the "K." The company adopted the name Circle K Food Stores in 1957 and, in 1963, made an initial public offering of common stock. Hervey built the company steadily, from 43 stores in 1961 to 423 stores by 1970. During the convenience store boom years of the 1970s, Circle K nearly tripled in size, and by 1980, operated 1200 stores in 12 states, as well as 3 in Japan. Recognizing the increasing importance of gasoline sales and hoping to ensure a stable supply of it, in September 1980, Circle K purchased a 13.2 percent stake in Nucorp Energy, Inc., an oil and gas exploration company. The following year, Circle K was reorganized into a holding company to permit greater flexibility in acquiring other oil and gas companies, although none were ever purchased. In 1982, Nucorp filed for Chapter 11 bankruptcy, and Circle K took a $30 million write down on their investment, resulting in a loss for the fiscal year ending April 30, 1982. By the end of the next fiscal year, the company operated 1221 stores in Arizona, California, Texas, New Mexico, Idaho, Oregon, Montana, Oklahoma, Washington, Utah, Colorado, and Nevada. In July 1983, founder Fred Hervey, at age 73, turned over the company to Karl Eller, a long-time friend and business associate, stating:

> I have put 32 years into the development of Circle K, and it is time for me to turn things over to someone who can carry the company into its next generation of growth. I don't know anyone who has demonstrated better ability to manage growth and expansion than Karl Eller.[1]

Karl Eller

Karl Eller was an Arizona native and born entrepreneur. As a student at the University of Arizona in the early 1950s, he sold other students class notes for $4.00. He began his career selling billboard space and then as an account supervisor before becoming president of Eller Outdoor Advertising. In 1968, he began acquiring small outdoor advertising, broadcasting, and publishing companies, which he formed into Combined Communications Corporation. During this venture, he met and teamed up with Carl Lindner, a Cincinnati, Ohio, financier, who was to play an important role in

---

[1] Circle K Corporation, *1983 Annual Report*, 3.

Eller's tenure at Circle K. By the time Eller sold Combined Communications to the Gannett Company in 1979, it had become one of the country's largest outdoor advertising companies. After a short stay with Gannett, Eller went to Charter Company, an oil corporation wanting to build up its media division. In February 1981, he became president of the communications division of Columbia Pictures Industries and initiated the talks which eventually led to CocaCola Co.'s acquiring Columbia. From 1982 until he became president of Circle K, he ran Karl Eller Company Financial Consultants in Phoenix.

The Competitive Environment in the Early 1980s

By 1980, there were 35,800 convenience stores throughout the U.S., nearly half of which sold gasoline. These stores accounted for 5.6 percent of grocery sales overall, and up to 12 percent in some markets. However, some markets were becoming saturated with convenience stores, especially southern states with warm weather and heavy tourist traffic. Consequently, convenience stores began to compete with each other, as well as with companies in the grocery, gasoline, fast food, and other retail sectors of the economy. Clearly the boom years for convenience stores were ending.

Supermarkets had begun to strike back by increasing hours of operation and installing "express" lanes. Some supermarket companies, using their food merchandising expertise, began to open and operate their own convenience stores, although they usually did not offer gasoline. In addition, discount department stores and drugstores were attempting to grab some grocery dollars by carrying selected food items.

By 1982, convenience stores accounted for 8 percent of the total amount of gasoline pumped in the U.S.[2] Despite this significant inroad convenience stores were making in marketing gasoline, oil companies had made only feeble attempts to add convenience store operations to their facilities. By 1982, six oil companies operated convenience stores at only 2000 locations. Oil companies lacked the necessary marketing expertise to merchandise the thousands of products carried in a convenience store. Yet they retained many prime corner locations, usually with garages that could be converted into stores, and they certainly had deep pockets.

In theory, the demographics for convenience stores looked strong. The increasing number of time-constrained, dual-income households appeared to be building a solid base of convenience store customers. Yet the typical customer was an 18-to-34-year-old male in a blue-collar occupation. Convenience stores recognized the need to attract more women and upscale customers, but they faced an image problem. Shoppers considered the stores to be dirty, high-priced (except for gasoline), and crime-infested. Indeed, many stores had never been refurbished and looked run down and cluttered. So companies began extensive, expensive remodeling programs to improve lighting, brighten colors, and increase street visibility in hopes of attracting more women and upscale customers. To combat their high-priced image, many convenience stores began offering staples at competitive prices and advertising these and other special promotions aggressively. The combination of more expensive sites, increased capital expenditures for remodeling, reduced prices on staples, and aggressive advertising began to impact profits for convenience stores.

Convenience stores were also facing potential trouble with their product mix (see Exhibit 2). Pinball machines, delicatessen and sandwich counters, fountain drinks, microwave ovens, and self-service fast foods had been introduced in the 1970s. During the 1980s, convenience stores began offering car washes, videocassette rentals, automatic teller machines, upscale merchandise, and extensive fast-food service. Still, in 1983, four products accounted for 66 percent of sales: gasoline, tobacco, alcoholic beverages, and soft drinks. Of these categories, only soft drinks appeared immune to increasing regulatory or legislative pressure. The Environmental Protection Agency had begun to study the effects of underground gasoline storage tanks and lines. Sales of alcoholic beverages, especially through outlets that also sold gasoline, were coming under attack from groups such as Mothers Against Drunk Driving. The tobacco industry was facing intensified pressures, especially regarding advertising, and the number of smokers continued to decline. Even fast-food

---

[2]"Look Who's a Champ of Gasoline Marketing," *Fortune*, 1 November 1982, 150.

operations, predicted to be the growth vehicle for the 1980s (much like gasoline was in the 1970s), were becoming more labor intensive and often included on-site preparations, subject to local health regulations (see Exhibit 3).

Karl Eller Takes Over At Circle K

By the time Karl Eller arrived at Circle K, the easy growth years had ended. The company's rate of sales growth had slowed due to the 1980 and 1981-1982 recessions and increased competition. To boost sales, in early 1983, Circle K launched "an aggressive marketing and advertising program...designed around a more competitive pricing posture on selected items such as milk, cigarettes, and beer plus an increase in seasonal promotions and advertising."[3] Circle K had just opened its own commissary to produce sandwiches and other fast foods for its stores, and, with its own distribution system, was better positioned than many to ride the fast-food wave. Eller announced ambitious expansion plans. He predicted the company would grow 15 to 20 percent per year and would become a national chain operating 5000 stores by 1990 (see Exhibit 4).

His first acquisitions came within five months when he purchased two outdoor advertising companies in Texas and Idaho. He explained that these acquisitions would benefit a convenience store chain because of "logical synergism--for every corner where a Circle K is located, there is the potential for an outdoor billboard."[4] In fact, the company's 1984 10K report announced Circle K's intentions to "seek acquisitions of additional outdoor advertising or other media or communications businesses." In October 1983, Circle K issued $50 million in debentures to finance its growth.

Rumors of Circle K's becoming another media conglomerate quieted when, in December 1983, Eller acquired the UtoteM Corp. from American Financial Corporation, the company run by his friend, Carl Lindner. UtoteM, headquartered in Houston, Texas, operated 959 convenience stores in 12 states and was a major competitor of Circle K in some states. The acquisition almost doubled the number of Circle K stores and expanded operations into seven new states: Alabama, Arkansas, Florida, Kansas, Kentucky, Missouri, and Ohio. UtoteM stores were located primarily in single or multi-family residential areas or along heavily traveled local streets. Although 64 percent of these stores sold gasoline, they did so primarily on a consignment basis. UtoteM's dairy and snack foods businesses had been sold earlier by AFC, but UtoteM continued to operate three ice plants (see Exhibit 5).

The total cost of $226.8 million consisted of $100 million in cash, $75 million in 12.5 percent installment notes, $50 million in newly issued Circle K preferred stock, and $1.8 million in common stock purchase warrants. The consignment gasoline operations at 395 stores were purchased for approximately $12 million. Four months later, 370 UtoteM stores were sold to and subsequently leased back from AFC for $98.6 million, part of which paid off the $75 million note. Circle K retained, among others, three top-level executives from that chain, including the president, James Williamson, Jr., who was named president of Circle K Convenience Stores.

In October 1984, Eller purchased the chain of Little General Stores from General Host Corporation. Little General operated 435 convenience stores in 6 southern and southeastern states, primarily in Florida. The acquisition pushed the company into four new states: Georgia, Louisiana, Mississippi, and North Carolina. Little General's stores were located in dense residential areas, primarily along homeward bound routes, and 52 percent sold gasoline. Little General operated one ice plant, but did little warehousing. The purchase price of $132.2 million consisted of $112.3 million in cash and $19.9 million in assumed liabilities. None of the senior management of Little General was retained (see Exhibit 6).

By January 1985, the three top executives from UtoteM had left Circle K. To fill the critical gaps in his executive offices, Eller appointed three outsiders including Robert Reade, from the outdoor advertising division of the Gannett Company, who was named senior vice president of real estate.

---

[3] *1983 Annual Report*, 2.

[4] "Seems Like Old Times," *Forbes*, 5 December 1983, 58.

The 1985 Annual Report noted that the company's "growth has been a quality growth of manageable proportions." Economies of scale were being realized for distribution, buying, and administrative functions as acquired businesses were integrated into the Circle K system. The company launched an extensive remodeling program and announced plans to become a leader in new product and service introductions. The commissary was beginning to supply all newly acquired stores, thus reducing dependence on local distributors for fast-food products.

In September 1985, Circle K acquired Shop & Go, Inc., for $166.6 million in cash. Shop & Go operated 406 convenience stores in central Florida and 40 stores in southern Georgia. Stores were located on the outskirts of rapidly growing cities, with some in strip shopping centers. Approximately 74 percent of Shop & Go stores sold gasoline, and one-third were located on corner sites. The company operated ice and sandwich manufacturing facilities and distributed some items under its own label. Shop & Go's founders and majority stockholders, Robert and Lorena Jaeb, were 74 and 65 years old, respectively, when they sold their shares to Circle K (see Exhibit 7).

Although internally generated funds still covered portions of the acquisition costs, Circle K increasingly began to rely on outside sources of capital. The bond market in the early and mid 1980s was eager to lend money. High-yield, speculative bonds (later known as "junk" bonds) were a fashionable and readily available means of raising capital. In May 1985, the company issued $100 million in 8.25 percent convertible subordinated debentures and, in October 1985, issued $125 million in 12.75 percent senior subordinated debentures. Both offerings were rated by Moody's in the Ba category, as containing speculative elements.

In March 1986, Circle K acquired 224 convenience stores, including 38 closed stores, from National Convenience Stores, Inc., of Houston, Texas. National Convenience was facing difficult times due to the oil bust in its largest market, Houston, and had decided to concentrate its resources on fewer markets where it had a strong presence. Circle K purchased stores in Arkansas (23), Texas (53), Louisiana (24), Oklahoma (8), Colorado (23), Mississippi (31), and another new state for the company, Tennessee (25). The purchase price was $51.8 million in cash plus $5.6 million in assumed obligations. The president of National Convenience Stores announced later that he had sold Eller "a bunch of crap."[5]

Circle K's 1986 Annual Report admitted it "was not an easy year." The company blamed poor economic conditions in Texas and the Gulf Coast states, acquisition-related expenses, and increased liability insurance premiums. Circle K stated that it would "maintain a competitive edge by providing our customers with as many different products and services as possible--even those items infrequently purchased." In November 1986, Robert Reade, senior vice president of real estate, became president (see Exhibit 8).

In terms of acquisitions, 1987 was a comparatively quiet year, although Eller did pick up 123 stores in California, Texas, and Oklahoma. The company raised the capital by issuing bonds and selling and leasing back stores (see Exhibit 9).

In April 1988, Eller was presented with an irresistible opportunity. Circle K's chief competitor had always been the Southland Corporation, operators of 7-Eleven stores, the largest convenience store chain in the nation. In December 1987, Southland had been acquired by the founding family through a leveraged buyout. Struggling under a huge debt burden, the company was forced to sell assets to raise cash. Southland agreed to sell Circle K all of its stores in Alabama, Arkansas, Georgia, Louisiana, and South Carolina, as well as stores in Arizona, Florida, North Carolina, Tennessee, and Texas. The total transaction involved 473 stores and 90 closed facilities and cost Circle K $151.4 million. This acquisition had a dilutive effect on Circle K's earnings. Still, Eller insisted these stores would be profitable once personnel duplications were eliminated, once they were supplied with Circle K manufactured products, and once the company's increased volume purchasing power was realized.

In September 1988, Eller made his final acquisition, Charter Marketing Group, from Charter Co., where he had previously worked. Charter had recently emerged from three years of bankruptcy proceedings, which had left Carl Lindner as chairman of the board and AFC holding the majority of stock. Charter operated 538 convenience stores primarily in the

[5]"Stop N Go's Van Horn Wants to Reinvent the Convenience Store," *Wall Street Journal*, 6 February 1991, A10.

Southeast, but also in 6 states new for Circle K: Michigan, Indiana, Maine, New Hampshire, Connecticut, and Massachusetts. Although in 1986 Eller had said he didn't envision the company "going into the Upper Midwest or Northeast because our path has always been here in the Sunbelt,"[6] the 1988 Annual Report claimed this acquisition took Circle K into the "economically attractive New England area." The purchase price of $125.6 million consisted of $75.6 million cash and $50 million in newly issued preferred stock and left AFC owning 38.4 percent of Circle K (see Exhibit 10).

At the end of fiscal 1988, Circle K appeared to be riding the crest of the wave, with earnings at a record $60.4 million. With Southland now privately held, the company could proclaim itself to be the largest publicly owned convenience store operator in the U.S. and an industry leader and pacesetter as well. A joint venture in branded fast foods with Dunkin' Donuts appeared successful and was slated for expansion. Circle K continued testing new products and services including a microwavable ice cream sundae and Federal Express drop boxes. The company's videocassette rental program was available in 65 percent of stores, and Circle K attributed its mixed results to temporary supplier problems (see Exhibit 11).

In short, from 1983 to 1988, Circle K had grown from 1221 stores in 12 states to 4685 stores in 32 states, and sales had increased from $750 million to nearly $3.5 billion. In February 1989, Eller proposed hiring an investment banker firm to assess the company's value for possible sale. On that news, the company's stock price jumped, eventually trading at $16.25. In May 1989, Circle K officially announced that it was for sale, and Eller indicated that he was considering purchasing the company himself in a leveraged buyout. Financial analysts estimated the company's value at between $16.00 and $18.00 per share, despite Circle K's disclosure that it expected to post a loss for the fourth quarter ending April 30, 1989 (see Exhibit 12).

Problems Begin To Surface

As the investment bankers scrutinized Circle K, they discovered more problems with the company than had been previously suspected. In August, when Circle K released its Annual Report for the year ending April 30, 1989, the outside community became aware of some of these problems.

Circle K was strapped for cash. The acquisition binge and store construction and remodeling program had skyrocketed the company's debt from $40.5 million in 1983 to more than $1.1 billion by 1989. Nearly one-third of this debt was subject to fluctuations in interest rates, and rates had risen. The company had been forced to renegotiate credit lines and loan terms with its banks and faced suspension of its dividend should profitability requirements not be met. In addition, late in 1988, the Environmental Protection Agency had tightened regulations on underground storage tanks, and Circle K estimated it would need $150 million to comply.

The company was attempting to generate funds, but options were becoming limited. The junk bond market, particularly in the depressed convenience store industry, collapsed. In October 1988, the company was able to raise $200 million in a private placement of notes, but only by putting up 425 stores and an office complex as collateral. Circle K was running out of assets to divest. The two outdoor advertising companies had been sold for $16.2 million. (Eller was one of the buyers.) The ice manufacturing and distribution operations brought in $32 million. The commissary was sold for $28 million, although Circle K immediately entered into an agreement to purchase its products at market prices. The company even sold the future rights to its name in Japan for $55 million. In addition, the majority of Circle K stores already had been sold and leased back.

Increased competition made funds from operations scarce. Oil companies finally had launched their own strategic assault on convenience stores, and accounted for virtually all of the growth in the industry since 1986.[7] By 1989, oil

---

[6] "Circle K Breaking New Ground with Acquisitions, Fast Foods," *National Petroleum News*, February 1986, 48.

[7] "Why C-Store Chains Are Getting Squeezed," *National Petroleum News*, September 1988, 41.

companies owned 7 of the 20 largest convenience store chains. Their stores were newer and more attractive, and often they would discount food items to sell more gasoline. Even their small kiosk and mini-mart operations stole profitable sales from convenience stores. In addition, other retailers such as Blockbuster Video (which had 17 stores in 1985 and 1079 in 1989) had devastated many convenience stores' videocassette rental programs. Despite heavy investments in these programs, convenience stores were unable to compete with the specialty retailers' wide selections.

Most importantly, Circle K suffered serious operating problems. The company's decision to carry all items, even infrequently purchased ones, left many slow-moving products on the shelves. Many stores even carried multiple brands of these unwanted items, ranging from hair nets to dog food. In addition, the company did not even know what was in many of its stores. During the 1970s and 1980s, many retailers had invested heavily in electronic technology to help their merchandising operations. Scanning equipment, for example, reduced checkout time and allowed merchants to monitor product sales by store, enabling them to tailor product mixes to individual markets. However, most convenience stores, including Circle K, had not invested in technology, believing it was unnecessary since their stores offered quick enough service and sold many "unscannable" items such as fast foods and fountain drinks. Due to obsolete inventory management systems, Circle K did not know what was selling in its stores and had no cost-effective way to find out.

Because Circle K had retained none of the senior executives from any of the chains it had acquired and the company's top officers had no experience in convenience store management, operations had been essentially neglected. Needing someone to handle day-to-day operations, Eller turned to another business associate, Richard Smith, chairman of Steve's Homemade Ice Cream, Inc. Eller designated Smith an "unpaid consultant" to Circle K and gave him far-reaching authority. Smith was allowed to set company policy on purchasing, marketing, advertising, pricing, personnel training, and vendor negotiating. This highly unusual arrangement raised conflict-of-interest questions, since Smith's company sold ice cream to Circle K and Eller owned 16.6 percent of Steve's.

Smith convinced Eller that Circle K could improve its operating performance by getting tough with suppliers, raising prices, reducing promotions, and eliminating regional deviations by centralizing marketing efforts. In its 1989 Annual Report, the company announced plans to do those things. Circle K felt it wielded enough volume purchasing power to justify putting additional pressure on vendors to lower their prices. Although Smith's negotiations brought discounts from some suppliers, others were antagonized. The company believed that raising prices and reducing promotions would generate more cash, which was needed desperately to cover debt payments. Once prices were uniformly raised, the reasoning went, then promotions could be offered more selectively and would be more successful. Prices were raised approximately six percent at all stores, and gross margins did improve. However, sales began to drop, slowly at first, but as customers flocked to competitors, sales plunged.

By September 1989, no one, including Eller, had stepped forward with an offer to buy Circle K. The investment advisers indicated that no one probably would, due to the depressed junk bond market and Circle K's weak financial performance and severe operating problems. When it became clear that no one was interested, Circle K announced it was no longer for sale and suspended its common stock dividend. As the jilted company revealed plans to devote its full energies to strengthening operations, the stock price fell to $7.75.

Postscript

Circle K's troubles did not end with its failure to locate a buyer. The bills for the acquisition binge were coming due, despite frantic negotiations with creditors for time to sell off assets and develop a strategic plan. The Board of Directors began to assert themselves, particularly the major stockholder, Carl Lindner. Smith was "fired" and Lindner brought in another AFC executive, Robert Dearth, to manage operations. Dearth immediately moved to slash prices, revamp the product mix, and return authority to local managers--but it was too late. By March 1990, Circle K stock traded at $1.75. Eller admitted "when you look back, we probably grew too fast at the time...I did the best I knew how. Somebody has to be the hero when you're doing good, and the fall guy when things are going bad. I deserve all the credit, and all the woes."[8] A final plan to swap junk bond debt for common stock fell through at the last minute when lenders decided to cut their losses in Circle K, apparently not confident that the company could continue as a viable firm in the intense retail competitive environment.

In April 1990, the company reported a loss of $772.9 million for the year. In May, Eller resigned. One week later, Circle K filed for protection under Chapter 11 of the U.S. bankruptcy code.

Questions for Discussion

1. What were the major changes in consumer, channel, and competitor trends that influenced the growth of convenience food stores?

2. When did it become evident that Circle K was headed for financial trouble? What were the danger signs? What measures of financial performance would have provided management with additional useful information?

3. What were the primary causes of the bankruptcy of the Circle K Corporation?

---

[8] "Karl Eller of Circle K, Always Pushing Deals, May Have Overdone It," *Wall Street Journal*, 28 March 1990, A1.

Exhibit 1
Growth of the Convenience Store Industry

Year	Number of Convenience Stores	Number of Convenience Stores Selling Gasoline	Convenience Store Sales (millions)	Convenience Store Gasoline Sales (millions)	Number of Service Stations
1960	2,500	N/A	$400	N/A	220,200
1965	6,000	N/A	$990	N/A	221,000
1970	13,250	N/A	$2,600	N/A	222,000
1975	28,500	5,871	$7,100	$500	189,480
1980	44,100	17,861	$24,500	$6,800	158,240
1981	47,900	20,693	$31,200	$9,600	151,250
1982	51,200	23,706	$35,900	$12,200	144,690
1983	54,400	28,288	$41,600	$15,800	136,570
1984	57,300	28,650	$45,600	$16,300	132,080
1985	61,000	33,550	$51,400	$18,200	124,600
1986	64,000	38,400	$53,900	$17,900	120,510
1987	67,500	39,825	$59,600	$20,500	115,870
1988	69,200	40,828	$61,200	$22,000	112,000
1989	70,200	45,630	$67,700	$27,100	N/A

Source: National Association of Convenience Stores and Dollars per Day Survey.

Exhibit 2
Convenience Store Sales by Product Category

Product Category	1975	1980	1981	1982	1983	1984	1985	1986	1987	1988	1989
Tobacco Products	14.2%	10.5%	10.2%	11.0%	10.9%	11.6%	11.5%	13.2%	13.6%	13.8%	14.0%
Alcoholic Beverages	14.8	9.4	9.3	10.4	9.7	9.6	9.8	10.1	9.8	8.5	8.9
Fast foods	4.6	5.2	4.9	4.9	4.2	4.7	6.8	7.2	7.0	7.8	5.3
Soft drinks	9.4	7.9	7.8	7.7	7.3	7.3	6.6	6.9	6.4	5.7	5.9
Dairy Products	8.9	7.1	6.7	4.9	4.3	4.4	4.3	3.9	3.8	3.5	3.1
Candy & gum	3.8	3.8	3.7	3.3	3.0	3.1	3.2	3.3	3.5	3.2	3.2
Groceries	10.5	6.7	6.4	6.5	5.7	5.8	3.8	3.7	3.7	3.2	2.3
Fountain Drinks	0.4	0.5	0.6	1.1	1.3	1.5	1.7	2.4	1.6	1.8	2.2
Health & beauty aids	4.0	3.7	3.3	2.2	2.1	2.1	2.2	2.0	2.0	1.7	1.4
All other	22.4	17.4	16.3	14.1	13.4	14.0	14.8	14.0	14.4	14.7	13.7
Total merchandise sales	93.0%	72.2%	69.2%	66.0%	62.0%	64.3%	64.6%	66.8%	65.6%	64.0%	60.0%
Gasoline sales	7.0	27.8	30.8	34.0	38.0	35.7	35.4	33.2	34.4	36.0	40.0
Total sales	100.0	100.0	100.0	100.0	100.0	100.0	100.0	100.0	100.0	100.0	100.0

Source: National Association of Convenience Stores and Distribution Research Program, The University of Oklahoma.

Exhibit 3
Convenience Store Gross Margins on Selected Products (1985)

Hot Beverage	61%	General merchandise	39%	Wine and liquor	30%
Fountain drinks	58%	Ice cream	39%	Beer	27%
Ice	53%	Health and beauty aids	37%	Eggs	23%
Frozen beverages	44%	Groceries	35%	Dairy products	22%
Delicatessen	43%	Cookies and snacks	35%	Magazines	21%
Candy and gum	41%	Soft drinks	32%	Gas (company-owned)	8%
Sandwiches	39%	Tobacco products	30%	Gas (on consignment)	5%

Source: National Association of Convenience Stores

Exhibit 4
Increase in Number of Circle K Stores

Fiscal Year (4/30)	Number of Stores at End of Fiscal Year	Number of Stores Acquired During Year	Number of Stores Opened During Year	Number of Stores Closed During Year	Number of Stores Selling Gasoline
1970	423	*	81	2	—
1975	1024	*	89	12	516
1980	1200	3	61	22	726
1981	1194	2	19	28	741
1982	1211	16	9	8	768
1983	1221	12	8	10	798
1984	2185	985	10	31	1436
1985	2669	456	61	33	1719
1986	3372	632	166	95	2293
1987	3507	123	161	149	2433
1988	4077	573	252	255	3011
1989	4685	557	163	212	3600

* Included in number of stores opened during year.

Exhibit 5
UtoteM, Inc.

	12/31/80	12/31/81	12/31/82
Sales	$321,817	$387,709	$438,968
Net profits	$4,324	46,533	$14,093
Total assets	$168,391	$163,999	$177,386
Net worth	$78,102	$80,835	$89,510
Number of states	12	12	12
Number of stores	931	949	959
Number of stores selling gasoline	558	600	618

Exhibit 6
Little General Stores

	12/26/81	12/25/82	12/31/83
Revenues	$177,745	$181,791	$205,769
Operating profits	$8,331	$11,552	$14,298
Identifiable assets	$49,287	$56,245	$71,012
Number of states	7	6	6
Number of stores	462	431	435
Number of stores selling gasoline	208	208	226

Exhibit 7
Shop & Go, Inc.

	3/31/83	3/29/84	3/28/85
Sales	$201,956	$254,183	$294,868
Net profits	$6,421	$8,944	$10,205
Total assets	$52,400	$71,006	$81,910
Net worth	$32,258	$39,653	$48,036
Number of states	2	2	2
Number of stores	415	430	446
Number of stores selling gasoline	286	307	328

Exhibit 8
Summary of Circle K Bonds Issued

Date	Type of Bond	Amount (millions)	Yield	Moody's Initial Rating
Oct 83	Convertible subordinated debentures	$50	9%	Ba-3
May 85	Convertible subordinated debentures	$100	8 1/4%	Ba-3
Sep 85	Convertible subordinated debentures	$75	8 3/4%	—
Oct 85	Senior subordinated debentures	$125	12 3/4%	Ba-2
Nov 85	Convertible subordinated debentures	$150	7 1/4%	Ba-3
Dec 87	Junior subordinated debentures	$72	13%	B-1
Oct 88	Senior secured notes	$200	10.7%	—

Exhibit 9
Summary of Stores Sold and Leased Back

Date	Number of Stores	Price (millions)
Apr 84	370	$98.6
Mar 85	122	$38.4
Apr 85	132	$39.1
Oct 85	97	$38.0
Apr 86	238	$80.0
Apr 87	250	$100.0
Fiscal 88	147	$106.0

Exhibit 10
Charter Marketing

	12/26/85	12/31/86	12/31/87
Revenues	$552,179	$482,964	$506,396
Operating profits	$9,329	$21,043	$8,957
Identifiable assets	$103,084	$92,920	$114,860
Number of states	9	9	13
Number of stores	411	407	538

Exhibit 11
Summary of Circle K Major Acquisitions

Date	Company	Number of Stores	Price (millions)
Dec 83	UtoteM	959	$226.8
Oct 84	Little General	435	$132.2
Sep 85	Shop & Go	446	$166.6
Mar 86	(from) National Convenience	224	$57.6
Apr 88	(from) National Convenience	563	$151.4
Sep 88	Charter Marketing	538	$125.6

Exhibit 12a
Circle K Corporation Selected Financial Data (1983-1989)

	4/30/83	4/30/84	4/30/85	4/30/86	4/30/87	4/30/88	4/30/89
Operating Statement							
Merchandise sales	$460.5	$646.7	$1,090.0	$1,368.4	$1,558.2	$1,649.2	$1,962.4
Gasoline sales	$287.3	$382.2	$592.1	$742.9	$731.2	$964.6	$1,479.0
Other revenues	$5.9	$6.3	$14.2	$20.2	$27.3	$42.9	$53.5
Total revenues	$753.7	$1,035.2	$1,696.3	$2,131.5	$2,316.7	$2,656.7	$3,494.9
Cost of sales	$573.1	$783.1	$1,252.7	$1,551.5	$1,649.5	$1,893.1	$2,580.4
Operating and administrative expense	$149.7	$205.9	$362.3	$467.1	$537.4	$627.6	$822.3
Interest and debt	$5.6	$7.9	$21.8	$36.6	$41.6	$56.6	$95.9
Operating profit (loss)	$25.3	$38.1	$59.6	$76.3	$88.3	$79.5	($5.5)
Gain on sale of assets	—	—	—	—	$5.9	$8.2	$32.3
Other expenses[a]	($3.7)	—	—	($6.7)	—	—	—
Earnings before income taxes	$21.6	$38.1	$59.6	$69.6	$94.3	$87.7	$26.8
Income taxes	$5.8	$17.7	$25.9	$30.4	$44.9	$32.8	$11.4
Gain from change in accounting method	—	—	—	—	—	$5.5	—
Net earnings	$15.8	$20.4	$33.7	$39.2	$49.4	$60.4	$15.4

[a] Expenses related to Nucorp sale and litigation.

Exhibit 12b
Circle K Corporation Selected Financial Data (1983-1989)

	4/30/83	4/30/84	4/30/85	4/30/86	4/30/87	4/30/88	4/30/89
Balance Sheet							
Assets							
Cash	$12.3	$16.5	$22.3	$19.9	$24.8	$44.2	$38.5
Accounts receivable	$3.5	$7.2	$11.1	$12.5	$25.7	$34.4	$36.3
Inventory	$42.3	$79.0	$107.1	$135.8	$160.2	$191.0	$239.9
Other current assets	$22.1	$20.6	$39.5	$108.9	$148.2	$109.9	$94.3
Total current assets	$80.2	$123.3	$180.0	$277.1	$358.9	$379.5	$409.0
Fixed assets	$91.6	$189.4	$252.5	$345.7	$451.8	$708.3	$1068.5
Intangibles[b]	$0.0	$67.2	$109.0	$173.1	$235.2	$247.1	$405.8
Other assets	$2.9	$32.3	$38.3	$59.9	$90.6	$200.9	$161.6
Total assets	$174.7	$412.2	$579.8	$855.8	$1,136.5	$1,535.8	$2,044.9
Liabilities							
Notes payable[c]	$15.9	$14.7	$6.1	$56.6	$18.0	$65.4	$98.9
Accounts payable	$23.8	$42.3	$61.1	$77.1	$84.6	$112.1	$134.9
Other current liabilities	$14.6	$42.6	$48.0	$54.2	$66.8	$103.1	$116.6
Total current liabilities	$54.3	$99.6	$115.2	$187.9	$169.4	$280.6	$350.4
Long-term debt	$40.5	$157.0	$269.4	$382.9	$536.6	$844.1	$1,103.8
Other long-term liabilities	$8.2	$12.1	$20.4	$34.9	$73.0	$80.1	$212.8
Preferred stock	$0.0	$50.0	$50.0	$50.0	$47.5	$47.5	$47.5
Stockholder's equity	$71.7	$93.5	$124.8	$200.1	$310.0	$283.5	$330.4
Total liabilities and equity	$174.7	$412.2	$579.8	$855.8	$1,136.5	$1,535.8	$2,044.9
Dividends on common stock	$8.2	$8.4	$8.9	$9.9	$13.0	$13.0	$12.2
Dividends on preferred stock	$0.0	$1.0	$4.0	$4.0	$4.0	$3.8	$5.1
Capital expenditures	$18.9	$56.9	$95.4	$150.8	$264.1	$268.9	$193.3

[b] Intangibles include excess costs over acquired net assets and favorable leases acquired.

[c] Notes payable include due to bank and current portion of long-term debt and capital lease obligations.

Source: Circle K Corporation Annual Reports.

JCPenney: WEATHERING THE WINDS OF CHANGE*
By Deborah Zizzo, University of Oklahoma

The historical trail of retailing is littered with the carcasses of once-thriving enterprises. Few companies manage to endure, much less flourish, for almost 100 years, but the JCPenney Company is one such survivor. Its longevity may be attributed, in part, to a commitment to continual renewal, as well as to timing and good luck. Trying to redirect a large institution is formidable enough, but knowing how and when to change a successful one presents even more challenges, and JCPenney did both. Although sometimes the company was incredibly slow to respond to changes in the market, occasionally that delay worked to their advantage. The strategic transformation required a constant balancing act of retaining old customers while enticing new ones, and sometimes these efforts faltered. The story of how JCPenney survived to become one of the oldest and largest retailers in the country begins at the turn of the century.

Setting Up Shop

James Cash Penney opened his first store in 1902 in Kemmerer, Wyoming, a small mining town. His Golden Rule Store sold clothing, shoes, accessories, notions, and piece goods on a low-price basis. It was open seven days a week from 7:00 a.m. (8:00 a.m. on Sundays) until midnight, or until James Cash saw no potential customers walking down the street. Many expected he would fail, because of his one-price, cash-only policies. At that time, small-town consumers usually bought from local general stores, which sold on credit, or from mining company operations, which paid employees with coupons and ran their own stores that accepted those coupons. James Cash, however, believed people would pay cash for lower prices, and the store's success proved him right. By 1909, he had bought out his partners and began to build his own chain of Golden Rule Stores. James Cash's plan for expansion was based on his theory of "enlightened selfishness"[1], which offered lucrative partnerships to carefully selected, highly motivated men who demonstrated they could train others. After incorporation in Utah in 1911, the company expanded rapidly, primarily taking advantage of the huge population growth in the western part of the country. (Exhibit 1)

In the late 1920s, the two giant mail-order companies, Sears and Montgomery Ward, noticed that many of their customers were moving from rural communities to larger cities. In response, Sears rapidly began opening full-line retail stores in urban areas, with Wards soon following suit, although not as aggressively. Penney also noted the population shift at this time, but thought it was probably a temporary trend--that people would tire of city life and return to small towns, and Penney would be there to serve them better than ever. Besides, most of Penney's store owner/operators were small and did not have the capital, much less the desire, to enter urban areas. Although the company's loose, highly decentralized structure enabled it to grow extremely quickly, lack of central operations began to present major disadvantages, and in 1927, the organization underwent a major structural overhaul. By 1929, Penney operated 1395 stores with sales of $210 million. The Company began trading on the New York Stock Exchange on October 23, 1929. Six days later the market crashed.

When Earl Sams took over the presidency from James Cash in 1917, he moved to rid Penney of the "junkiness" that existed in the company's stores and to pick some more attractive facilities.[2] Otherwise, however, for the next three decades Penney stuck pretty much with its original plan--providing basic soft goods for middle-class working families. Stores were clean, "no frill" facilities, still located primarily in small towns, where the company felt most comfortable. By 1950, Penney was the third-largest general merchandise retailer in the country behind Sears and Wards. Unlike the other

---

* Used with permission of Deborah Zizzo

[1] Main Street Merchant: The Story of the JCPenney Company, Norman Beasley, McGraw-Hill, 1948, p. 60.

[2] Beasley p. 102.

two, Penney had accomplished this by selling soft goods, on a cash-only basis, with no catalogs. The company's yellow and black signs were a familiar part of small-town America, sales and profits continued to increase steadily and the company carried virtually no debt. Such a successful business did not appear to be in desperate need of change. However, William M. Batten, assistant to the president, thought otherwise and told this to the Board of Directors in 1957.

All You Need is . . . Appliances

In his now famous memorandum, Batten examined the company, analyzed the competitive environment, and called for systematic strategic planning for the future. He was concerned that Penney was not keeping pace with changing consumer markets and called for a company-wide reevaluation to clearly define the Penney mission. Batten cited that changes such as rising living standards had spawned a new middle-income mass market that demanded fashion goods more than utility goods. He noted shoppers' increasing time constraints and yet another population shift from the cities to the suburbs. Batten also foresaw an increasingly difficult retail environment due to traditional competitors like Sears and Wards as well as others moving into lines the company had previously dominated. In addition, consumer demand for credit could no longer be ignored.

For his trouble, Batten was named president and CEO in April 1958. As he noted: "It is often more difficult to make changes in a very successful company than in one not doing so well. People . . . ask, 'Why change a winning combination? If it ain't broke, some say, why fix it?"'[3] Skeptics argued Penney might be risking a great deal by trying to change its well-established image. Batten replied: "It costs money to change and that cost can be computed. It costs money not to change and that cost cannot be computed."[4] He began to reinvent Penney gradually, through diversification, improved internal structure, a new location strategy, a revamped merchandise mix, and new customer services.

The new Penney goal was to be a "complete" general merchandise retailer, where the entire family could shop for everything. This meant adding hard goods and developing lines in major appliances, furniture, hardware, sporting goods, and automotives virtually from scratch. These new lines required bigger stores and a larger customer base. Store size increased from approximately 20,000 to 50,000 square feet to more than 175,000, with about one-third of the space in new stores allocated to hard goods. To find more customers, Penney began to explore urban sites. When Sears and Wards had moved to cities earlier, they had gone in with freestanding stores or in strip malls. By the 1960s, however, malls were expanding and becoming regional shopping centers. Penney's late entry into cities may have been fortuitous, as it allowed them to open their new stores as anchors in these malls. In addition, more upscale, fashionable apparel was an important part of the strategy. Although Penney kept their functional "housedress" type clothing, these staples were relegated to the back of the store.

Penney's move to big-ticket hard goods and higher-priced apparel forced it to introduce credit services. While Sears and Wards had had successful credit programs since the 1920s, Penney finally offered it chainwide in 1962. That was despite one dissenting vote from James Cash himself. Again, coming late to the game worked to Penney's advantage as they were able to start off with a computerized system. To protect its small town market share, Penney offered its new hard lines through catalog desks in stores too small to carry that merchandise. Lateness paid off again, as catalog operations arrived fully automated through the acquisition of a small catalog business in 1962. Penney also decided to diversify into other areas.

By 1975, Penney operations included 31 Treasury discount stores, 255 Thrift drug stores, 24 supermarket operations, 96 company-owned and 211 franchised food/general merchandise stores in Belgium and Italy, and an insurance business. In addition, Penney had 1289 soft-line stores primarily in small towns. Still, the 354 full-line department stores located throughout the country accounted for about one-half of the company's nearly $7 billion in sales. Penney had moved

---

[3] Creating an American Institution: The Merchandising Genius of JCPenney, Mary Elizabeth Curry, Garland Publishing, Inc. 1993, p. 308.

[4] "How They Minted The New Penney," John McDonald, *Fortune*, July 1967, p. 111.

from its small-town soft goods beginnings to a full-line international retailer. Analysts of the time dubbed Batten's work "one of the most dramatic refurbishings in American corporate history."[5] In 1974, Batten retired as chairman and Donald V. Seibert stepped in--right into the recession and a new set of challenges.

To Change or Not to Change

The retail landscape of the mid 1970s looked much different from the boom years of the 1950s and 1960s. Weakened fair trade price laws in 1951 had spawned the discount department store, which forced radical changes in the entire retailing industry, especially during the 1960s and 1970s. In fact, by the mid-1970s, Kmart had overtaken Penney as the nation's second-largest general merchandiser behind Sears. Waning fair trade laws also started a wave of national advertising by manufacturers seeking to protect equity in their brands. Also during this decade, the tremendous growth of shopping centers began to level off.

The recession of 1974-1975 was an economic electric chair for many companies. It shocked everyone else to attention. The "Big 3," Sears, Penney, and Wards, were hit especially hard, since they carried huge inventories, bought far in advance, and subsequently were forced to take more markdowns. All three companies already had begun to question the viability of pursuing a mass marketing strategy in what was becoming an increasingly diverse and segmented society. Population growth had slowed and women had entered the workforce in large numbers. More leisure time had given consumers more options. Inflation; high interest rates; and rising energy, construction, and real estate costs made growth by expansion more difficult than in the boom decades. In addition, markets were becoming saturated. Many retailers believed that future growth would depend on more efficient and productive use of existing store space. In 1975, Penney set up a task force to study these challenges and put William R. Howell in charge.

Since the big restructuring launched in 1958, Penney had worked hard to project a more fashionable image. In the late 1950s, they began to advertise in national magazines and to explore television advertising opportunities, partly for the "cachet" of being seen next to top manufacturer brands. In the 1960s, they hired Mary Quant as a designer. In the late 1960s, *Fortune* magazine proclaimed Penney to be a leader in the "mass merchandising of fashion," a somewhat contradictory title at best[6] Yet the company's bread and butter sales remained in private labels and in less exciting lines--work clothing, underwear, children's clothing, sheets, and towels.

To help dimension the changes and better understand the market of the 1970s, the company undertook a survey of 7000 customers in 1975. They learned that women bought lingerie and underwear at Penney, but went to department stores for dresses, coats, and sportswear. In other words, the Penney customer was not different from the department store shopper, but still viewed Penney as a place to buy staple goods, not fashionable clothing. The survey also identified three distinct customer segments: young fashion-conscious juniors; "contemporaries," the largest group, who spent the most on high quality clothing; and "conservatives," the traditional customer who wanted comfort and value. Unfortunately for Penney, the highly-desired "contemporary" segment saw Penney as old-fashioned and catering to a lower class of customer. Only one-third of these shoppers rated Penney as being "very good" or "excellent" in apparel.[7]

Still, women's fashionable apparel, with its high gross margins and potential to generate store traffic, remained an attractive area and Penney decided to pursue more vigorously their upscale strategy. The 1976 Annual Report stated this goal to offer merchandise of "character and fashionability of the traditional department stores, but with a price edge of 10 to 20 percent."[8] The "Women's Fashion Project" was launched to increase the company's market share in women's apparel. Some stores were remodeled with softer lighting and carpeting. The Company, never keen on owning property when it

---

[5] "JCPenney: Getting More From the Same Space," *Business Week*, August 18, 1975, p. 83.

[6] *Fortune* Minted p. 110

[7] "JCPenney's Fashion Gamble," *Business Week*, January 16, 1978, p. 68.

[8] JCPenney Company, Inc., Annual Report 1976, p. 7.

could be leased, purchased their headquarters building in New York City to remain near the "natural center" for their main merchandise groups, apparel and soft lines. The new fashion thrust still presented potential problems such as a quicker buying and selling schedule and a continuing need for suitable suppliers. Some manufacturers were reluctant to "dilute" their image by selling to Penney; others did not want to upset their department store customers by selling to Penney; still others lacked the capacity to supply such a huge company.

Over the next few years, Penney plowed ahead with its fashion update program, despite early pronouncements by critics that the program had, at the very least, "stumbled."[9] Critics charged that although advertising dollars were being spent to project a fashion image, stores didn't always reflect that when high-dollar goods were placed next to candy counters or popcorn machines. Some charged that prices had been hiked too high, and the company's traditional customers were fleeing to discounters. Still, Penney persevered and said in its 1981 Annual Report that it planned to allocate even more space to apparel, especially women's, and to home furnishings and leisure merchandise.

By 1982, the company had closed or sold the marginal businesses--the Treasury discount stores, supermarket operations, and stores in Italy--which some felt consumed too many resources anyway. Besides its 1631 Penney stores, the company still operated 353 drug stores and 62 stores in Belgium. The catalog division, which had become profitable ahead of schedule, had 1815 locations. Nearly one-half of sales were made on credit. However, hard good lines, which took up about one-third of the space in full-line stores, were operating barely at break even. Still, Penney looked relatively healthy financially, especially when compared to Sears, Wards, and other types of retailers. (Exhibit 2) As in 1958, did the time seem right to tinker with a successful company?

The Two Billion Dollar Bet

In January 1983, Penney took what seemed to be a bold step--announcing plans to drop nearly $1 billion in hard lines merchandise including major appliances, paint, hardware, lawn and garden, fabrics, and automotive operations. Some hard lines such as sporting goods, electronics, and housewares would be continued and updated. But Penney believed customers just weren't comfortable buying fashions and hammers at the same store. The emphasis would be on apparel and accessories, home furnishings, and leisure goods, toward the new goal of becoming a national department store. This new merchandise mix would command higher markups, better margins, and faster inventory turn. It also would require less in accounts receivable, unlike some hard lines such as appliances, which was a low-margin, low-turn, high-credit operation.

The new JCPenney Stores Positioning Statement, issued about that time, stated the company's mission: to offer quality, fashionable merchandise at a lower price. Specifically, stores would look "85 percent" like department and specialty stores but carry a wider range of prices and sell comparable merchandise at 10 to 20 percent less. The emphasis would still be on private brands, but with manufacturer labels added to increase consumer perception of quality. A key part of the plan was creating that elusive trendier image. Customers still saw Penney as "functional, institutional, unattractive, unexciting, and dull, and the stores were dark."[10] Apparently, Penney customers shopped at department stores almost twice as often as at Penney stores, due, primarily, to women's apparel. The goal was to get current customers to buy items at Penney that they normally would walk down the mall to a department store to buy.

To do this, Penney budgeted $1 billion for 1983 to 1987 for major store remodeling, with new fixturing, wider aisles, carpeting and parquet, and more updated colors. Additional dollars went to advertising, too, to communicate this new image. One success in the quest to attract national brands came when Penney finally obtained Levi Strauss merchandise. In response, Macy's, the department store, promptly dropped its Levi lines. In pursuit of exclusive designer names, the company hired Halston and Lee Wright.

---

[9] "Can Ward Break Upgrading Barrier," *Chain Store Age General Merchandise Edition*, September 1980, p. 51.

[10] "Better Slow Than Never," Jeff Blyskal, *Forbes*, October 10, 1983, p. 151.

Several upper management changes also occurred, with Howell taking over as chairman and CEO in September 1983. New incentive pay plans for store managers and sales personnel were instituted, although 9300 of the 160,000 employees were scheduled to lose their jobs.

In 1985, sales were still slow and earnings were declining. A concurrent slowdown in consumer spending led to high inventories for many retailers which, in turn, forced heavy markdowns. The early 1980s also marked the beginning of rapid growth in specialty stores such as The Limited and Gap in apparel, and Toys "R" Us and Home Depot in hard goods. Also a new breed of competitor, the off-price apparel store, threatened department stores and the "Big 3." Off-price retailers such as Marshalls, T.J. Maxx, and Loehmann's, sold department store apparel and soft goods at prices discounted from 20 to 60 percent. Despite substantial concern over whether they were pursuing the right course, Penney felt they had the right strategy and committed even more resources to the plan.

Full Speed Ahead

In October 1987, the company announced it was dropping its remaining hard goods from the stores. These lines, primarily home electronics, sporting goods, and photographic equipment, represented another $500 million dollars in sales, but had been decimated by the consumer electronics "category killer" stores like Circuit City and Best Buy. Studies indicated women accounted for 80 percent of all merchandise bought in regional shopping centers, so Penney aimed to better reflect what that shopper wanted in malls--clothing, not bicycles.

Space was not a problem, since abandoning all hard lines freed 20 million square feet, which was used primarily to expand women's apparel departments. Although since 1983 more than 200 stores had been closed and nearly that many more would be shut by 1993, total selling space had not dropped dramatically. In fact, the overall ratio of selling to gross space increased from 50-50 to 70-30.[11] Internal restructuring brought marketing and merchandising operations together in four categories: women's (which accounted for 42 percent of sales), men's (27 percent of sales), children's (13 percent), and home furnishings (18 percent). After Halston's last collection in 1988, Penney decided to concentrate on upgrading its own private label items and emphasizing department store brands instead of exclusive designer names. Promotional dollars were shifted from advertising to visual merchandising.

At the same time, to bring their executives closer to their middle market customers, Penney decided to move its headquarters from New York City to Plano, Texas. Cost savings were estimated at $30 million per year. However, the move to Texas left 2100 of the 3300 New York employees behind, many of them senior buying staff. Many of the new buyers were inexperienced and didn't buy enough for the 1988 Christmas season, leaving stores without inventory at that important time.

Penney made other substantial changes during 1987. Operations in Belgium were sold to concentrate on U.S. businesses. An experiment into interactive home shopping, Telaction, was launched and the company invested in four small specialty retail ventures. These experiments were short-lived, however, as Telaction was discontinued in 1989 and the specialty retail operations were closed two years later to focus on core operations.

By early 1990, many analysts were pleased with Penney's performance and prospects, saying the company had "quietly pulled off a major restructuring."[12] Penney was (still) the largest seller of private label soft goods and the largest children's apparel retailer in the world, getting 11 cents of every dollar spent in that category. The mix in apparel settled in at about 75-25 private labels to national brands. A big boost in upgrading came with the 1989 addition of the Van Heusen label. That manufacturer decided Penney's shoppers finally matched the demographics of its customers. Penney also softened its commodity image by holding fewer sales and increasing emphasis on special events marketing.

---

[11] JCPenney Company, Inc., Annual Report 1989, p. 2.

[12] "JCPenney Takes On A Bright New Shine," Patricia Sellers, *Fortune*, September 25, 1989, p. 26.

Some of the company's strengths were not so obvious, including the use of information systems. They were connected electronically to 200 of their largest suppliers representing half of merchandise volume.[13] In 1985, they had been one of the first retailers to use Direct Broadcast Satellite (DBS) to allow stores to select part of their merchandise to suit local taste. The DBS had also been used for consumer market research as well as employee training and international buying. Catalog operations included the largest privately-owned telemarketing network in the country, with 90 percent of orders reaching customers within two days. Also, Penney remained in sound financial shape. The 1980s brought mergers, acquisitions, LBOs, and heavy debt loads for many retailers. Many department stores were under extreme financial pressure. Campeau's bankruptcy in 1990 undoubtedly made some department store suppliers more willing to consider selling to Penney. After all, the company had an unusual reputation for paying bills on time and seemed to be at least relatively stable financially.

Unfortunately, Penney's latest upgrading push coincided with the Persian Gulf War, the recession, and reduced consumer spending in late 1990 and 1991. At the same time, department stores were cutting prices heavily to raise cash to pay debt. Another group of off-price apparel retailers, including Burlington Coat Factory, Ross Stores, and Syms, were also hurting many traditional retailers. Penney seemed to be caught in the middle--not the highest quality apparel and not the lowest prices either. Traditional customers began disappearing, because they thought Penney was getting too expensive for them, primarily since all the staple merchandise had been moved back against the walls to showcase the fashions. Howell admitted that fashion levels and prices may have been pushed too far too fast during this time.[14]

Again, the strategy had to be refined. As consumers became more "value"-oriented at the beginning of the 1990s, Penney began to emphasize what has been a long-standing strength--private labels. Penney continues efforts to upgrade their image while trying to maintain the delicate balance between fashionable merchandise and retaining basic goods for core customers. One moral victory of sorts came when Macy's began carrying Levi Strauss goods again in 1993. However, May Department Stores decided to drop its Ultima cosmetic line when Penney began selling it.

Return to Ground Zero

In some ways, Penney has come full circle. The company began at the turn of the century by selling apparel and soft goods to middle-class America. To become a more "complete" retailer, hard goods were added in the early 1960s, which put the company into larger stores in urban areas. These hard lines were dropped in 1983 and 1987, and the large stores in regional malls are now stocked again with apparel and soft goods.

Penney would not be in its current position without a founder willing to step aside so others could make key strategic decisions and a series of leaders who each recognized and implemented needed changes. Some changes such as moving into urban areas and offering credit were made nearly 30 years after the competition. But, in some cases, lateness worked to the company's advantage.

For more than three decades, Penney has been trying to upgrade its image, although they are finding it extremely difficult to change 90 years of perceptions. The upscaling process will always be evolving, as long as standards of living and consumer taste levels continue to rise. Penney continues to walk the tightrope between attracting new fashion-oriented shoppers and keeping old basic goods customers.

In 1993, discounter Wal*Mart passed Sears to become the largest retailer in the country. Penney is currently the fourth largest general merchandiser, behind those two companies and Kmart. The company has just recorded two years of sales and earnings growth. It appears well-positioned for the 1990s. Could this be the perfect time for another strategic overhaul?

---

[13]"JCPenney Grows in Furniture," Les Gilbert, *HFD*, January 15, 1990, p. 8.

[14]"NRF Honors William R. Howell," Penny Gill, *Stores*, January 1992, p. 70.

Questions for Discussion

1. Describe some of the risks a company takes when it decides to reposition itself by changing its image, merchandise mix, etc. How can a business know when it is time to reposition?

2. What are some of the vulnerabilities of the niche Penney is trying to serve?

3. Considering Penney's financial performance from 1982 to 1986 (Exhibit 3), would you have continued the strategy begun in 1983 to drop hard lines? Does their financial performance since 1987 reflect the success or failure of this strategy?

4. What are some of the demographic, social, legal, technological, and competitive changes occurring now that Penney should consider when deciding on a strategic direction for the year 2001?

Exhibit 1
Number of Stores and Sales
"JCPenney Stores, Inc."
(1902-1993)

Year	Stores	Sales (In millions except for 1902)
1902	1	$28,898
1909	6	$.3
1915	86	$4.8
1920	312	$42.8
1925	674	$91.1
1929	1,395	$209.7
1935	1,481	$225.9
1940	1,586	$304.5
1945	1,602	$549.1
1950	1,612	$949.7
1955	1,666	$1,220.0
1960	1,695	$1,468.9
1965	1,669	$2,289.2
1970	1,647	$3,747.0
1975	1,651	$6,278.0
1980	1,682	$10,290.0
1985	1,482	$12,165.0
1990	1,312	$14,616.0
1993	1,246	$16,846.0

Exhibit 2
Strategic Profit Model Ratios
"Big 3" Retailers, Other Retailers, and All Retailers
1981/1982

Strategic Profit Model Ratios	J.C Penney (1-30-82)	Sears (12-31-81)	Montgomery Ward (12-30-81)	Department Stores	Specialty Stores	Discount Department Stores	All Retailers
Net profits/Net sales	3.3%	1.9%	(2.2)%	3.3%	2.2%	1.8%	1.9%
Net sales/Total assets	1.9×	2.8×	1.4×	1.5×	2.2×	3.1×	2.3×
Net profits/Total assets	6.2%	5.4%	(3.0)%	5.0%	4.9%	5.7%	4.4%
Total assets/Net worth	2.12×	1.5×	2.5×	1.7×	1.9×	2.7×	2.5×
Net profits/Net worth	13.2%	8.3%	(7.5)%	8.5%	9.3%	10.9%	10.9%

Source: Company Annual Reports, National Retail Merchants Associaton, Cornell University, Federal Trade Commission and Distribution Research Program, The University of Oklahoma.

Exhibit 3
JCPenney Company, Inc.
Income Statement (In Millions)
1981-1993

	1/30/82	1/26/85	1/25/86	1/31/87	1/30/88	1/28/89	1/27/90	1/26/91	1/25/92	1/30/93	1/29/94
Income Statement											
Retail Sales	$11,860	$13,451	$13,747	$14,740	$15,332	$14,833	$16,103	$16,365	$16,201	$18,009	$18,983
Finance Charge Revenue								$674	$647	$570	
Other Revenue						$463	$302	$371	$447	$506	$595
Total Revenue	$11,860	$13,451	$13,747	$14,740	$15,332	$15,296	$16,405	$17,410	$17,295	$19,085	$19,578
Cost of Goods Sold	$8,101	$9,030	$9,240	$9,786	$10,152	$9,717	$10,492	$10,969	$10,841	$12,040	$12,997
Selling, General and Administrative Expense	$2,875	$3,374	$3,454	$3,679	$3,783	$3,815	$4,129	$4,999	$4,924	$5,160	$4,508
Interest Expense, net	$227	$350	$370	$350	$300	$307	$303	$301	$308	$258	$73
Other Income						$222[5]					
Other Expense[1]					$172[4]	$487	$311[6]	$309	$754	$368	$446
Income Taxes	$289	$290	$297	$428	$356	$385	$368	$255	$204	$482	$610
Other Income[2]	$31	$28	$11	$33	$39						$51[8]
Other Expense	$12[3]			$52					$184[7]		$55[9]
Net Income	$387	$435	$397	$478	$608	$807	$802	$577	$80	$777	$940

Notes:
1. Primarily from costs of other businesses.
2. Other income from 1/30/82 to 1/30/88 is from unconsolidated subsidiaries, insurance, real estate and bank. These operations were consolidated in 1/28/89 fiscal year.
3. Repositioning Belgian operations (net of gain from an exchange of stock for debt).
4. Provision for relocating corporate headquarters to Texas, mostly personnel relocation costs and severance.
5. Sale of New York City headquarters building.
6. Includes discontinuing Telaction.
7. Accounting charge for postretirement health care benefits.
8. Accounting change for income taxes.
9. Charge on debt redemption.

Exhibit 3 (Continued)
JCPenney Company, Inc.
Balance Sheet (In Millions)
1981-1993

	1/30/82	1/26/85	1/25/86	1/31/87	1/30/88	1/28/89	1/27/90	1/26/91	1/25/92	1/30/93	1/29/94
Balance Sheet											
Cash	$123	$43	$158	$639	$112	$670	$408	$137	$111	$397	$173
Accounts Receivable	$1,617	$1,864	$4,504	$4,614	$4,536	$4,233	$4,353	$3,837	$3,525	$3,161	$4,679
Inventories	$1,578	$2,383	$2,298	$2,168	$2,350	$2,201	$2,613	$2,657	$2,897	$3,258	$3,545
Other Current Assets	$109	$134	$117	$111	$132	$142	$165	$168	$162	$154	$168
Total Current Assets	$3,427	$4,424	$7,077	$7,532	$7,130	$7,246	$7,539	$6,799	$6,695	$6,970	$8,565
Fixed Assets	$1,932	$2,608	$2,812	$2,919	$2,910	$3,034	$3,237	$3,500	$3,602	$3,725	$3,818
Other Assets	$857	$1,138	$633	$737	$802	$1,974	$1,922	$2,026	$2,223	$2,868	$2,405
Total Assets	$6,216	$8,170	$10,522	$11,188	$10,842	$12,254	$12,698	$12,325	$12,520	$13,563	$14,788
Notes Payable	$0	$25	$740	$1,081	$955	$100	$1,452	$979	$708	$907	$1,632
Accounts Payable	$420	$398	$424	$555	$525	$646	$708	$663	$610	$944	$1,034
Other Current Liabilities	$1,282	$1,416	$1,559	$1,076	$1,206	$2,039	$1,240	$1,020	$1,091	$1,226	$1,217
Total Current Liabilities	$1,702	$1,839	$2,723	$2,712	$2,686	$2,785	$3,400	$2,662	$2,409	$3,077	$3,883
Long Term Debt	$1,126	$1,839	$2,865	$2,431	$2,395	$2,195	$1,947	$2,394	$2,685	$2,583	$2,929
Other Debt	$455	$680	$883	$1,705	$1,588	$3,317	$2,998	$2,875	$3,238	$3,198	$2,611
Net Worth	$2,933	$3,812	$4,051	$4,340	$4,173	$3,957	$4,353	$4,394	$4,188	$4,705	$5,365
Total Liabilities and Net Worth	$6,216	$8,170	$10,522	$11,188	$10,842	$12,254	$12,698	$12,325	$12,520	$13,563	$14,788
Dividends	$129	$175	$176	$183	$213	$266	$301	$335	$342	$342	$371
Capital Expenditures	$208	$505	$426	$348	$376	$481	$477	$637	$515	$453	$480

YAOHAN INTERNATIONAL HOLDINGS*

By Keri Davies, University of Stirling

Introduction

> "By studying and practicing the truth of life's philosophies, the Yaohan group of companies strives to create a company that will render better service to people all over the world and in so doing become a model for other companies."
>
> Yaohan credo

In just two decades, Yaohan has moved from being a second-tier Japanese retailer to a recognized pan-Asian name. Through Yaohan Overseas and Yaohan International, the group has one of the largest overseas store networks of any Japanese retailer. This case concentrates on Yaohan's expansion into the People's Republic of China and on Yaohan International Holdings (YIH), the company established primarily to act as an investment vehicle for that expansion. For background information, we will begin by looking at the Yaohan Group as a whole before concentrating on YIH.

The Yaohan Group

The company now known as Yaohan was established in 1928 as a small greengrocer's business in the hot spring resort of Atami, 60 miles southwest of Tokyo, by Ryohei and Katsu Wada, the parents of the current chairman Kazuo Wada. At the very beginning, the Wadas even peddled goods in the street--a common activity even now for small greengrocers and fruiterers. Kazuo Wada wished to become a diplomat after graduating from Nihon University in March 1951; but, as the eldest son, his parents insisted on his joining the family business. Kazuo's mother was a strong adherent to the teachings of "Seicho-no-Ie" ("House of Growth," a new religion established in 1929 by Masaharu Taniguchi), and Kazuo has followed her in these beliefs. These teachings have been very important in the history of Yaohan and the form that it has taken. To some extent, the cult still permeates the company. While there is no compulsion to adhere, the morning meetings are still called "morning prayers." It is also reflected in the uplifting mottoes of Yaohan, which according to commentators, are believed in by management.

The Wadas have always looked to the long run, buoyed up by their beliefs. Two anecdotes will show this. In the first, it is said that when a huge typhoon in the Atami area destroyed all the vegetable crops, every store but that owned by the Wada's pushed up its prices because of the shortage. The Wadi Shoji store did not cash in on the disaster but it did earn trust and respect, which were deemed to be more important in the long run. Secondly, in 1952 there was a major fire that devastated Atami and reduced the Wada's shop to ashes. They were not covered by insurance. In an almost melodramatic manner, Kazuo Wada is said to have declared, "Now we have been stripped naked. In the future we may be stripped naked again, but we will always persevere and survive."

By 1956 the rebuilt business had thrived enough for a small supermarket to be opened. Total sales averaged ¥156,000 per day and there were 20 employees. By 1960, sales totaled ¥310 million per annum and there were 140 employees. When Kazuo Wada became president of the company, one of his first acts, on July 1 1962, was to change the company's name from Wada Shoji to Yaohan Department store. 'Yaohan' is a Japanese term meaning "selling foodstuffs carried on one's back." This was a reference both to the company's past and to the self-sufficiency that was to characterize its future development.

While Yaohan expanded during the 1960s, it was unable to keep pace with its larger competitors. Rivals such as Daiei, Seiyu, and Ito-Yokado had established supermarkets earlier and were already expanding aggressively. In 1971,

---

* Used with permission of Keri Davies.

Wada realized that as a late comer with only six retail outlets exclusively in the Shizuoka area, he would always play second fiddle to these major retailers. He also faced another obstacle in the introduction of the large-scale Retail Store Law, which inhibited the construction of large supermarkets in local areas. Retailers needed either to have a prestigious name that might sway local opinion, or be large enough to persevere through the complicated procedures involved. Recognizing that he had little room to grow in Japan in the immediate future, Wada took Yaohan to Brazil.

Yaohan's Brazilian operation opened in 1971, with four supermarkets in Japanese-Brazilian neighborhoods in Sao Paulo. This choice of country illustrates the decision making typical of many Japanese retailers. At the time, Brazil had a strong economy and was forecast to be in line for retail expansion by a number of overseas retailers, including Sears Roebuck of the U.S. and Carrefour of France. It also had a substantial population of Japanese immigrants who had moved there before World War II whose presence would allow Yaohan to transfer its expertise overseas with less of an immediate culture shock. However, the crucial element in the choice of Brazil was the personal link, almost a recommendation, that is so important in Japanese business life. Wada's religious teacher had lived in Brazil and the positive impression Wada was given of the country was carried into his business dealings. While the stores looked likely to be successful in their own right at first, they were devastated by the currency changes consequent of the 1973 oil crisis. Wada sold them at a loss and, unable to get his cruzeiros out of the country, invested them instead in a Brazilian ranch. "I learned about country risk," he grimaces.

In the meantime, however, Wada had reflected upon his experiences and found other, more attractive locations to set up shop (Exhibit 1). The choice of countries to enter was based upon a number of factors, in addition to the usual business or marketing strategy reasons relating to size of market, expected growth in consumer demand, and so on. First, a number of these countries had become destinations for Japanese tourists. Many Japanese department stores had opened branches in Singapore and Hong Kong, for example, to tap into this market. They provided the security of a well-known name, facilities for Japanese speakers, and even for payment in yen on the spot or drawn from Japanese bank accounts. Finally, they could help put together the package of gifts that must be taken home for family, friends, and workmates. The appreciation of the yen during the 1980s made the purchase of many branded products overseas a very attractive proposition.

As we have already noted for Brazil, many Japanese live abroad. Expatriate Japanese working for financial institutions, car companies, or other manufacturing operations are commonly found in many countries throughout the world. In addition, there are many second or third-generation ethnic Japanese living in countries such as the U.S.. Many families emigrated in the late nineteenth or early twentieth centuries when Japan was seen as a source of cheap labor to work on the construction of the railway system in the U.S. or on farms in Brazil, for example. Yaohan focused on this group and built stores in locations patronized by local residents rather than tourists.

To achieve their goals, these Yaohan stores have a number of common characteristics:

- They provide food items not found in most local stores.

- They prepare foods differently (meat is cut thinner, for example).

- They have non-food categories similar to most supermarkets, but sizing, etc. within the categories is different. Says Yoshiya Watanabe, administrative manager for Yaohan's U.S. division, "Our clothing is directed toward the Japanese because the Japanese are a smaller build than the Americans. So, the sleeves, for example, are shorter than those you would find on garments in an American clothing store."

- They provide related services for their customers. The Yaohan store in London includes a Japanese travel agent, a Japanese estate agent (primarily for purchasing property in the U.K.), and an agent who can arrange schooling in either the U.K. or Japan.

However, other American units, such as that in Chicago, are located in areas where there are fewer Asians; therefore, the product mix is adjusted accordingly. "One of the Fresno stores caters to Latinos, another to the black community, and the third to caucasians. There are a minimum number of Japanese products in the stores where there is not a large Japanese or Asian population," says Watanabe.

There have been negative factors that have, until recently, constrained development in some of the countries geographically closest to Yaohan's home base. In the 1960s and 1970s, many Asian countries introduced controls over inward investment, particularly investment targeted at their domestic markets. While Japanese manufacturing plants producing items for export have been welcomed, ventures aimed at the home service or retail markets have been placed under strict control or even prohibited altogether. Controls over location, ownership of land, use of foreign employees, and the necessity for local equity participation have been commonplace. It has been only since the mid 1980s that domestic pressures from consumers wishing to see greater diversity and lower prices in the retail sector, and foreign pressures from countries such as the U.S. wanting to see more markets for their firms, have combined to force open more Asian markets.

It is not surprising, therefore, that Yaohan's development during the 1970s and early 1980s should have been concentrated upon countries that, in addition to supporting large numbers of Japanese shoppers, have been relatively open to foreign investment. Singapore and Hong Kong, in particular, have been used by Yaohan as testbeds for experiments in targeting their retail product at different groups of visitors, expatriates, and local shoppers. Their experience has been reflected in the manner in which Yaohan has approached other Asian markets in the 1980s and 1990s and the retail offering they have provided.

By this time, the Yaohan Group was split into three main sections: Yaohan Japan (formerly Yaohan Department store), Yaohan Overseas, and Yaohan International. Each of these subgroups was run by a member of the Wada family: Kazuo Wada controlled the group as a whole and was also chairman of Yaohan International with particular responsibility for Hong Kong, Macau and the People's Republic of China; Terumasa Wada was president of Yaohan Japan; and Mitsumasa Wada was director of Yaohan Overseas in Singapore and looked after operations in the rest of Asia, the U.S., and Europe.

The position the renamed Yaohan Group had reached by 1991 is shown in Exhibit 2. The number of overseas stores had grown from just 1 in 1976 (the stores in Brazil having been closed down) to 24 in 1991. While this was just one-fifth of the total number of stores in the group, they had half the sales area and accounted for half of the group's sales. The exhibits are slightly misleading, however, in that the new overseas stores are almost all large supermarket-cum-department stores; whereas the Japanese exhibits include electrical, DIY, and fast-food outlets. Nonetheless, the message seems to have been clear--Wada's original idea that expansion outside Japan would be easier and more profitable was correct. In 1991, Yaohan reached another milestone when it began to expand into the People's Republic of China.

Yaohan International Holdings

As he approached his sixtieth birthday in 1989, Kazuo Wada began to reflect on Yaohan's growth and on his plans for the future. During the 1980s, the growth in Yaohan's overseas operations had been concentrated in the Pacific Asia region (see Exhibit 1), where several countries were recording double-digit levels of economic growth. A noticeable absence was the immense yet underdeveloped market of the People's Republic of China. There had been major economic and social changes in this market following the "Four Modernizations" program instituted by Deng Xiaoping in 1978.

With the increase in their living standards, Chinese consumers, and particularly those in the big cities, had become more interested in buying foreign and imported manufactured goods. This change can also be attributed to the rejection by consumers of the outdated and shoddy products being manufactured by state enterprises. The foreign brands that attracted most Guangdong consumers, for example, tended to be the same ones that were across the border in Hong Kong. Virtually every household in the Pearl River Delta had erected a towering TV antenna to tune into the latest trends and advertisements from Hong Kong. The problem for Yaohan was that the Chinese government had been following a manufacture-for-export policy in its dealing with foreign companies, which protected the domestic market by excluding foreign retailers and imposed tariffs and quotas on foreign products.

Yet, by the late 1980s, it was beginning to look as if the Chinese government would soon be prepared to allow foreigners to enter the retail and wholesale markets. The country's distribution system needed outside investment and expertise if consumer demand was to be satisfied. A number of Japanese retailers such as Daiei had representative offices in Beijing or Shanghai as a means of sourcing products for Japan and obtaining market information, but they were not allowed to sell products in China. The only exceptions to the rule were foreign retailers who sold only products manufactured in China and a small number of Western style outlets, run mainly by Hong Kong companies, aimed directly at foreigners using "hard" currency.

Wada's strategy was to bypass China in the first instance and to concentrate on Hong Kong, which is due to return to Chinese rule in 1997. In setting up the current tripartite structure of Yaohan Group, Wada announced that the group's headquarters would be moved from Japan to Hong Kong, along with Yaohan International Co. Ltd. Even more importantly, in 1990, Kazuo Wada and his mother Katsu Wada moved to take up non-Japanese resident status in Hong Kong. Such a move attracted immense publicity at a time when most foreign companies were reassessing their position in Hong Kong. The Wadas were invited to meet the then Governor of Hong Kong, Sir David Wilson; were received by officials of the Chinese government in Beijing; and became players in the expatriate Chinese society of Hong Kong.

When the Wadas arrived in Hong Kong, local confidence had crashed with the stock market following the Tiananmen Square riots. Their arrival was a vote of confidence in the colony and won them friends in the closed ranks of the business community. With a clear and stridently stated mission, Kazuo Wada stood out from the materialistic local business community. His vision of a global role for his retailing group contrasted with the usual focus on short-term profitability. Wada cemented business relationships and displayed his confidence in the colony and China through property purchases and business acquisitions.

This expansion (which is detailed below) is being undertaken by Yaohan International Co. Ltd. This is a private company that acts as the investment vehicle of the Wada family (the family holds approximately 46 percent of the company), although nine banks also participate and provide finance. Wada shrewdly sold a percentage of the company to the influential Hong Kong and Shanghai Banking Corporation. The Wadas have injected their holding of Yaohan Japan into Yaohan International Co. Ltd, which has also acquired Yaohan Japan's stake in Yaohan Hong Kong. Apart from the general strategy to be defined below, these moves are plainly very tax-effective. Yaohan International Co. Ltd now has just a 6.6 percent stake in Tokyo-listed Yaohan Japan.

The move of Yaohan International Co. Ltd's main office to Hong Kong was part opportunism and part strategy. In the short term, high taxes and land and labor costs in Japan played a part in the move. Wada also wanted to get around a Japanese law forbidding the formation of a holding company. Under Hong Kong law, Wada was able to establish Yaohan International Holdings Ltd (YIH). Yaohan International Co. Ltd has a 75 percent stake in YIH, while the remaining 25 percent was made available to the public when the company was floated on the Hong Kong Stock Exchange in 1993.

In the long run, the move to Hong Kong reinforced the group aim of expansion overseas and, in particular, began preparing the ground for the move into China. At the time, Kazuo Wada is said to have believed that China would not be ready for international merchandising until per capita income reached US$1000 and that China would remain an area for development in the future. Nonetheless, as we have seen, he began immediately to lay the foundations for a move building *guanxi* or connections with the Chinese government, provincial governments, and businessmen. In 1992 he announced,

"In the three years that I have lived in Hong Kong, I have been for liberalization, the introduction of capitalism, and consumer development. I am positive that the twenty-first century will be the era of China."

What Yaohan and other foreign retailers have found is that the official statistics in China do not match the reality. Economic statistics show it to be one of the poorest Asian nations, with a per capita GNP of US$355, compared to Indonesia's US$666 or Thailand's US$1800. However, the economic reforms since 1978 have brought relative prosperity to many of the urban areas, particularly in the south of the country, and much wealth also appears to have been hidden from the official census-takers. Average per capita income in Guangdong and Shanghai were between two and three times higher than the national average in 1993. As a consequence, Wada soon revised his view of when Yaohan should enter China. While Yaohan Hong Kong consolidated its local position, YIH opened its first store in China in 1991. This has proven to be just the first of a variety of developments undertaken by the company.

The Organizational Structure of YIH in 1994

According to Kazuo Wada, YIH now has four pillars of growth--distribution, property development, catering, and processing and trading.

Distribution. YIH has responsibility for the Hong Kong, Macau, and Chinese operations. At first Yaohan concentrated on developing its position in Hong Kong.

- In 1989 Yaohan Hong Kong had three department stores in niche areas of Kowloon and the New Territories; by June 1994 there were eight department stores in Hong Kong (with two more under development) and one in Macau. Most Japanese stores in Hong Kong are located in the main shopping areas of Causeway Bay, Wanchai, and Tsimshatsui, appealing to tourists and high-spending Hong Kong residents. By way of contrast, Yaohan was one of the first foreign retailers to move into Hong Kong's new towns, including Tsuen Wan and Tuen Mun. These are not wholly invisible to Japanese visitors however; for example, its store in Tsuen Wan is built under a Japanese-run hotel. Nonetheless, the main aim has been to become a household name to those living and working in Hong Kong's suburbs.

- YIH has over 150 other retail outlets in Hong Kong including the Yaohan Best joint venture in electrical retailing; the Millie's group, which retails shoes, leather goods, and fashion wear; the Saint Honore bakery stores; and Chinese restaurants (see below).

- YIH operates a chain of indoor family entertainment centers under the Whimsy name.

YIH was listed on the Hong Kong Stock Exchange in October 1993, where it joined Yaohan Hong Kong, Yaohan International Caterers, and Yaohan Food Processing and Trading. The company plans listings for Yaohan Best, Whimsy, Millie's, and Saint Honore during 1994. The net result has been to reinforce the perception of Yaohan's commitment to Hong Kong and to the region in general.

The development of Yaohan in China has been rapid, aided by the Chinese government's decision to loosen controls on retailing beginning with small trials in the Shenzen Special Economic Zone (SEZ) near Hong Kong in 1991. Then, in 1992, the Chinese State Council established a scheme to allow foreign retailers to open joint ventures in Beijing, Tianjin, Shanghai, Guangzhou, Dalian, Qingdao, and the five SEZs. Under this scheme, 2 large Chinese-foreign joint ventures can be set up in each of these locations, a maximum of just 22 developments. The companies involved in this experiment enjoy special privileges regarding imported products. In 1994, the State Council gave permission for a number of Japanese retailers to establish supermarket chains in China, including Daiei and Nichii. However, it was also made clear that the experiment with department stores would not be expanded or extended to other parts of the country for a number of years.

Within this environment Yaohan's development has taken place in a number of steps:

- YIH opened its first store in China in Sha Tau Kok in Shenzen in September 1991. A total of HK$10m was invested, to which Yaohan contributed 49% in cash; the Chinese partner, Sha Tau Kok Pte Ltd, put up the other 51% in land. Sales already exceed those of the Yaohan store in Sha Tin in Hong Kong, and as 90 percent of sales are made in Hong Kong dollars, there is no problem repatriating the profits. It is said that Yaohan's Hong Kong base did make it easier to gain entry to the market.

- A joint venture between Yaohan International (36%), Yaohan Japan (19%), and the Shanghai No. 1 Department Store (45%) was the first store to be approved by the government following its relaxation of the rules on foreign investment in 1991-1992. The proposed new store on Zhang Yang Road in Pudong, Shanghai, will be called the Shanghai No. 1 Yaohan Department Store. Covering 20,000 square meters and with a total floor area of 80,000 square meters, it will be part of a 21-story office and commercial complex due to open in December 1995. The Board of Directors will consist of nine members, five from the Japanese side and four from the Chinese side. The chairman of the board will be a representative of the Chinese side, while the General Manager will be a member of the Japanese side. However, the store manager will be Chinese.

  Yaohan has also been granted the right to import up to 30 percent of the goods sold in the store. At the same time, to take advantage of Yaohan's extensive international distribution network, the joint venture can also conduct export business to achieve a balance of foreign exchange and export surplus. In the first 5 years of operation, the joint venture will enjoy a reduced income tax rate of 15 percent, as opposed to the regular 30 percent set by the state.

  Yaohan will have an outlet in the store but also plans to rent much of the space to other companies. Half of the first floor will be dedicated to an automobile dealership featuring cars from around the world; the other half will be used to sell an international selection of brands. Elsewhere in the store, YIH hopes to attract department stores from Japan, South Korea, Europe, and the U.S. to form the 'core' of each of the floors.

- In 1993, YIH entered into a joint venture agreement with China Venturetech International Co. Ltd (CVIC), a wholly-owned subsidiary of Beijing-based China Venturetech Investment Corporation and the Japanese Nippon Investment and Finance Co. Ltd, which is the venture capital arm of the Daiwa Securities Group and Niten Enterprises Ltd. (It is unlikely that such a prestigious joint venture would have been available to Yaohan without the positive signals about its faith in China that Yaohan's move to Hong Kong had been sending to the State Council.) The joint venture vehicle, CC&Y, will invest in consumer products, distribution, and retail companies. It already has two department stores cum supermarkets in Beijing and Shanghai. When the 19,000 square meter Beijing store started trading in December 1992, a queue a kilometer long waited for the doors to open!

- YIH, in conjunction with CC&Y, has announced plans to open 1000 stores in the Shanghai-Nanjing region by the year 2010. Yaohan has been granted a license to operate supermarkets in Shanghai and its first such store opened in May 1994, with a further three to follow by the end of the same year. The store was a joint venture between Liannong, a company controlled by the Shanghai City Agricultural Committee (whose shares are listed on the Shanghai Stock Exchange), and a company set up by YIH and Yaohan Japan. All the sales staff are Chinese because the cost of just one Japanese manager would have doubled the staff costs from 3 percent of sales to 6 percent. However, this meant that the company had to introduce a new operational system that can work without the presence of Japanese employees--a new practice within the group.

- In March 1994, YIH entered into an agreement with the American retailer Wal*Mart to join forces in a broad range of operations including retailing, wholesaling, and product development. Yaohan's stores will be able to sell Wal*Mart products. They began stocking Wal*Mart household products, stationery, bedroom linen,and cosmetics in November 1993. These goods came from factories commissioned by Wal*Mart in Hong Kong and other parts of Asia. Wal*Mart allowed Yaohan to sell the goods at between 30 percent and 50 percent below prices for similar products from other suppliers. Yaohan hopes that the tie-up will allow them to explore the development of discount stores in Asia. The agreement will also allow Yaohan Group to wholesale products supplied by Wal*Mart in Singapore, Hong Kong, Malaysia, Thailand, Indonesia, and the Philippines through its own sales network

- In May 1994, YIH signed a further deal with the Shanghainese government to redevelop a train station into a shopping center containing retail shops, restaurants, and souvenir shops. YIH plans to put retail and food shops into a number of station buildings in conjunction with the Shanghai Railway Bureau along the railway line between Shanghai and Nanjing. The basements of a few of these stores will be used as distribution centers.

- Yaohan International will open a large-scale computerized international distribution center in Shanghai in 1994 (a joint venture with the Minhang Municipal Government in Shanghai) and a similar center in Beijing in September 1995. These centers will be modeled on the IMM center developed in Singapore by Yaohan Japan. The project will precede the opening of the Yaohan department store in Shanghai and may be followed by up to 10 similar centers in other provinces. Kazuo Wada has been quoted as saying that Yaohan's experience at its existing Chinese stores is that it can take two to three months from placement of orders to delivery of popular merchandise. While the retail industry is managing to adjust to the new economic conditions, the wholesale industry continues to operate much as it did under central planning, he says. IMM Shanghai and any other distribution centers will be needed if Yaohan is to establish its planned retail network around Shanghai.

The partnership with CVIC demonstrates the strength of Yaohan's strategy. Following expansion in Hong Kong, Yaohan is looking for package deals in China where it can introduce restaurant and boutique businesses as well as department stores. The partnership will seek investments in distribution, manufacturing, production, and catering. Glenn Chan, founder and managing director of Yaohan International Caterers (YIC), says, "If you want to open a restaurant chain in China you need as many as 40 shops and you could be lucky to get approval within a year. For us, it will be much easier and may take only two or three months." YIC's subsidiary, Saint Honore, opened its first outlet in Shanghai in mid 1993, and hopes to expand aggressively by taking full advantage of its parentage. "If we were not partners with Yaohan and CVIC, we would have to offer 60 percent to 80 percent more in rental charges," boasts Chan.

In mid 1994 the large Japanese retailers Daiei, Nichii, and Jusco all announced plans to expand into China. Daiei plans to open 5500 stores and 4500 restaurants. While this dwarfs even YIH's plans, Kazuo Wada welcomed the move, officially saying that Daiei would contribute to the modernization of China's retail industry. However, Wada also took the opportunity to underline the difference between Daiei's strategy and Yaohan's. He said that Daiei has a nationwide strategy for China, whereas Yaohan is following a regional approach. Not only does this allow for the great diversity in culture in China, but it also lets Yaohan concentrate its efforts on the Shanghai-Nanjing area with its relatively high levels of income and spending power and openness to foreign investment. YIH plans to set up a holding company in Shanghai in 1994 to oversee its Chinese operations and will seek a listing on the Shanghai Stock Market within five years, reinforcing its efforts to gain insider status in China.

Property Development. This sector is closely related to the distribution sector. In the past, whenever Yaohan opened a store overseas, it would rent the space as a key tenant in a locally-developed shopping center. However, Yaohan's strategy aims at increasing profitability and strengthening competitiveness. For example, Wada has stressed the importance of the new business links he has acquired since his move to Hong Kong, bringing land deals in Hong Kong and other interesting propositions from Hong Kong Chinese businessmen. For example, Wada has purchased properties from Li Ka-Shing, Cheng Yu-Tung, the Kwok Family's Sun Hung Kai Properties, and Macau casino king Stanley Ho--possibly the four most important property developers in the Pearl River Delta.

Catering. Chinese restaurants constitute the core of this category. In addition, various types of new business have been introduced through acquisition such as Korean restaurants, cake shops, and coffee shops. These restaurants and shops are expected to form a franchise chain throughout the world. The operation is organized through Yaohan International Caterers (YIC), in which Yaohan International holds a 51 percent stake; YIC holds 80 percent in the bakery chain Saint Honore. As noted, it plans to expand both YIC and Saint Honore into the Chinese market.

Processing and Trading. Yaohan entered this sector by acquiring a Hong Kong company that had been the sole agent for exporting fish to and importing meat from China and which has a 65% share of the ham market in Hong Kong; YIH holds a 58 percent stake in the renamed Yaohan Food Processing and Trading company. In Hong Kong, YIH also acquired an entertainment company, Whimsy, and a leather goods chain, Millie's, both of which are to be listed on the HKSE in 1994. In March 1994, YIH took over Marumitsu Co., an Osaka-based general clothing wholesaler.

Once again, however, the main expansion of Yaohan in this area has been into China

- In 1993 the joint venture vehicle CC&Y announced plans to build production facilities in several Chinese cities for its own brand of shoes, ham, and biscuits. CC&Y also formed a joint venture, the Suzhou M&Y Cosmetics Co. Ltd, to manufacture and sell cosmetics in China. CC&Y has 14.5 percent of the company, along with Suzhou Yuezhong-gui Household Chemical Factory general, the leading Chinese government enterprise with 100 years experience in cosmetics production (3.3 percent), and the large Japanese cosmetics companies Nippon Menard Cosmetics Co (41 percent) and Milott Cosmetics Corporation (10 percent) among other investors. The products will be designed for the Chinese market, using modern Japanese technology. Production is due to begin in 1995, with the cosmetics being made available through the Yaohan Beijing and Shanghai department stores. Kazuo Wada will be honorary chairman of the new company.

- In December 1993, YIH acted as broker for a new Chinese printing venture, the Shanghai Furubayashi International Printing and Packaging Co. Ltd, which aims to capitalize on the shortage of high-quality printing and packaging materials in China. Yaohan will hold 20 percent of the joint venture together with the Shanghai No. 10 People's Printing Factory (40 percent) and the Japanese printing firm Furubayashi Shiko Co. (40 percent).

- In May 1994, YIH took a 20 percent stake in a new venture, the Shanghai Choya Fashion Company, which will manufacture and sell casual and dress shirts for the domestic and international markets. Yaohan has been instrumental in bringing together an existing Chinese clothing manufacturer, the Shanghai Garment Co. (which will hold 20 percent of the new company), and several Japanese companies: Choya Corporation (40 percent), Itochu Corporation (10 percent) and Nisshinbo Industries Inc. (10 percent).

The net effect of much of this expansion and reorganization is reflected in YIH's organizational chart (Exhibit 3). YIH's turnover trebled between 1991 and 1993, while profit rose by about five times over the same period (Exhibit 4). The core retailing business now accounts for just over half of the business's turnover (Exhibit 5), followed by catering and the food processing and trading subsidiaries. The cost of the expansion has been high however; the group has used its five listed vehicles, including YIH, to raise capital and plans further cash calls by listing several more subsidiaries. By 1997, the group should have two listings in Japan, eight in Hong Kong, and others in the U.S., Malaysia, Singapore, and Thailand.

Most expansion will be funded by banks; however, between 1992 and 1997 Wada expects the Yaohan group to invest ¥137 billion (US$1.2 billion), of which ¥93 billion (US$788 million) will come from loans. With sales projected to double over the next five years to ¥800 billion (US$6.8 billion)--only half coming from Japan--expansion is not expected to be hobbled by debt repayment. Net profit of ¥30 billion (US$254 million) in 1997 is seen as coming mainly from non-Japanese operations.

Estimates are for 65 percent of projected bank borrowing to be undertaken by Tokyo-listed Yaohan Japan. The Hong Kong-based operations are expected to require ¥59 billion (US$500 million) investment capital by 1997 of which ¥33 billion (US$280 million) will come from banks. Set against projected sales of ¥400 billion (US$3.4 billion) and profit of ¥20 billion (US$169 million) in 1997, the group balance sheet is likely to remain conservative.

Problems in the Chinese Market

Despite all the optimism expressed by Yaohan about China, there are still a number of problems that need to be addressed. These problems fall into three main areas:

- **Dealing with the Chinese bureaucracy and getting the requisite permissions to open stores.** To date, Yaohan's management has been quite astute in terms of the links that have been built with their Chinese joint venture partners. Kazuo Wada has also managed to handle the necessary personal and social links with the Chinese state, pulling off an early coup with the move of Yaohan Group's headquarters to Hong Kong. YIH was the first company to receive permission to develop a large department store in China and the first foreign company to be awarded a license to operate supermarkets by the Shanghai municipality.

  Nonetheless, there are still big problems that need to be faced on a day-to-day basis. When Yaohan opened in Beijing, French dolls were among the best-selling items. The store tried to reorder before all its stock was sold, but government officials told the management that no new order could be placed until all the existing stock was depleted. As the time between ordering and delivery was three months, it became impossible to maintain continuity of stock. Yaohan has had to enter into negotiations with the Beijing municipal government in an attempt to establish a new distribution system that will coordinate the gap between production and retailing.

- **Working with the over-stretched distribution system in China.** One of Yaohan Food's ventures, a meat processing plant in Shenzen, provides a good example of some of the difficulties faced in China. Because the rail system has no refrigeration units, processed meat is packed in ice, which has to be changed every 2 days during the 12-day journey from the processing works to the Harbin distribution point in northern China.

- **Dealing with cultural differences.** Not all Chinese are completely sure about the changes in the retail sector and many appear shocked by the displays of wealth represented by such stores. There were reports that when Yaohan's store in Beijing opened, the largest crowds were those gathered at the windows of the goldfish bowl-style swimming pool. There, rich parents sipped cocktails while their children splashed around in the pool below. This frivolity does not come without its critics. A circumspect *People's Daily* commentary in December 1992, focused on people standing outside high-class stores, reluctant to enter and be labeled a "coward" for not buying anything. The newspaper said officials fiddling expense accounts, newlyweds, and criminals had joined the *da kua* to form China's "consumer aristocracy."

Reflecting on the reasons why Japanese investment in China has lagged behind that from Hong Kong, Taiwan, and the U.S., Kazuo Wada in 1994 argued that many Japanese investors were still looking back to Tiananmen Square and saw China as a dangerous place to do business.

> "China is not a country where you need a consensus among the top management to make a decision; rather, you need a strong commitment by the top person that is logically supported and the decision has to be made top-down. I wish that more large-scale companies would begin operating in China, but I think that they lack this decision-making structure. Unless the decision is made in this top-down fashion, it will be difficult to succeed in China."

Conclusion

During a four-year period that has seen the Japanese economy in recession, Wada seems to have been successful in overcoming many of the barriers around the world's fastest growing retail market. He is convinced that within the next decade, he will fulfill an even more ambitious goal to bring international retailing standards to China--the newest, biggest, and most challenging of the world's emerging markets.

In his recent book *Yaohan's Global Strategy,* Wada describes Yaohan's business philosophy as based upon the *Seicho-no-ie* religion. From this viewpoint, he says, "Press hard with resolution and perform with strength and bravery." Whether or not his business strength comes from his religion, Wada has taken Yaohan from being many steps behind to the forefront of Japanese retailing.

Questions for Discussion

1. What is Yaohan importing, in terms of retail or management technology?

2. Is the company likely to succeed in carrying through its plans for China?

Exhibit 1
Establishment of Yaohan's International Operations*

Country	Year
Brazil	1971**
Singapore	1974
U.S.	1979
Costa Rica	1979
Hong Kong	1984
Brunei	1987
Malaysia	1988
Taiwan (R.O.C.)	1988
Thailand	1990
China (P.R.C.)	1991
Indonesia	1992
U.K.	1993
Macau	1994

* The company has also announced plans to open stores in Australia, France, and Germany.
** Yaohan withdrew from Brazil in the mid 1970s

Exhibit 2
The Growth of Yaohan Group, 1976-1991

	1976	1981	1986	1991
Sales (¥ million):				
Domestic	30,155	54,654	101,216	142,401
International	5,845	17,346	40,845	160,086
Total	36,000	72,000	142,061	302,487
Number of stores:				
Domestic	28	54	90	92
International	1	4	12	24
Total	29	58	102	116
Sales floor space (m^2)				
Domestic	58,800	71,300	133,990	222,784
International	13,760	25,776	67,084	213,787
Total	72,560	97,076	201,074	436,571

Exhibit 3
YIH's 1993 Organizational Chart

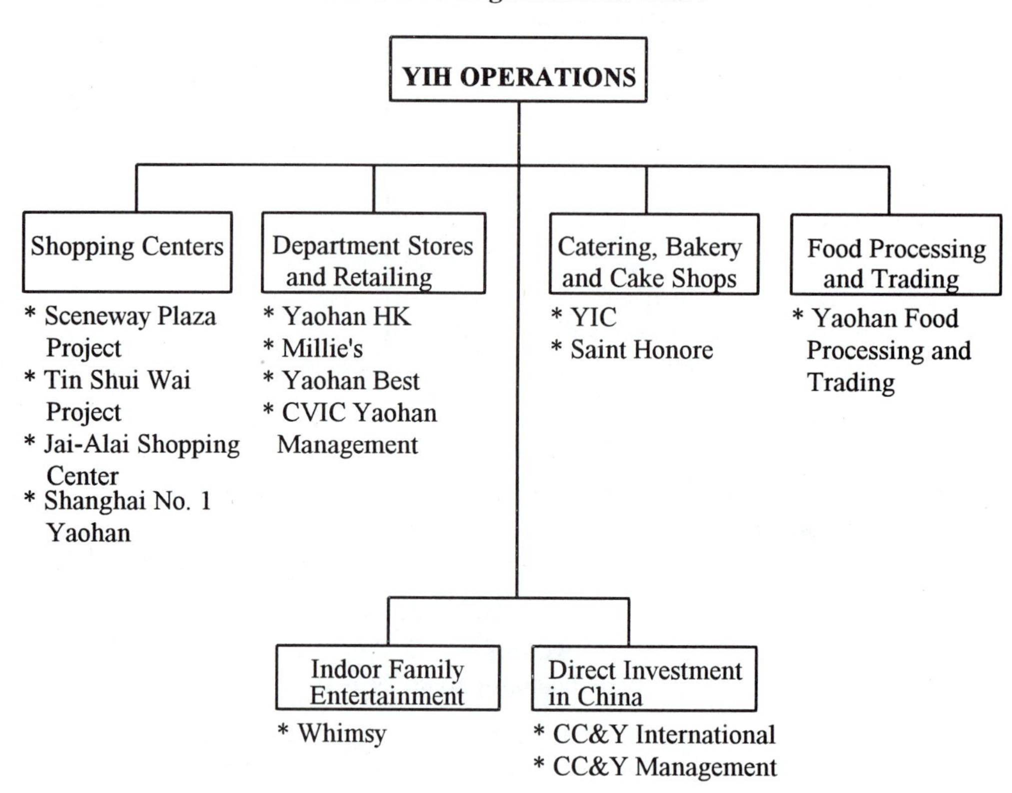

(Source: Yaohan International Holdings press releases)

Exhibit 4
Financial Performance of YIH, 1991-1994
(HK$ million)

Year	Turnover	Profit Attributable to Shareholders
1991	1,467	31.2
1992	3,081	51.9
1993	4,423	149.7
1994		265.0*

* projected
(Source: Yaohan International Holdings press releases)

Exhibit 5
YIH's Turnover by Business, Year ended March 31, 1993

Sector	Turnover (%)
Department Stores and Retailing	57.6
Catering and Bakeries	15.5
Food Processing and Trading	13.8
Properties and Property Based Investments	8.9
Indoor Family Entertainment	4.0
Others	0.2
Total	100.0%
Total	HK$4,423 million

(Source: Yaohan International Holdings press releases)

REFERENCES

Anon, "Retailing - The New Era, Yaohan Chief Gives His Views on Asian Prospects," *Asian Retailer*, November 1991, 7.

Davies, K., "Foreign Investment in the Retail Sector of the People's Republic of China," *Columbia Journal of World Business*, Winter 1994, 56-69.

Davies, S., "Opening Doors in China. Yaohan's 1,000 Store Vision," *JapanScope* (Tokyo), Spring 1993, 18-22.

Foster, A., "Profile: Yaohan. A Move Against the Migrant Tide," *Financial Times*, 12 June 1990, Hong Kong Supplement, 5.

Fredman, L., "Hong Kong-based Yaohan Plans Shanghai Holding Company," *The Nikkei Weekly*, 27 June 1994, 26.

Goldstein, C., "Shopping Spree," *Far Eastern Economic Review*, 19 September 1991, 80-81.

Hattori, S., *Yaohan Department Store*. Tokyo : Yamaichi Investment Report, August 1991.

Hendry, S., "Consumer Revolution," *China Trade Report*, February 1993, 5.

Lim, J., "Yaohan Goes Fast Forward Into Global Retailing," *Retail Asia*, March/ April 1992, 13-15.

Ozawa, K., "The Yaohan Group. New Globalization and a Touch of Dogma," *Tokyo Business Today*, December 1989, 57(12), 60-62.

Ozawa, K.., "The Vision of Chairman Kazuo Wada, Cosmopolitan Retailer," *Tokyo Business Today*, August 1990, 58(8), 38-41.

Robins, B., "China: Japanese Retailer Gets a Head Start - Yaohan," *Business Review Weekly*, February 25, 1994, 55.

Tan, L.H., "How the Japanese are Winning the Retailing War," *Asian Finance*, January 1989, 26-27.

Tanzer, A., "Southeast Asia's Missionary Retailer," *Forbes*, 21 March 1988, 120 & 122.

Tanzer, A., "Selling the Japanese Way of Life," *Forbes*, 3 September 1990, 58 & 60.

Wada, K., *Yaohan's Global Strategy. The 21st Century is the Era of Asia.* Hong Kong : Capital Communications Corporation.

Wada, K., "Stage Set for Yaohan's Global Expansion," *Retail Asia*, March/ April 1992, 16-17.

Wada, K., "Business Operations in Asia: How to Deal with China," *The Nikkei Weekly*, September 26, 1994.

Yaohan International Holdings, various press releases.

HOMEWORLD-AMERICA: PART A*
By Virginia Newell Lusch

This scene takes place during the 1992 board meeting of HomeWorld-America. HomeWorld-America was started by two brothers in 1956 and has steadily grown over the years from one small general store in Ohio to a highly profitable national chain of 518 stores in medium to small towns, selling mostly American-made products for the home and family. A profit and loss statement for last year is shown in Exhibit 1.

Although there is no standard store format or type, the stores have some common characteristics. They range in size from 40,000 to 85,000 square feet, a typical store is 55,000. Each store employs between 75 and 125 full and part-time people. The average number of full-time equivalent employees per store is 83, with 41 of them full time and 84 part time. Of the nonmanagement, nonsupervisor staff, 70 percent are female. The average work week for this level of employee is 26 hours for part time and 40 hours for full time. The managerial and supervisory level is composed of one manager, three assistant managers, and eight supervisors per store. The male/female ratio at this level varies by location but averages 65 percent male and 35 percent female. All workers at this level are full time, and their average work week is close to 60 hours. In the last few years, managers have been reporting problems with low employee morale, absenteeism, and high turnover of workers. A committee was assigned to look into this problem and its head, Ms. Jacoby, Human Resources Director, presents the following report.

Ms. Jacoby:

As you all know, our committee has been studying the problem of low morale, absenteeism, and turnover among company employees. In doing so, we discovered the following:

1. Ninety-six percent of employees who quit during the last six months stated personal or family problems as their reason for leaving HomeWorld - America. On further investigation, the problems were found to fall into five major categories.

    a. not enough time for career and family
    b. child care expenses
    c. inflexibility of employer when dealing with personal issues
    d. money (needing more money to fulfill needs)
    e. personality conflicts

2. HomeWorld's employee turnover rate of 61 percent percent is very high compared to national averages for our line of business. What is most interesting is the fact that for women between the ages of 25 and 44 with one or more children under 13, our turnover rate is 87 percent. Stated alternatively, this employee group is likely to stay with the company only a little over one year.

3. Absenteeism was reported in all age groups with the highest three groups being college-age, part-time employees; full-time, women employees with children under age 5; and full-time, male employees over age 60.

---

* Used with permission of Virginia Newell Lusch

Mr. Hayes (Chief Operating Officer):

May I interrupt a minute, Ms. Jacoby? I don't see what you are getting at. Your committee was told to find out why people are quitting and why they are unhappy here at HomeWorld-America not to figure out **WHO** is unhappy. We already know who is unhappy...the people who quit.

Ms Jacoby:

If you please, Mr. Hayes, I am getting to that...

Mr. Watson (Vice President of Merchandising):

We don't need to hear about baby sitters and class schedules. Get down to the meat. What are the employees upset about? Not enough coffee breaks? Are the shelves too high for women to stock easily? Should we quit hiring so many working mothers? Is the lunch hour too short? Don't they like the color of the smocks? You know...the basics.

Mr. Simpson (Chairman of the Board):

I think you are thinking too small, Bob. There are big issues here that we need to address. We promote our company as being family oriented and socially and environmentally conscious. We go out of our way to sell recyclable products, buy American, support the local economy and schools, and reward excellence among our employees. Isn't it time to address family problems as they conflict with career choices? Please gentlemen and ladies, let's allow Ms. Jacoby to finish.

Ms. Jacoby:

Thank you, Chairman Simpson. As I was saying, the problems among our workers at all levels of employment seem to be centered around family vs. career struggles. We therefore suggest that a new department be created to handle these problems. This is something that needs more than just a committee or task force. The employees need to know that management understands and wants to help them solve their problems. Exhibit 2 contains some suggestions and costs for beginning to deal with the problems of low morale, absenteeism, and high turnover. We must realize that this is an ongoing and ever-evolving situation and that it is only going to get more serious as fewer people enter the service industries. A higher proportion of those available will be working mothers, older adults, and working adult children who are caring for aging parents.

Questions for Discussion

1. As the general population and workforce gets older, what long-term problems do you foresee for retailers? What solutions might HomeWorld-America be ready to offer?

2. Construct an employee survey to measure the problems of and concerns about the quality of work life of HomeWorld - America employees.

3. Is the creation of a special department for family/career concerns a good idea? Why or why not?

4. What possible short-term solutions might HomeWorld-America offer its employees?

5. One member of the board of directors, Mrs. Jane Juarez, has come out strongly in favor of HomeWorld-America's building on-site child care facilities. As chairman of the board, write her a letter explaining why you can or cannot support these suggestions.

Exhibit 1
HomeWorld-America
Profit And Loss Statement
December 31, 1991

Sales	$ 6,104,321,000
Cost of Merchandise	4,803,491,000
Gross Profit	1,300,830,000
Less: Operating Expenses	
Salaries/Wages/Fringe Benefits	622,641,000
Occupancy/Utilities	214,973,000
Advertising	108,190,000
Depreciation	57,418,000
Other	56,810,000
Total	1,060,032,000
Net Profit (Before Tax)	240,798,000
Less: Taxes	94,634,000
PROFIT	$ 146,164,000

Exhibit 2
Possible Actions to Overcome Low Morale, Absenteeism, and High Turnover

- On-site child care facilities--child care centers set up and maintained by the company at each store location for the children of employees. The estimated setup cost of such a facility would be $500,000 per store and the annual operating costs between $130,000 and $180,000 per facility depending upon its location (the average being $155,000). Each facility would have the capacity to handle 40-60 children age 3 months to 12 years.

- Newsletter containing employee suggestions and concerns and company suggestions. We already have a company newsletter so we would only need to add a new section to it at minimal cost.

- Flexible time, in which employee works up to his or her own weekly schedule as long as the total number of hours stays constant. There is no added cost for doing this and it allows employees flexibility within their week so they are more productive when they are working.

- Job sharing--two employees work part time to share one full-time position. Benefits are shared as well, and some companies have actually saved money because they don't have as much turnover and training costs when employees are happier with their jobs.

- Creation of a permanent department for career/family concerns. This would be a top-management level department for coordinating all the career/family concerns of all employees in all the stores with an assistant manager in each store to carry company policy to employees and employee concerns back to top management. Costs of the creation of this department would include hiring or promotion of new staff, office expenses, etc., but it should pay for itself in a short time.

- Seminars for employees on family matters, career counseling, fitness and health matters--these can be conducted at a minimal cost by having volunteer agencies present the programs. Yet, the contribution to employee morale is high, because employees feel the company cares about them as people.

- Weekly personal time--up to 2 hours per week of time to take care of personal matters that can only be handled during the employees' regularly scheduled work week. Time not used can be accumulated and applied toward an extended annual vacation.

- Family resource center of books, tapes, and videos on family issues--annual costs of $300 to $1,000 per location.

- Before-and after-school programs for children of employees--a safe place for school-age children of employees to stay before and after school so employees need not worry about their children getting to and from school safely and on time. Average cost of the program ($50 per month per employee) could be paid by employees.

- Summer "camperships"--the company could provide vouchers to children of employees for summer camps in the area. Costs would vary depending upon location, but the company could offer $300 camper vouchers for employees who have worked over 1 year and $500 camperships for employees who have worked over 5 years.

- Extended maternity/paternity/family leave--mother or father could receive up to one year of leave to care for babies or other family members needing full-time care, and return to pre-leave level position.

- Biweekly working parent exchange groups where employees can interact and discuss problems and solutions of trying to juggle careers and families--minimal cost to stores, who simply provide a meeting place.

HOMEWORLD-AMERICA: PART B
By Robert F. Lusch, University of Oklahoma

Introduction

HomeWorld-America is a national chain that was started by two brothers in 1956 and has steadily grown from one store in Ohio to over 600 stores at yearend 1993. Currently, the company is struggling with revising its store manager compensation plan.

Ms. Helen Jacoby, Human Resources Director, had an uneasy feeling when she reviewed the annual salary and bonus adjustments for the over 500 store managers. Helen couldn't help but reflect that some of the store managers that performed the best in the HomeWorld-America's two-week Leadership Development Program were getting the poorest salary adjustments and bonus payments. For the last several years, she always had this uneasy feeling when it came time to set the new compensation levels. Unfortunately, she always had so many projects and deadlines to meet, that she kept putting off addressing the store manager compensation program. However, the problem was getting worse as evidenced by the over one dozen store managers that protested their last salary adjustment and bonus payment. Because she felt it necessary to support her regional managers, she did not override their decisions during the 1992 performance review. However, it was quite disquieting to her that four of the five store managers that protested resigned their positions within several months and all of them went to work for the competition. This was the year she had to do something; thus she wrote a memo to Mr. Hayes, the Chief Operating Officer, who quickly charged her with reviewing and offering recommendations for a new store manager compensation system.

Past and Current Compensation Plans

In the early years (pre 1984) of HomeWorld-America, when it had less than 100 stores, almost all management and merchandising decisions were centralized. In addition, all stores were within a 250-mile radius and consequently received constant attention from management. This was a time when everyone was treated equally regardless of store performance. The system worked well. The company had a high level of "espirit de corps" and everyone saw themselves as an important part of a team. Even though they may have been operating a 40,000 square foot store they viewed themselves and were treated as someone running a 65,000 square foot store. This egalitarian attitude was reflected in the store manager compensation system. For example, in 1983, all store managers received a base salary of $26,000 and year-end bonus based on two factors. First, for each year they had been a store manager they received an extra $1000. Second,the store managers as a group would share equally in 5 percent of the pre-tax net profit. For example, in 1983, the company earned $14,800,000 in pre-tax net profit. Thus, the store managers, as a group, received $740,000. In that year there were 94 stores at year end and each manager received a bonus of $7872.

In 1984, HomeWorld-America had a major change in its store manager compensation system when Mr. Hayes was recruited as Chief Operating Officer. The system was revised to include three components: base salary, managerial performance bonus, and store performance bonus. Each of these components will be reviewed.

Base Salary

The base salary a store manager receives is based on the size of store being managed. There are three categories of store size: A = 40,000 to 54,999; B = 55,000 to 69,999; and C = 70,000 square feet and over. Currently the base salary for a size-A store is $34,000; for a size-B store it is $37,000; and for a size-C store it is $40,000. Also, if a store manager has a manager trainee in the store, they receive an additional $200 for each month the trainee is under their guidance. When the company recruits college graduates, they are placed in an existing store as a manager trainee for between 18 and 36 months. This is an important part of HomeWorld's human resource development system; thus, store managers are rewarded to encourage their active participation. Finally, a store manager with a tenure of more than five years receives an additional $2500 in base pay.

Managerial Performance

HomeWorld-America has found that managerial performance is a function of the proper behavior in four broad areas: people management, operations management, communication skills, and behavioral characteristics. Each district supervisor rates each of its store managers twice a year on these areas. The rating form in Exhibit-1 is used for this purpose. In addition, the district supervisor makes an unannounced store visit monthly and rates the store manager on three broad areas: store management, marketing management, and merchandise management. Exhibit 2 presents the store visit rating form.

Toward the end of each fiscal year (usually early June since the new fiscal year starts July 1) the regional supervisor sits down with the rating forms that have been completed during the year and develops composite ratings for each of its store managers. Composite ratings can fall into five categories:

Exceptional. Managerial performance is consistently far in excess of goals and standards. Only the exceptional store manager should be in this category; generally 5 percent to 10 percent of store managers will receive an exceptional rating.

Superior. Managerial performance often exceeds goals and standards. Generally 25 percent to 30 percent of store managers will receive a superior rating.

Fully Competent. Managerial performance regularly meets goals and standards and occasionally exceeds these goals/standards. Most store managers (50 percent) will receive this rating.

Needs Improvement. Managerial performance is often marginal and below standards/goals. Consistency of performance is lacking. Up to 10 percent of store managers will fall in this category.

Unsatisfactory. Managerial performance is not suitable for continued employment. Performance must be improved rapidly to maintain employment. Up to 10 percent of store managers will fall in this category.

The managerial performance bonus is only available for the top three categories. A manager rated fully competent would receive a 3 percent bonus; a manager rated superior would receive 6 percent; and a manager rated exceptional would receive a 10 percent bonus.

Store Performance

At the end of each fiscal year the profit of each store is computed accordingly:

Gross Sales	$
Less: Sales Returns & Allowances	________
Net Sales	$
Less: Cost of Merchandise Sold	________
Gross Margin	$
Less:	
Salaries & Wages & Benefits	
Rent/Occupancy Costs	

Advertising/Promotion	
Corporate Overhead Charge	
Operating Profit	$

A store performance bonus is granted for all stores that exceed a 4 percent operating profit as a percent of net sales. Five percent of the operating profit that exceeds this amount is paid to the store manager as a bonus. For example, a store with $7,500,000 in annual net sales that has an operating profit of $405,000 would be eligible for a bonus. This is because any amount over 4 percent of $7,500,000, or $300,000 would qualify for the bonus. The amount of operating profit in excess of $300,000 is $105,000 and the manager would receive 5 percent of this amount or $5250.

Recap

In summary, a store manager who manages a 80,000 square foot store, who has been a store manager for 6 years, who receives a managerial performance rating of superior, and who obtains 6 percent operating profit as a percent of $8,000,000 net sales would receive the following compensation.

Standard Base Salary	$40,000
Addition to Base for 5+ years of service	2,500
Managerial Performance Incentive*	2,550
Store Performance Incentive**	8,000
Total Compensation	$53,050

* 6 percent of $42,500

** Incentive kicks in after 4 percent of $8,000,000 or $320,000 in operating profit. Operating profit was 6 percent of $8,000,000 or $480,000. Incentive is 5 percent of ($480,000 - $320,000) or $8,000.

Current Weaknesses

Helen took the opportunity to put the current store manager performance system on the agenda of her quarterly meeting with her 28 district supervisors. When she introduced the agenda item, she was sure to not mention her preconceived thoughts about how the system might be flawed. Helen wanted to have an open discussion, thus she served as the discussion leader and did not offer any of her comments. Below is a summary of some of the more salient points made during the half-hour discussion.

- I find it interesting that some of our more senior store managers have been able to position themselves to operate large C-level stores in less competitive nonmetro areas. They clearly know what they are doing--cost of living is less in these areas and their compensation goes further. Because competition is less severe, it is easier to achieve a operating profit in excess of 4 percent of sales. Often, some of these stores do over 7 percent in operating profit as a percent of sales.

- I often wonder if my ratings of managerial performance are truly reflective of the store manager's behavior. Since I am constantly reviewing the weekly, monthly, quarterly, and annual financial results on each store and especially overall sales, gross margin, and operating profit, I find it difficult to rate a store manager as having poor managerial performance if indeed his or her store is performing spectacularly on a financial basis. After all, I only visit the store once a month and that is usually for a half-day; how do I really know managerial performance? Nonetheless, numbers don't lie and I certainly know if the store is performing well financially.

- I have never understood why a manager of an 80,000 square foot store should get a higher base pay than one managing a 40,000 square foot store. In fact, when I was in store management, I managed all three size of stores and the smaller stores were more difficult because you only had one assistant store manager to delegate to; whereas in a 80,000 square foot store, you have three assistant store managers (two day time and one night manager).

- There clearly are some market areas where we can't seem to do anything wrong. These tend to be markets where we have a high proportion of households that characterize our primary target market. If a manager has a store in one of these markets, he or she is going to benefit because of something not under their control. I wonder if this is fair.

- The biggest complaint I receive from store managers regarding their compensation is equity-related. It seems that managers are always concerned with the pay they get in relation to the effort or work they put into operating their store and often perceive that other managers receive more compensation for less effort.

In addition to the preceding salient points, Helen felt that too high a proportion of the total compensation for a typical manager was salary and not incentive base. For the most recent fiscal year, 81 percent of compensation was salary and 19 percent was incentive-related. She felt that managers would work both smarter and harder if more of their compensation was at risk. Her tentative thinking was salary should be no more than 70 percent to 75 percent company wide for store managers. In a recent conversation with Mr. Hayes, he suggested that consideration be given to a 50-50 split between salary and incentive compensation.

Helen thought her next step would be to put together a task force of five to seven individuals to help her work on developing some recommendations for a revised store manager compensation system. During her recent quarterly meeting with the district supervisors, she was especially impressed with the comments and interest expressed in the topic by Harold Clark, Tina Horrell, and Tom Hirschman. Harold had seven years of store management experience and was promoted to district supervisor last year. Tina started with HomeWorld as an assistant buyer and moved on to be a buyer for toys for three years, she then served in store management for four years before being promoted to a district supervisor in 1987. Finally, Tom was with a competing retail chain where he had 10 years of store management experience. After only two years as a store manager for HomeWorld, he was promoted to a district supervisor in 1991. Helen especially liked his familiarity with the store manager compensation system of a major competitor where he worked for 10 years.

Since HomeWorld had been emphasizing cross-functional teams for all task forces, she was required to put two people on the committee from other functional areas in the firm. She decided to put Nicole Boyt, the head buyer for the automotive area, and Henry Rodriquez, the director of new store development, on the task force. Initially, she did not see the logic of Henry serving on the committee. When having lunch with him in the company cafeteria, Helen mentioned her work on reviewing the store manager compensation program and Henry expressed a strong interest in serving on the task force. He said he had some thoughts on how his research on new store site selection might be helpful in developing a store manager compensation system. Helen really didn't see the connection, so she asked him to send her a brief memo outlining some of his thoughts. After she read his memo (see Exhibit 3) she got very excited and immediately called him and asked him to serve on the task force.

The first meeting of the task force is scheduled for a week from Friday. In preparation for the meeting, Helen asked Tina Horrell to prepare a summary of the 25 store managers she has in her district. Helen felt that Tina's district was one of the most representative districts in the company. Helen asked Tina to provide for each store and its manager the following data: (1) name of manager, (2) managerial performance rating for fiscal 1993, (3) net sales, (4) operating profit, and (5) size of store in square footage. At the same time Helen asked Henry Rodriquez to provide for each of these stores data on several of the variables mentioned in his recent memo. Helen asked for the competing retail space per thousand households in the trade area and the percent of the households in the trade area that match HomeWorld's desired target market. Exhibit 4 provides this combined data for the 25 stores in Tina's district.

Questions for Discussion

1. Evaluate the current store manager compensation system. What are some of its weaknesses?

2. Assuming the current system is not altered, but only the way it is implemented, how could it be better implemented?

3. Offer some ideas on how the current system could be improved.

Exhibit 1
Evaluation of Managerial Performance

Store Number ______
Name of Manager ______________________
Name of Rater _________________________

Date of Evaluation ______________________
Period Evaluated ______________________

Instructions. Please evaluate each store manager on each of the following attributes. Each manager should receive a rating of either exceptional (E), superior (S), fully competent (FC), needs improvement (NI), or unsatisfactory (U) on each attribute.

People Management

Leadership. Moves individuals and the group in the desired direction without using coercion. Develops within subordinates the desire to want to achieve organizational goals.

E S FC NI U

Motivating. Motivates subordinates to strive for high levels of performance. Uses positive feedback, gives credit when deserved, empowers employees.

E S FC NI U

Team Oriented. Achieves a high level of "espirit de corps" among all employees. Requests subordinate input and allows employees to broaden their skills by cross-functional activity.

E S FC NI U

Conflict Management. Settles in a satisfactory manner disagreements that arise on a daily basis within the store. Is honest and fair in resolving conflicts.

E S FC NI U

Operations Management

Problem Solving. Effectively uses time to solve problems as they arise in day-to-day management. Proactively anticipates and reacts to problems.

E S FC NI U

Planning. Develops good plans based on objective data. Sets both short and long-range objectives. Follows through to implement plan and keep the plan on course.

E S FC NI U

Priority Setting. Assesses which problems need the most urgent attention and addresses those first. Is flexible in changing priorities based on changing circumstances.

E S FC NI U

Technical Knowledge. Applies and uses up-to-date techniques and methods to improve the store operations.

E S FC NI U

Communication Skills

Oral Communication. Clearly and effectively expresses oneself in a verbal manner. Verbal communication is timely, positive, and constructive.

E S FC NI U

Written Communication. Clearly and effectively expresses oneself in a written manner. Written communication is timely, positive, and constructive.

E S FC NI U

Information Sharing. Shares information with subordinates and superiors that they need to effectively perform their job.

E S FC NI U

Listening. Is open in all communication. Objectively listens to the ideas and thoughts of others and accepts criticism when it is due. Is open to input from subordinates and superiors.

E S FC NI U

Behavioral Characteristics

Initiative. Exercises self initiative in pursuing business opportunities. Constantly seeks ways to improve store performance.

E S FC NI U

Integrity. Sets a high standard for ethical conduct and does not compromise values. Has high respect for people of all backgrounds and ages.

E S FC NI U

Self Awareness. Is able to assess own strengths and weaknesses and seeks to improve as a manager and individual. Welcomes feedback and assistance in regard to professional development.

E S FC NI U

Commitment. Positively supports the organization, its mission, and its goals.

E S FC NI U

Exhibit 2
Store Visit Evaluation

Store Number ______
Name of Manager ______________________
Name of Rater _________________________
Date of Evaluation ______________________

Instructions. Rate the store manager on each of the following areas. Provide a rationale for each rating. Each manager should receive a rating of either exceptional (E), superior (S), fully competent (FC), needs improvement (NI), or unsatisfactory (U) on each attribute.

Store Management. This reflects the extent to which the manager operates a well organized, clean, safe store.

E S FC NI U

____
____
____

Marketing Management. This area reflects how well the manager is doing with displays, endcaps, graphics, signage, sales promotions, and lighting.

E S FC NI U

____
____
____

Merchandise Management. This area reflects how well the manager is doing at markdown management, merchandise mix, inventory levels, receiving and transfers, and ordering of merchandise.

E S FC NI U

____
____
____

Exhibit 3
Management Memo

To: Helen Jacoby, Human Resources Director
From: Henry Rodriquez, Director of New Store Development
Topic: Taskforce on Store Manager Compensation System
Date: July 13, 1994

It was good to have lunch with you the other day and hear about some of the problems you are having with developing a valid store manager compensation system. HomeWorld-America has experienced substantial growth since 1984 when the compensation system was last revised and I am sure you will identify some ways it can be improved. Back in 1984 when we had less than 100 stores, things just seemed to work better; but now with over 500 stores, we need to look at how we approach all areas of our business and how we can improve. We have been doing exactly that in the real estate and new store development department. I want to share with you some of our findings because I think they have relevance for what you are doing.

In the past when we opened new stores, our market entry and site selection techniques were quite primitive. Essentially, what we would do is look at towns or cities within a few hours of our distribution centers. If the community looked attractive based on our subjective judgment, we would begin to look for a vacant parcel of land upon which to build a store.

Several years ago, we began to notice that our new store location decisions were not working as well as in the past. I think part of the reason was that we were opening over 60 stores a year--more than 1 new store every 7 days, and frankly competition was more intense than in the past. As a result, we hired a location consultant who took us through an exercise in which we identified our top 25 performing stores and our bottom 25 performing stores. We found that three variables tended to distinguish these stores. The high performance stores were larger, faced less competition, and were more likely to be in a trade area where there were a large number of households that matched HomeWorld's ideal target market. As you are aware, our target household earns between $22,000 and $46,000 with at least one child, and the head of household is between 26 and 45 years of age. Below is a summary of what we found:

	Low profit stores	**High profit stores**
Average store size	46,000 sq. ft.	76,000 sq. ft.
Square feet of competitive space per thousand households	5,125	3,229
Percentage of households that match HomeWorld's target market	20.9%	40.1%

The consultant then worked with our information systems department and developed an equation to help us select new trade areas to enter. The equation was developed by including data not only on the top 25 and bottom 25 stores in terms of financial performance, but on all of the stores in the company. The equation is used to predict the operating profit per square foot of selling space. At the end of each fiscal year, we enter new data into a statistical package and get an updated equation. The equation for fiscal year 1993 is as follows:

$Y = .81 + .00011(F) - .00084(C) + .112(M)$

where:

Y = operating profit per square foot of selling space
F = square feet of selling space
C = square feet of competing retail space per thousand households in trade area
M = percent of trade area households that match HomeWorld-America's target market

How the equation works is fairly straight forward. Let's assume we have a store of 65,000 square feet of selling space and it is operating in a trade area with 4188 square feet of competitive retail selling space per thousand households in the trade area and 31 percent of households in the trade match our target market. This store would be expected to have the following performance:

$Y = .81 + .00011(65{,}000) - .00084(4188) + .112(31)$
$Y = .81 + 7.15 - 3.52 + 3.47$
$Y = \$7.91$

What this tells us is that, holding all else constant, a store of 65,000 square feet of selling space operating in a market where there is 4188 square feet of competing space per thousand households and where 31 percent of the households match our target market, will be expected to generate $7.91 in operating profit per square foot. Now let's say we locate this same size store in a market with 7000 of square feet of competing space per thousand households and where only 20 percent of the households match our target market. The predicted store performance would be:

$Y = .81 + .00011(65{,}000) - .00084(7000) + .112(20)$
$Y = .81 + 7.15 - 5.88 + 2.24$
$Y = \$4.32$

or $4.32 in operating profit per square foot. Since we expect our stores to generate $200 in annual sales per square foot of selling space, the $4.32 would not be very attractive. This would equate to a operating profit margin of .0216 or 2.16 percent; (4.32/200) = .0216.

You are probably wondering at this point how this relates to your task force on store manager compensation. When we had lunch, you mentioned that a common problem was that some store managers receive very good compensation without much effort because of the environment their stores are located within. The preceding equation seems to further support the point that there are certain things beyond the control of the manager (store size, competitive intensity, and the extent of the presence of the target market) that have a major impact on store performance.

Frankly, I am not exactly sure where we go from here but clearly we need to talk about how we can reward store managers for what they have influence over vs. those things that are uncontrollable. I will look forward to hearing from you regarding when the first meeting of the task force will be held.

Exhibit 4
Summary of Performance Factors
For 25 Stores in Tina Horrell's District*

Store Manager	Performance Rating	Net Sales (1,000)	Operating Profit (1,000)	Store Size	Competitive Intensity	% Market Match
Alford	FC	7,957	239	47,500	3450	21
Barnes	S	8,490	337	51,300	3890	30
Benett	FC	18,300	691	80,000	4450	26
Brown	E	13,902	502	67,300	4100	23
Cooksey	NI	4,123	103	52,400	6840	10
Copeland	S	8,491	338	46,700	3340	38
Dizzo	FC	17,053	763	78,800	4100	35
Earl	S	10,302	598	84,000	7800	29
Estes	S	17,448	741	83,000	5340	30
Evans	U	3,909	47	58,000	4160	28
Ezzell	NI	10,812	325	65,000	5930	18
Fabro	FC	6,564	348	46,500	4250	42
Fader	FC	7,696	324	45,000	2880	34
Field	FC	8,616	363	67,300	5890	27
Gesel	NI	14,900	396	65,800	6190	33
Lee	FC	8,607	241	48,400	5870	24
Liddy	FC	5,627	296	42,000	4550	28
Pfaff	E	19,171	820	83,300	4300	32
Pless	S	11,074	595	82,000	6540	24
Roach	FC	13,752	670	75,800	5240	37
Santos	FC	8,941	355	55,000	3680	23
Schultz	FC	7,603	320	51,400	2990	19
Sylvia	E	5,829	415	41,200	2800	39
Tustin	FC	13,089	543	78,900	6780	27
Whalen	S	17,622	725	83,000	5870	33

*Note: Performance rating is the 1993 composite rating of managerial performance where: E = excellent, S = superior, FC = fully competent, NI = needs improvement, and U = unsatisfactory. Store size is square feet of space. Competitive intensity is square feet of competing retail space per thousand households in trade area. Percent market match is the percent of trade area households that match HomeWorld-America's target market.

PRODUCE-ING PROFITS: THE MARSH SUPER STUDY*

By Stephen Bennett

There probably would be produce displays in every aisle of every Marsh supermarket if Jim Richter could have his way. Richter, director of produce merchandising for the Indianapolis-based chain, is intent on "broadening the reach" of his departments.

What's more, he has statistics to back up his wish list. Exhibits 1-4 present these statistics.

The exhaustive Marsh Super Study (a 65-week study of sales, profits, promotion, space, and productivity, published in *Progressive Grocer* in December 1992) shows that 85 percent of shoppers who enter the produce department make a purchase. That is a better success rate than other fresh perishable departments such as deli, bakery, and meat.

Richter would like to improve upon that success rate by extending the produce department's presence to other parts of the store. Cross-merchandising produce items in other departments is one of the key ways of achieving his goal.

For example, bunches of bananas, preweighted and prepriced, are displayed periodically on a table in the cold cereal aisle; fresh berries are displayed next to the ice cream case; and popcorn is merchandised in either the general merchandise section or in video rentals. The idea is to snare shoppers who aren't regular visitors to the produce department, Richter says.

Cross-merchandising serves another purpose: It gives produce more space, which leaves more room in the produce department for the top performers.

Ritcher found another way to increase space for produce performers after the Super Study revealed that nonperishable items (dried fruit, bird seed, etc.) occupied 23.1 percent of department display space, but generated only 11.35 percent of sales. "We've divested ourselves of those items and moved them into either grocery or the general merchandise sections," says Richter.

Those changes also fit with the growing emphasis on freshness in the produce department. To highlight that image, juice bars featuring fresh-squeezed juice and fresh-cut fruit have been installed in approximately half of the chain's 84 stores. Richter concedes that the direct product profit from juice bar items isn't as great as that from "unprepped" fruits and vegetables, but "it pays off by further defining quality and freshness issues."

In addition, in terms of trying to broaden our sales reach, "the juice bars are effective because they appeal to convenience-minded shoppers," he says. Time-pressed shoppers who might not purchase regular produce items might look kindly on the juice bar's ready-to-eat offerings, which include fruit and vegetable kabobs, cut pineapple, mixed melon chunks, cut strawberries and citrus fruit, watermelon sections, and combination fruit-and-vegetable trays.

The juice bars aren't the only section of the produce department that can appeal to shoppers' needs for ready-to-eat or convenience items. Pre-cut, packaged salad items containing lettuce, cabbage, and carrots "have taken off like a rocket," says Richter. Marsh carries one and three-pound packs of the Fresh Express brand. Working couples and other time-pressed consumers tend to buy these items. "They may not be able to eat a head of lettuce in a week," says Richter. The prepacked item provides an alternative.

The salad pack appeals on the price front, too. Processors usually have a locked-in price that prevents change caused by crop fluctuations. When supply is short, "they normally don't take a price swing," he says. The one-pound pack retails at $1.49; the three-pounder, at two for $5.

The popularity of salad packs has brought about some changes in the handling of regular lettuce, which is no small issue given the importance of lettuce in the overall produce mix. Lettuce is the third best seller in the entire department (behind only bananas and potatoes) and is the most profitable item in the department with a direct product profit return on inventory dollars of $117.62. (The sum is the annual return in DPP dollars on every dollar of inventory investment.) Grapefruit is the second most profitable produce item, with a DPP return on investment of $75.24.

---

* Reprinted, by permission, from *Progressive Grocer* Magazine.

Despite the strong performance lettuce turns in, "We have reduced [display space for] lettuce somewhat to give pre-cut, packed lettuce the first position in the refrigeration rack," says Richter. "That really has paid excellent dividends."

Other moves have shown similar benefits and in many cases those improvements are documented by the Super Study.

For example, according to the study, the vegetable side of the department accounts for nearly 48 percent of produce sales. The top 10 sellers among vegetables are, in descending order: potatoes, lettuce, onions, tomatoes, celery, carrots, broccoli, peppers, mushrooms, and cauliflower.

While the presence of peppers and mushrooms among the top 10 might surprise some observers, it is no shock to Richter. The numbers provide him with a sense of accomplishment at a promotional job well done.

"We have aggressively promoted red, orange, yellow, and Holland peppers," he says. Marsh prices them at $1.99 per pound, "which means you can get a nice pepper for 85 cents to 90 cents." (Green bell peppers are normally priced at two for $1.)

Peppers respond dramatically to promotion, Richter says. That claim is supported by the number of annual inventory turns generated by peppers—333.59.

Work with the Margin

Making pepper sales a success required some unconventional thinking on Richter's part. "Where people get in trouble is when they try to make normal margins and get normal sales [on such an item]. If they just work with the margin a little bit" the result will be strong movement, sales, and some profit—without cannibalizing another produce category, says Richter.

The Marsh numbers make a good case for the emphasis on peppers. Peppers rank eighth in dollar sales among all vegetables and they place third in DPP return on investment ($44.83). Marsh promotes peppers by featuring them in circulars and giving them extra space in an end display. A promotion of peppers and mushrooms, ideal for kabobs, worked wonderfully, says Richter. That promotion was supported with an end display that featured both items.

Among vegetables, mushrooms rank ninth in both sales and DPP return on investment ($14.34). Marsh produce departments offer a wide variety that includes whole and sliced mushrooms, a bulk presentation of large mushrooms that can be used to make stuffing, and 7 to 10 varieties of exotic mushrooms in Marsh's newer-format "European" stores. All of the varieties are displayed together. "We are big advocates of family commodity groupings," says Richter. (Marsh's so-called European stores feature some 400 items in the produce department, which is the first department customers see in the traffic pattern. In contrast, produce is located in second or third place in older Marsh stores and in those units the departments feature about 250 items.)

Another noteworthy performer among vegetables is broccoli, which ranks seventh in sales, second in DPP return on investment, and second in sales per foot of display space. Marsh supports this traditionally strong item with a buy-one, get-one-free offer. To give broccoli a special look, the product is displayed upright, with the stalks planted in a bed of crushed ice. "It looks like a putting green," says Richter.

The "Five a Day" program (for suggested produce consumption) has also helped get shoppers to recognize the health benefits of eating broccoli, says Richter. To generate even more sales and profit, display space for broccoli has been extended by two feet. Space was taken from the sections for other vegetables such as cabbage, bunch beets, and greens, which tend to be seasonal or slow movers. "Broccoli sells real well year-round," says Richter.

In every department there is at least one item that is priced so aggressively that it is a guaranteed money loser. Corn is that item among the vegetables. Just as Marsh prices ground beef to match the competition and to keep shoppers coming in, corn, on a seasonal basis, is priced as a big drawing card. The summer picnic holidays —Memorial Day, Independence Day, and Labor Day—are the times when corn is promoted especially heavily. The impact of the price promotions helps corn, a highly seasonal item, run such a high number of annual inventory turns: 231.25

The impact of the promotional activity isn't all positive, however. According to the Super Study, corn's DPP return on inventory is a negative $149.19. In addition to the promotions, the negative DPP is partially caused by the labor, time, and expense Marsh puts into packaging corn. Packaged corn, consisting of five shucked ears to a tray, "is a very important part of our program in spring and summer." Richter says.

Willing to Pay a Premium

When Richter joined Marsh, about three months into the Super Study, the chain was displaying about 25 percent of its corn in trays. He increased it to 50 percent in hopes of boosting sales and profits. (Because of the timing, the impact of the changes would be muted in the Super Study findings.)

Richter believes that corn in trays carries added appeal for shoppers who are looking for convenience and want to see the product's quality immediately. Richter says shoppers are willing to pay a premium for that. The corn in trays, priced at five ears for $1.49, is displayed next to the bulk corn, priced at four for $1.

Pricing strategy also has a powerful impact on bananas, the best selling of all fruit and vegetable items in Marsh stores. (Fruit, overall, accounts for nearly 41 percent of produce department sales.)

Bananas carry an everyday price of 49 cents per pound, which helps drive the item to the most annual inventory turns, 450, of any produce item. Bananas also rank high in terms of the amount of display space they occupy. Their DPP return on inventory is $29.26—fourth among all fruit items and ninth among all produce items.

In promotional periods, Richter sets the price at 3 pounds for $1 or 39 cents per pound. "It depends on the competition," he says. However, Richter practices caution in his price cuts, noting that "deep price cuts on promotions aren't always necessary to meet profit objectives." Going too far with price cuts can backfire, he says.

Richter says he notices a difference in the movement of bananas depending on the promotional strategy used. The 39-cents-per-pound promotion "drives more sales and profits" than when the price is 3 pounds for $1. Because bananas are such a big volume item to start with, "they don't need a big price discount to drive sales," he says.

"If you sell bananas at 4 for $1 or 5 for $1, you can run yourself out of a period or a quarter by over-promoting the item," says Richter. "Because you promoted it at such an aggressive price, you didn't get the sales you hoped for and you didn't get the profits you wanted to make budget."

This is where the challenge of pricing comes in, Richter says. In setting the most advantageous price for many produce items, "a lot depends on seasonality. You also have to study your competition and try to figure out what they're likely to do."

The strategy can change from item to item. For example, the handling of apples, another staple item in produce, has undergone sweeping changes. With 10 SKUs, the category is one of the few in produce that has an appreciable variety. The apple variety at Marsh today includes items from New Zealand that are fairly new in the U.S., such as Royal Gala, Fuji, and Braeburn. "Those items have really taken off with our customers," says Richter.

Marsh tries to make use of this wide variety. For its "Apple-rama" promotion, the chain gave all 10 varieties of apples special attention. The company's circular featured all 10 varieties, with copy points for each item and general copy providing information on the nutritional properties of apples.

However, more than variety has changed in the apple category. While fall and winter remain the seasons for the strongest sales, apples are steady year-round sellers, he says. This helps the overall performance of the produce department in summer, for example, because "there's a little less shrink in apples than for the traditional summer fruits," says Richter.

An everyday price for the most popular varieties of apples—red Delicious and golden Delicious—is 99 cents per pound during the spring.

Apples ran second in sales among all fruit items (fourth in the whole produce department). Their DPP return on inventory investment is a respectable eighth among all produce items. The apple category is supported heavily. In terms of display space, measured as the number of linear shelf feet given each item, apples trail only potatoes among all produce items. Of course, the large space and low prices combine to keep apples out of the top 10 items in terms of sales per square foot. (Similarly, top-selling bananas place only tenth in sales per foot.)

Grapes...Out-Perform Bananas

Significant display space is also given to grapes, the third best performer in dollar sales per week among fruit items. However, grapes get most of their attention from June through August—the item's peak season. "California grapes, when they're in season, outperform bananas in sales and profits," says Richter.

The popular grapes—seedless red, white, and black—typically retail at $1.29 to $1.39 per pound. On special, the price drops to 88 cents or 99 cents per pound. Those promotions get strong support. One recent merchandising effort, featuring several varieties of grapes and eight varieties of plums, was given two color pages in the chain's inserts, says Richter.

One of the difficulties of selling grapes is the potential shrink. Richter has been at work on that problem since the Super Study showed that grapes had 7.5 days of supply on shelf with an inventory cost of $1,169.73. Richter says he has devised a system to speed up the turns (48 annually at the time of the Super Study) and reduce inventory, but he won't reveal it for competitive reasons. Even with the inventory problems before Richter's adjustments, the DPP inventory return on investment for grapes was $5.78, eighth among all fruit items.

Performance statistics among produce items can vary as much as the products themselves. Strawberries, for example, ring up the fourth highest dollar sales among fruit items (seventh overall in produce). Yet, strawberries post some startling differences from bananas, apples, and grapes, the items that sell at a greater clip.

Unlike those items, strawberries register spectacular sales per foot of $295.32--more than 10 times the average for all produce items. Nectarines are a distant second among fruit items, fourth in the whole department. Strawberries also show a healthy number of annual inventory turns, 248.37.

Big packs bring sales

Strawberries are sold packaged and in bulk. Richter finds that packaging the berries minimizes handling and helps increase unit sales. Marsh produce departments feature strawberries in two, three, and five-pound packs. "Consumers will pick up a big pack instead of picking them out one at a time, so why not merchandise toward that?"

In addition, the retail price is the same on the berries whether they are displayed in packages or bulk. "We don't upcharge the packaged strawberries because we don't do anything to them," says Richter. "We don't remove the stems, or trim the tops, or anything."

It's a far different picture for oranges, which are aggressively priced and lose money. Oranges rank seventh in dollar sales among fruit items, and "in fall and winter, they are big drawing cards," says Richter. From the end of October through March, when navel oranges are in season, a 72-size fancy orange will normally be priced at 59 cents per pound. A hot price is 39 cents per pound, says Richter. The result is a negative figure in DPP return on inventory investment.

Kiwis are another item that Marsh deliberately lost money on during the study period. However, that was part of a company strategy to turn kiwis from a specialty item into a staple item. Using deep price cuts to aid sales, Marsh built up strong unit movement on kiwis, then eased back on the price promotions (after the Super Study). Marsh produce personnel report that kiwis are sustaining strong unit movement and are returning a profit.

Questions for Discussion

1. Jim Richter has commented to the data processing center that he would like them to develop a way to more compactly present the information in Exhibits 1-4. Jim believes that all of this information is useful, but a bit redundant and overburdensome. The data processing center has asked Jim to suggest a more compact format for reporting the statistical data in Exhibits 1-4. If you were Jim, what would you recommend?

2. If you were Director of Information Systems for Marsh Supermarkets, what additional data do you think would be helpful to help management make pricing and promotion decisions?

Exhibit 1
Sales: Weekly Dollar, Profit, and Unit Movement

Producer	Weekly Dollar Sales[1]	% of Total Produce Dept.	Weekly Gross Profit[2]	% of Total Produce Dept.	% Gross Margin	Weekly Unit Sales	% of Total Produce Dept.
Vegetables							
Artichokes	$7.19	0.03	$3.37	0.04%	46.88%	6.13	0.02%
Asparagus	125.50	0.53	36.06	0.40	28.74	79.53	0.30
Beans	132.26	0.56	41.04	0.45	31.03	160.26	0.59
Beets	0.19	*	0.04	*	19.52	0.19	*
Broccoli	657.89	2.80	246.73	2.71	37.50	531.21	1.97
Brussel Sprouts	9.90	0.04	3.78	0.04	38.18	10.35	0.04
Cabbage	169.91	0.72	56.98	0.63	33.53	506.42	1.88
Carrots	658.36	2.80	264.88	2.91	40.23	790.12	2.93
Cauliflower	432.80	1.84	157.27	1.73	36.34	246.01	0.91
Celery	702.21	2.99	263.10	2.89	37.47	629.10	2.34
Corn	197.15	0.84	44.97	0.49	22.81	644.82	2.39
Cucumbers	324.85	1.38	116.47	1.28	35.85	721.03	2.68
Eggplant	13.89	0.06	5.53	0.06	39.79	17.01	0.06
Kale	5.13	0.02	2.95	0.03	57.44	5.35	0.02
Lettuce	1,848.25	7.85	760.92	8.37	41.17	2,209.97	8.22
Mushrooms	507.01	2.16	200.85	2.21	39.62	436.12	1.62
Mustard	0.50	*	0.25	*	49.54	0.61	*
Okra	1.85	0.01	0.68	0.01	36.93	1.30	*
Onions	948.32	4.03	400.88	4.41	42.27	1,328.74	4.93
Parsley	8.86	0.04	4.65	0.05	52.43	15.52	0.06
Peppers	519.50	2.21	229.15	2.52	44.11	936.61	3.48
Persimmons	0.26	*	0.13	*	48.96	0.37	*
Potatoes	1,906.65	8.10	941.93	10.37	49.40	1,354.99	5.03
Radishes	130.01	0.55	43.34	0.48	33.33	178.28	0.66
Rhubarb	0.16	*	0.04	*	26.24	0.10	*
Slaw	67.33	0.29	35.95	0.40	53.40	59.27	0.22
Spinach	58.53	0.25	25.93	0.29	44.31	54.51	0.20
Sprouts	11.78	0.05	5.90	0.06	50.12	10.80	0.04
Squash	119.78	0.51	53.16	0.58	44.38	147.02	0.55
Tofu	21.82	0.09	9.57	0.11	43.86	15.68	0.06
Tomatoes	885.37	3.76	382.03	4.20	43.15	1,027.22	3.81
Turnips/yams	117.89	0.50	62.03	0.68	52.62	247.99	0.92
Vegetables, mixed	5.72	0.02	2.11	0.02	36.86	4.22	0.02
Misc. vegetables	628.69	2.68	221.75	2.44	35.27	508.48	1.89
Total vegetables	$11,225.51	47.71%	$4,624.42	50.86%	41.20%	12,885.33	47.84%

Exhibit 1 (Continued)
Sales: Weekly Dollar, Profit, and Unit Movement

Produce	Weekly Dollar Sales	% of Total Produce Dept.	Weekly Gross Profit[2]	% of Total Produce Dept.	% Gross Margin	Weekly Unit Sales	% of Total Produce Dept.
Fruit							
Apples	$1,668.68	7.09%	$813.22	8.95%	48.73%	1,670.81	6.21%
Apricots	23.23	0.10	8.16	0.09	35.11	10.93	0.04
Avocados	22.81	0.10	8.00	0.09	35.09	15.25	0.06
Bananas	1,912.29	8.13	612.09	6.73	32.01	4,154.00	15.43
Blueberries	14.15	0.06	5.11	0.06	36.09	7.31	0.03
Cherries	30.15	0.13	10.54	0.12	34.95	15.26	0.06
Coconuts	0.72	*	0.25	*	34.88	0.98	*
Grapefruit	298.91	1.27	119.58	1.32	40.01	525.90	1.95
Grapes	1,572.89	6.69	482.32	5.31	30.66	1,265.14	4.70
Kiwis	50.86	0.22	9.07	0.10	17.83	244.43	.91
Lemons/limes	92.54	0.39	30.65	0.34	33.12	200.30	0.74
Melons	763.10	3.25	252.00	2.77	33.02	899.82	3.34
Nectarines	257.96	1.10	90.50	1.00	35.08	222.10	0.82
Oranges	312.24	1.33	113.60	1.25	36.38	1,168.46	4.34
Papayas	1.19	0.01	0.34	*	28.35	0.82	*
Peaches	363.28	1.54	126.72	1.39	34.88	349.94	1.30
Pears	234.00	1.00	93.60	1.03	40.00	343.26	1.27
Pineapples	206.41	0.88	74.98	0.82	36.33	139.52	0.52
Plums	154.14	0.66	43.08	0.47	27.95	126.06	0.47
Raspberries	22.49	0.10	6.39	0.07	28.41	10.88	0.04
Strawberries	885.96	3.77	345.61	3.80	39.01	644.81	2.39
Tangerines	27.86	0.12	11.15	0.12	40.02	37.05	0.14
Misc. fruit	705.65	3.00	239.79	2.64	33.98	594.22	2.21
Total fruit	$9,621.51	40.94%	$3,496.75	38.47%	36.34%	12,647.25	46.97%
Other produce							
Candy	275.51	1.17	82.49	0.91	29.94	139.85	0.52
Dried fruit	338.48	1.44	115.16	1.27	34.02	180.13	0.67
Juices & drinks	839.11	3.57	220.50	2.42	26.28	490.95	1.82
Nuts & snacks	136.58	0.58	58.45	0.65	42.80	66.59	0.24
Popcorn items	881.60	3.75	412.70	4.54	46.81	373.83	1.39
Sauces/salads/fixings	160.46	0.69	64.41	0.71	40.14	109.93	0.40
Misc. other produce	36.89	0.15	16.36	0.17	44.35	42.44	0.15
Total other produce	$2,668.63	11.35%	$970.07	10.67%	36.35%	1,403.72	5.19%
Total produce	$23,515.65	100.00%	$9,091.24	100.00%	38.66%	26,936.30	100.00%
Total composite store	$302,155.16		$80,065.27		26.25%	191,860.23	

[1]Composite weekly average of five Marsh supermarkets for 52 weeks ended 3/31/91.
[2]Gross profit includes all markdowns due to retail reduction or manufacturer allowances applied to specific products. (Does not include unassigned payments, market development funds, etc.)
*Less than 0.01%.

Exhibit 2
Profitability: Gross Margin and DPP

Produce	% Gross Margin	% DPP Margin[1]	$ Avg. Retail Price Per Unit Sold	$ Avg. Gross Profit Per Unit Sold	$ Avg. DPP Per Unit Sold[2]	Gross Profit Return on Inventory Dollars[3]	DPP Return on Inventory Dollars[4]
Vegetables							
Artichokes	46.9	25.9	1.17	0.55	0.30	15.64	8.65
Asparagus	28.7	14.1	1.58	0.45	0.22	23.16	11.36
Beans	31.0	4.3	0.83	0.26	0.04	78.12	10.71
Beets	19.5	8.6	1.00	0.20	0.09	0.17	0.08
Broccoli	37.5	20.9	1.24	0.46	0.26	129.50	72.07
Brussel Sprouts	38.2	10.6	0.96	0.37	0.10	4.62	1.28
Cabbage	33.5	-24.0	0.34	0.11	-0.08	97.69	-69.89
Carrots	40.2	10.2	0.83	0.34	0.09	43.42	11.04
Cauliflower	36.3	18.7	1.76	0.64	0.33	17.06	8.76
Celery	37.5	17.5	1.12	0.42	0.20	59.58	27.81
Corn	22.8	-49.8	0.31	0.07	-0.15	68.34	-149.19
Cucumbers	35.9	-17.0	0.45	0.16	-0.08	66.53	-31.49
Eggplant	39.8	8.3	0.82	0.32	0.07	24.36	5.09
Kale	57.4	8.8	0.96	0.55	0.08	15.64	2.39
Lettuce	41.2	22.3	0.84	0.34	0.19	217.36	117.62
Mushrooms	39.6	7.1	1.16	0.46	0.08	79.99	14.34
Mustard	49.5	-6.2	0.83	0.41	-0.05	1.72	-0.22
Okra	36.9	-2.8	1.43	0.53	-0.04	2.19	-0.16
Onions	42.3	12.1	0.71	0.30	0.09	42.38	12.18
Parsley	52.4	12.5	0.57	0.30	0.07	37.06	8.83
Peppers	44.1	7.5	0.55	0.24	0.04	263.28	44.83
Persimmons	49.0	36.8	0.69	0.34	0.25	4.15	3.12
Potatoes	49.4	30.9	1.41	0.70	0.44	57.28	35.85
Radishes	33.3	-13.0	0.73	0.24	-0.09	33.59	-13.12
Rhubarb	26.2	22.7	1.50	0.39	0.34	0.24	0.21
Slaw	53.4	24.3	1.14	0.61	0.28	73.57	33.55
Spinach	44.3	20.1	1.07	0.48	0.22	46.98	21.31
Sprouts	50.1	13.4	1.09	0.55	0.15	11.75	3.13
Squash	44.4	13.6	0.81	0.36	0.11	22.43	6.86
Tofu	43.9	3.7	1.39	0.61	0.05	6.64	0.56
Tomatoes	43.1	14.4	0.86	0.37	0.12	61.52	20.50
Turnips/yams	52.6	-1.0	0.48	0.25	0.00	95.46	-1.86
Vegetables, mixed	36.9	14.8	1.36	0.50	0.20	2.67	1.07
Misc. vegetables	35.3	21.6	1.24	0.44	0.27	37.38	22.91
Total Vegetables	41.2%	15.4%	$0.87	$0.36	$0.13	$56.25	$21.01

Note: Due to further calculation of inventory value, some adjustments have been made to the numbers in this section compared with the Marsh Super Study published in December 1992.

Exhibit 2 (Continued)
Profitability: Gross Margin and DPP

Procedure	% Gross Margin	% DPP Margin	$ Avg. Retail Price Per Margin[1]	$ Avg. Gross Profit Per Unit Sold	$ Avg. DPP Per Unit Sold	Gross Profit Return on Inventory Dollars[3]	DPP Return on Inventory Dollars[4]
Fruit							
Apples	48.7%	34.4%	$ 1.00	$0.49	$0.34	$47.03	$33.20
Apricots	35.1	19.5	2.13	0.75	0.41	7.32	4.07
Avocados	35.1	5.5	1.50	0.52	0.08	5.95	0.94
Bananas	32.0	4.4	0.46	0.15	0.02	211.85	29.26
Blueberries	36.1	10.6	1.94	0.70	0.21	8.94	2.63
Cherries	34.9	10.0	1.98	0.69	0.20	15.23	4.35
Coconuts	34.9	-52.5	0.73	0.25	-0.38	1.52	-2.28
Grapefruit	40.0	19.8	0.57	0.23	0.11	151.96	75.24
Grapes	30.7	8.3	1.24	0.38	0.10	21.44	5.78
Kiwis	17.8	-41.3	0.21	0.04	-0.09	16.71	-38.74
Lemons/Limes	33.1	6.5	0.46	0.15	0.03	12.46	2.44
Melons	33.0	10.7	0.85	0.28	0.09	43.12	14.02
Nectarines	35.1	10.5	1.16	0.41	0.12	52.01	15.62
Oranges	36.4	-7.4	0.27	0.10	-0.02	76.54	- 15.57
Papaya	28.4	-19.5	1.45	().41	-0.28	0.84	-0.58
Peaches	34.9	3.7	1.04	0.36	0.04	131.73	14.05
Pears	40.0	6.9	0.68	0.27	0.05	22.45	3.89
Pineapples	36.3	-6.2	1.48	0.54	-0.09	45.99	-7.81
Plums	28.0	-1.8	1.22	0.34	-0.02	17.66	- 1.16
Raspberries	28.4	8.8	2.07	0.59	0.18	9.35	2.88
Strawberries	39.0	17.3	1.37	0.54	0.24	158.86	70.42
Tangerines	40.0	8.2	0.75	0.30	0.06	13.19	2.71
Miscellaneous fruit	34.0	8.8	1.19	0.40	0.11	142.64	37.13
Total Fruit	36.3%	12.1%	$0.76	$0.28	$0.09	$46.93	$15.60
Other Produce							
Candy	29.9	23.2	1.97	0.59	0.46	4.42	3.43
Dried Fruit	34.0	26.0	1.98	0.64	0.49	12.83	9.81
Juices and drinks	26.3	19.7	1.71	0.45	0.34	23.51	17.60
Nuts and snacks	36.5	10.6	2.00	0.70	0.20	16.16	4.68
Popcorn items	46.8	39.6	2.36	1.10	0.93	19.09	16.15
Sauce/salad/fixings	40.1	32.6	1.46	0.59	0.48	6.19	5.04
Miscellaneous other produce	44.3	28.2	0.87	0.39	0.25	3.29	2.09
Total Other Produce	36.4%	29.2%	$1.90	$0.69	$0.56	$11.45	$9.20
Total Produce*	38.7%	15.6%	$0.87	$0.34	$0.14	$48.60	$19.61
Total composite store	26.3%	14.1%	$1.57	$0.41	$0.22	$8.61	$4.64

[1]Gross profit dollars minus direct product profit costs measured.
[2]DPP dollars divided by units.
[3]Annual return in gross profit dollars on every dollar of inventory investment.
[4]Annual return in DPP dollars on every dollar of inventory investment.

Exhibit 3
Productivity: Items, Packout, Turns, DPC, and Supply

Produce	Number of SKUs	% of Total Produce Dept.	Unit Capacity/ Packout[1]	Annual Inventory Turns	On-shelf Inventory at Cost	Avg. Direct Produce Cost/Unit Sold	Days of Supply on Shelf*
Vegetables							
Artichokes	1	0.2	18	17.72	$11.21	$0.25	—
Asparagus	2	0.4	72	57.44	80.96	0.23	6.34
Beans	1	0.2	48	173.62	27.32	0.22	2.10
Beets	1	0.2	14	0.72	11.27	0.11	—
Broccoli	2	0.4	128	215.80	99.07	0.21	1.69
Brussel Sprouts	1	0.2	72	7. 48	42.59	0.26	—
Cabbage	4	0.7	136	193.63	30.33	0.19	1.88
Carrots	4	0.7	637	64.50	317.23	0.25	5.64
Cauliflower	3	0.6	428	29.89	479.36	0.31	—
Celery	2	0.4	329	99.43	229.64	0.22	3.66
Corn	3	0.6	145	231.25	34.22	0.22	1.57
Cucumbers	4	0.7	315	119.03	91.04	0.24	3.06
Eggplant	1	0.2	24	36.86	11.79	0.26	9.87
Kale	2	0.4	24	11.59	9.81	0.47	—
Lettuce	7	1.3	370	310.59	182.04	0.16	1.17
Mushrooms	6	1.1	186	121.93	130.57	0.38	2.99
Mustard	1	0.2	18	1.76	7.52	0.46	—
Okra	2	0.4	18	3.75	16.23	0.57	—
Onions	6	1.1	1,194	57.87	491.93	0.22	6.29
Parsley	1	0.2	24	33.63	6.52	0.23	—
Peppers	5	0.9	146	333.59	45.26	0.20	1.09
Persimmons	1	0.2	5	4.33	1.59	0.08	—
Potatoes	7	1.3	1,201	58.67	855.11	0.26	6.20
Radishes	3	0.6	138	67.18	67.09	0.34	5.42
Rhubarb	1	0.2	8	0.68	8.83	0.05	—
Slaw	1	0.2	48	64.21	25.41	0.33	5.67
Spinach	1	0.2	48	59.05	28.70	0.26	6.16
Sprouts	2	0.4	48	11.70	26.13	0.40	—
Squash	6	1.1	272	28.11	123.26	0.25	—
Tofu	2	0.4	96	8.49	74.98	0.56	—
Tomatoes	6	1.1	659	81.06	322.91	0.25	4.49
Turnips/yams	2	0.4	150	85.97	33.79	0.26	4.23
Vegetable mix	2	0.4	48	4.57	41.09	0.30	—
Miscellaneous vegetables	15	2.7	388	68.15	308.50	0.17	5.34
Total Vegetables	108	20.5%	7,455	89.79	$4,273.30	$0.23	4.05

[1]Packout is a fully stocked shelf.
[2]DPC includes warehouse and store transport, occupancy, inventory, and direct labor costs. Does not include indirect labor such as management.
Note: Due to further calculation of inventory value, some adjustments have been made to the numbers in this section, compared with the Marsh Super Study published in December 1992. .

Exhibit 3 (Continued)
Productivity: Items, Packout, Turns, DPC, and Supply

Produce	Number of SKUs	% of Total Produce Dept.	Unit Capacity/ Packout[1]	Annual Inventory Turns	On-shelf Inventory at Cost	Avg. Direct Produce Cost/Unit Sold	Days of Supply on Shelf*
Fruit							
Apples	10	1.9	1,756	49.48	$899.07	$0.14	7.36
Apricots	1	0.2	42	13.53	57.96	0.33	—
Avocados	2	0.4	72	11.02	69.91	0.44	—
Bananas	2	0.4	480	450.02	150.24	0.13	0.81
Blueberries	1	0.2	24	15.83	29.71	0.49	—
Cherries	2	0.4	28	28.35	35.98	0.49	—
Coconuts	1	0.2	18	2.83	8.55	0.64	—
Grapefruit	2	0.4	120	227.89	40.92	0.12	1.60
Grapes	5	0.9	1,357	48.48	1,169.73	0.28	7.51
Kiwis	2	0.4	165	77.03	28.22	0.12	4.73
Lemons/limes	1	0.2	414	25.16	127.93	0.12	—
Melons	7	1.3	535	87.46	303.88	0.19	4.16
Nectarines	6	1.1	120	96.24	90.48	0.28	3.78
Oranges	5	0.9	454	133.83	77.18	0.12	2.72
Papayas	1	0.2	20	2.13	20.80	0.70	—
Peaches	2	0.4	74	245.90	50.02	0.32	1.48
Pears	2	0.4	530	33.68	216.77	0.23	—
Pineapple	2	0.4	90	80.61	84.78	0.63	4.52
Plums	4	0.7	144	45.52	126.86	0.36	8.00
Raspberries	1	0.2	24	23.57	35.52	0.41	—
Strawberries	1	0.2	135	248.37	113.13	0.30	1.47
Tangerines	4	0.7	98	19.76	43.97	0.24	—
Miscellaneous fruit	12	2.1	111	277.12	87.43	0.30	1.31
Total Fruit	76	14.4%	6,811	96.45	$3,869.04	$0.19	3.77
Other produce							
Candy	77	14.2	668	10.89	969.57	0.14	33.42
Dried fruit	55	10.2	383	24.45	466.57	0.15	14.89
Juices and drinks	18	3.4	387	65.97	487.60	0.11	5.52
Nuts and snacks	32	6.0	485	7.12	558.56	0.13	51.13
Popcorn items	65	12.0	903	21.53	1124.45	0.17	16.91
Sauces/salads/fixings	70	13.1	612	9.35	540.65	0.11	38.95
Miscellaneous other produce	33	6.2	445	4.77	258.55	0.15	76.35
Total Other Produce	350	65.1%	3,883	18.80	$4,405.95	$0.13	19.36
Total Produce**	534	100.0%	18,149	77.11	$12,548.29	$0.20	4.72
Total Composite Store	17,496	—	419,388	23.79	$478,906.76	$0.19	—

**Differs from December 1992 due to removal of florals from produce.

Exhibit 4
Space: Performance by Shelf Feet

Produce	Number of Shelf Feet[1]	% of Total Produce Department	Sales $/Foot
Vegetables			
Artichokes	0.5	0.1%	$14.39
Asparagus	2.3	0.2	54.56
Beans	2.0	0.2	66.13
Beets	0.3	*	0.77
Broccoli	9.9	1.0	66.45
Brussel Sprouts	1.0	0.1	9.90
Cabbage	10.4	1.1	16.34
Carrots	30.9	3.3	21.31
Cauliflower	15.6	1.6	27.74
Celery	17.6	1.9	39.90
Corn	17.0	1.8	11.60
Cucumbers	8.5	0.9	38.22
Eggplant	1.5	0.2	9.26
Kale	2.9	0.3	1.77
Lettuce	38.6	4.1	47.88
Mushrooms	11.6	1.2	43.71
Mustard	0.5	0.1	1.01
Okra	1.5	0.2	1.24
Onion	37.0	3.9	25.63
Parsley	1.5	0.2	5.91
Peppers	7.0	0.7	74.21
Persimmons	0.1	*	1.99
Potatoes	82.2	8.8	23.20
Radishes	6.2	0.7	20.97
Rhubarb	0.3	*	0.62
Slaw	1.3	0.1	51.79
Spinach	4.5	0.5	13.01
Sprouts	3.4	0.4	3.46
Squash	8.5	0.9	14.09
Tofu	5.1	0.5	4.28
Tomatoes	34.5	3.6	25.66
Turnips/yams	12.0	1.3	9.82
Vegetables, mixed	0.3	*	19.07
Miscellaneous vegetables	13.4	1.4	46.57
Total Vegetables	389.9	41.3%	$28.77

[1]Linear measure of shelf space, i.e. 5 shelves in a 4-foot section equals 20 feet.
*Less than 0.1%.

Exhibit 4 (Continued)
Space: Performance by Shelf Feet

Produce	Number of Shelf Feet[1]	% of Total Produce Department	Sales $/Foot
Fruit			
Apples	60.2	6.4%	$27.72
Apricots	1.0	0.1	23.23
Avocados	10.0	1.1	2.28
Bananas	41.5	4.4	46.08
Blueberries	1.0	0.1	14.15
Cherries	2.0	0.2	15.08
Coconuts	1.5	0.2	0.48
Grapefruit	7.5	0.8	39.86
Grapes	41.3	4.4	38.08
Kiwis	1.5	0.2	33.91
Lemons/limes	9.1	1.0	10.17
Melons	35.0	3.7	21.80
Nectarines	3.0	0.3	85.99
Oranges	28.3	3.0	11.03
Papayas	1.0	0.1	1.19
Peaches	10.5	1.1	34.60
Pears	30.0	3.2	7.80
Pineapples	20.0	2.1	10.32
Plums	9.0	0.9	17.13
Raspberries	0.4	*	59 97
Strawberries	3.0	0.3	295.32
Tangerines	12.0	1.3	2.32
Miscellaneous fruit	6.8	0.7	104.54
Total Fruit	335.6	35.6%	$28.67
Other Produce			
Candy	25.0	2.6	11.02
Dried Fruit	17.8	1.8	19.07
Juices and drinks	33.4	3.5	25.13
Nuts and snacks	26.5	2.8	5.16
Popcorn items	43.8	4.7	20.13
Sauces/salads/fixings	31.0	3.1	5.18
Miscellaneous other produce	44.2	4.6	0.83
Total Other Produce	221.7	23.1%	$12.04
Total Produce**	947.6	100.0%	$24.82
Total Composite Store	13,475.1	—	$22.47

1. Linear measure of shelf space, i.e. 5 shelves in a 4-foot section equals 20 feet.
* Less than 0.1%.
**Differs from December 1992 due to removal of florals from total produce.

Food4Less STORES, INC. *
By Ray R. Serpkenci, University of Toronto

In September 1985, Bob Allison, Senior vice president of store operations and corporate planning, and his newly hired staff specialist, Richard Wold, assistant marketing controller, were listening to final details of a major market research study being presented by the consultants. The two-day session, with all the other senior executives of Food4Less present, had been a draining exercise. The *Market and Performance Assessment Project* was easily the most ambitious study ever undertaken by the Food4Less organization. The year-long research, commissioned in late 1984, had two key objectives--in the short run, the research findings would be used to establish guidelines for the rehabilitation of ailing stores; and for the long run, the results of the study would provide new strategic insights for new store development and market positioning.

This last meeting with the consultants was especially important for Messrs. Allison and Wold, since they had been assigned the task of organizing the upcoming "store owners meeting" that was scheduled for November 14, 1985. At that time, the Food4Less senior management was expected to report on the results of the *Market and Performance Assessment Project*, and to present the general outlines of a new strategic plan for the Food4Less operation for the 1990s.

After the consultants' presentation, Mr. Allison turned to Rick Wold and commented:

> We have to get the findings of the consultants organized quite tightly for the November meeting. I think we should get together later this evening for a planning meeting. I am very disturbed at some of the findings, and we will have to put together a consistent program for the owners. As these guys [consultants] presented their stuff, things are all over the map. This surely won't go well with the owners.

Food4Less Organization

Though the individual Food4Less stores and their owners had been in business for a fairly long time, Food4Less Stores, Inc. in its present form was a relatively young operation. The supermarket chain had acquired a "cooperative" status early in 1980, following the initiative of several independent operators who decided to band together for buying, merchandising, and marketing efficiencies.

The *retailer-sponsored voluntary groups*, or *co-ops*, as they were commonly known in the trade, have become a major force in retail distribution, especially in the supermarket industry. The original concept had emerged as a response to the appearance and rapid growth of corporate chains in the early 1940s. At that time, (corporate) chain stores, with their massive scale in buying and distribution efficiencies, had been a major dislocative force in food retailing, forcing independents to realign themselves considerably. Later in its life cycle, however, the scope of voluntary group operations had been significantly expanded to include a vast number of integrated programs such as centralized consumer advertising and promotion, store design, location and layout expertise, employee and member training programs, financing and accounting systems, and, in some cases, a complete package of support services.

Food4Less Stores Inc. was a cooperative that exhibited many of the more advanced elements of this form of channel organization. The individual operators of Food4Less stores not only owned their wholesale company (and several distribution centers), but also used a uniform and standardized storefront and logo, and generally adhered to common advertising, promotional, and operating practices. They had, for example, a vigorous private label and generics program in place, a centralized equipment and store fixture procurement system, and a real estate and store engineering staff that all members could turn to for assistance from time to time.

---

* This case was prepared by Ray R. Serpkenci as a basis for class discussion rather than to illustrate either effective or ineffective handling of an administrative situation.

The executive group in the corporate office coordinated all of these activities of the voluntary group, and were appointed by the co-op general assembly. Executives in the corporate office reported directly to the Board of Directors, which included a number of Food4Less store owners as well as members appointed from the outside. Through the years, the corporate office had grown to become a source of innovative ideas and a driving force in the formulation of major strategic decisions for the voluntary group.

As of the end of fiscal year 1985, there were nearly 200 affiliated Food4Less stores located in several Eastern states, with combined revenues close to $2.0 billion and a work force of nearly 14,000 full and part-time employees. (Some of the key elements from their financial and operating profile are provided in Exhibits 2-4.)

The individual Food4Less stores were a mixed breed in terms of their size and physical configuration. Some of the affiliated stores were as small as 10,000 square feet, while others were much larger at 40,000 square feet of gross space. Furthermore, not all member stores had all the major departments in their stores. Newer units, for example, had added fresh-fish and bakery departments, which most of the smaller units could not support. Also, depending on local ordinances, some stores could not carry wine or beer while others chose not to do so. Predictably, the smaller Food4Less stores carried a narrower assortment of grocery items of nearly 10,000 to 12,000 SKUs, while larger stores were very much like superstores with nearly 20,000 to 25,000 SKUs. Exhibits 2 and 3 provide some of the key operating statistics and outline the sales contribution and gross margins by individual departments for all the Food4Less stores.

Except for the largest stores, most Food4Less members were located in strip centers, typically in high-density, urban locations. Most of the larger stores, on the other hand, were stand-alone units with ample customer parking spaces. Also, a few of the operators had recently switched to a 7-days-a-week, 24-hour format. Most Food4Less stores, however, were open about 16 hours per day, 8:00 a.m. until midnight.

Despite the common themes in advertising, promotion, sales support, and training, Food4Less stores at the local level were fairly independently run. In part due to their entrepreneurial spirit, and in part due to the considerations unique to their immediate market environment, Food4Less stores had historically operated, at times, according to the whims of their owners. A few of the operators did own more than one store. However, by and large, the independent owner/operator was the norm rather than the exception in the Food4Less operation.

Food Store Competition On The Eastern Seaboard

As in most other parts of the country, the food store competition on the East Coast was intense. Following the "oil bust" and the heavy reverse migration from the Sunbelt in the early to mid 1980s, several national chains had either expanded their existing stores and/or opened new stores in the region. Though there was certainly a new vigor in the marketplace, the level and nature of competition in this region was not particularly different from those found in other regions of the country. Notwithstanding this general observation, it was also true that some of the Food4Less stores operated in relatively mature markets of the Eastern seaboard, while others were in sprawling new suburbs. Shoprite and Pathmark, the two key competitors of the Food4Less organization, had larger, and in some cases, newer stores in or near Food4Less stores' trading areas. These and other competitors also had sharp pricing policies in the market, which Food4Less had tried to counter with double couponing since early 1982.

Given the high density of population in the Eastern seaboard, it was inevitable that most competitors had overlapping trading areas. Hence, it was not unusual for competing stores to be located within a one to three-mile radius of each other. Also in this region, the food stores typically had higher sales per store compared to conventional stores in other parts of the country. This was, in major part, a reflection of the higher cost of living in this region in general. (Exhibits 5 and 6 summarize some of the key measures of market and competitive structure in the Primary Trading Areas (PTAs) of Food4Less stores.)

There was also some "leakage" of food dollars away from the traditional supermarkets toward the local green grocers, and fresh meat/butcher shops. Especially in the more heavily ethnic neighborhoods, where there are traditionally stronger store loyalties, these small independents posed a threat to all supermarket operations.

Motivation for the Market and Performance Assessment Project

Each year, the affiliated members got together for a general business meeting to discuss the plans for the coming year, exchange data, and swap stories. According to Bob Allison:

> In our last year's meeting, a general consensus emerged that we should undertake a major research effort to reassess the status quo, with an eye on the future. Some of the owners were getting really nervous upon hearing stories about warehouse or PriceClub type concepts making inroads onto the East Coast. At the time, there did not appear to be a significant penetration [from these new-wave competitors]. But given the small size of some of our member operators, they are naturally quite concerned. For many, the investment in a Food4Less is their entire life savings. In any case, none of us wanted to be caught with our pants down.

With these thoughts and other considerations in mind, in late 1984, the corporate office hired a group of consultants, and for the next few months an intense research planning activity ensued. One of the key questions that Food4Less corporate, and the individual operators were asking was whether there were certain vital conditions, either internal or external, that resulted in superior operating performance; and conversely what, if any, were the conditions that impacted a store's performance adversely. Coming to grips with such factors was significant for several reasons:

1. To the extent such determinants could be isolated, store location or relocation decisions could be augmented considerably. If, for example, certain demographic and competitive conditions, in themselves or in combination, generally resulted in poor sales or profit performance, such market areas could be avoided in future store location decisions. Conversely, those areas with superior performance potential could be more actively sought.

2. If such parameters could be found, the corporate office would have a much easier time providing guide lines for improvement to those members who had negative contribution to the group. Or, if there were significant barriers for improvement, a case could be made for closing or relocating a store.

To the extent that an affiliated member was not performing well, it impacted the more profitable operators since they would be contributing more than their fair share of the group overhead. For a typical Food4Less, the current contribution rate for corporate overhead averaged about two to three percent of gross store sales.

Presently, there were a number of Food4Less members who had been consistently losing money over the past several years, while others were generating sales per foot in excess of $1,000--equaling or exceeding the highest quartile performers in the industry. This disparity in operating performance was one of the key reasons for the group members to push for a major research effort. Given the favorable economics of the region in recent years, there was also the fear that, if some of these stores could not be turned around, they probably would be unable to survive in an increasingly more competitive environment. This situation, of course, could potentially have an adverse effect on all Food4Less stores, because some of the efficiencies and scales realized by the corporate organization would be eroded significantly.

The Research Plan

To provide some answers to these and other questions, a significant amount of information on financial and operating characteristics of each store, as well as data on a number of market-based factors were needed. Working with the consultants, the following research plan and associated instruments were devised:

1. **A survey of store operations** was to be implemented at the store level for every member. This survey would include a complete income statement for each store for its most recent fiscal year, and a balance sheet for the corresponding year end. Also, this instrument would break down sales by individual departments and provide margin information for each of the departments in the store. Furthermore, an operating profile of the stores including such items as the number of customer checkout counters, part and full-time employees, annual staff turnover, parking spaces available to the customers, and a host of other variables would also be obtained for each store in the group.

2. **A competitive audit** was also to be implemented for each store, with the purpose of collecting information on all the competitors in the primary and secondary trading areas. Thus, for each Food4Less location, there would be information on the size of each of the competitors, their weekly and yearly volumes, and their location and distance to the focal Food4Less. Furthermore, a qualitative evaluation of the top 3 competitors on 20 dimensions would be obtained, comparing each competitor with the Food4Less store of interest. These measures could then be used to better understand the competitive position of each store vis-à-vis their major competitors, in their respective market areas.

3. **A demographic survey** of each store's trading area was also to be undertaken. The data for this purpose would include the standard socio-economic scales (e.g., income, occupation, ethnic composition, etc.), as well as population and household count and size distribution, level of employment, and mobility (migration) into or out of the trading area. Also to be included as part of this survey was a Housing profile, including such information as the number of housing units, average values of homes or rents, and vacancy rates.

4. **A consumer research study** was to be implemented to gather information on primary and secondary customers' store choice criteria in the general market area where Food4Less stores were clustered. Given the number of stores and the required sample sizes to make reasonable inferences, it was decided that it was best to gather this data for a limited number of stores in key states and in those market areas where Food4Less had significant membership.

Execution Of Research

Following the establishment of basic research objectives and parameters, all effort was directed, for the first six months in 1985, toward collecting and verifying data.

For the research effort to have a uniform basis for comparison at the store level, consultants, along with the corporate staff, carefully reviewed each store's trading area. An exit study of shoppers in each Food4Less, sampled randomly, was used to determine the primary trading areas (PTAs) of each of the stores. Operationally, PTA was defined as the geographical boundary within which the focal store drew 80 percent or more of its revenues. Predictably, many stores had quite distinct trading area shapes and boundaries, which in some cases, closely approximated a circle with a one or two-mile radius, while for others quite diverse shapes and sizes emerged. Ultimately, these boundaries were used to complete the competitive audit and the population and housing surveys. In this fashion, the competitive audit data and the demographic data could be merged to produce new measures of interest such as retail space per household, or aggregate household income, or population per square mile (see Exhibits 5 and 6).

By early August 1985, the consultants had finished their work on data collection and analyses. Throughout the months of August and September, a number of executive briefing conferences were set up to discuss the findings of the research with the senior executives (and a few key owners sitting on the Board). Today's meeting attended by Messrs. Allison and Wold was the last briefing conference in the series. The next meeting, which was to take place in mid

November, was the annual owners conference, where the key conclusions from the research undertaken had to be communicated to the affiliated members, and a new strategic plan had to be unveiled for the next five years.

Monday Night Meeting

After a long and exhaustive day, Bob Allison and Rick Wold got together in their hotel suite to discuss the game plan for the upcoming annual meeting. Throughout the year, Rick Wold had been gathering a variety of reports from the *Market and Performance Assessment Project* , but he was especially keen on a series of exhibits that the consultants had prepared for the meeting earlier in the day. (Some of key elements from these exhibits are reproduced here as Exhibits 2-6.)

In these exhibits, each Food4Less store was assigned into one of four space-productivity groups (calculated on sales area of each store) from very low to low, and from high to very high. In effect, each of these columns contained a "profile" of the *poorly performing* ($450/feet or less), *low performing* ($451 to $600/feet), *good performing* ($601 to $699/feet), and *excellent performing* ($700/feet or more) Food4Less operations. Also included in each exhibit was a column representing *All Food4Less Stores* that could be used as a "baseline case" for all figures to be compared.

Though such breakdowns were available based on many other performance criteria, Rick Wold wanted to limit the discussion to sales per foot as the critical dependent variable. According to Wold's reading, nearly all of the other measures such as net or gross profit as a percentage of sales, profits per foot, or Return on (Controllable) Assets [ROCA], appeared to support similar conclusions.

Though Mr. Allison was in general agreement, he thought one of the limitations of these exhibits was that they had no information from the consumer research study [of Food4Less customers]. Wold was quick to point out, however, that the consumer research in six Food4Less regions had indicated that the store choice behavior among the Eastern seaboard consumers was quite consistent with research results already widely reported in various trade and academic journals. There was, according to Wold, no "new" news there for the owners. Mr. Allison agreed, but he still believed that some the implications of this research should be tied to the information presented in the exhibits Wold had put together. (Some of the highlights from the Consumer Research Study are summarized in Exhibit-1.)

Looking at these exhibits and other results from the consultants' work, Mr. Allison was decidedly more enthusiastic: "There may be a simple story line to all this mass of data after all" he mused to himself. Looking at the reams and reams of data, and listening to the consultants early in the day, he had become increasingly disturbed, and at times, utterly confused as to what to make of this "stuff." The exhibits Rick Wold had gathered certainly made it easier to put together a comprehensive and consistent action plan that hopefully would be well received by corporate and the owners. As it passed midnight, Mr. Allison turned to Rick Wold:

> Rick, I think we have here the beginnings of a dynamite report for the owners. I also think we can make a strong case as to why some stores are doing well while others are doing so miserably. Since you seem to have made more headway in putting these things together, you should generate a first draft of an *Executive Briefing Document* that we can circulate to the senior people at Corporate, before we go "public" with it to the owners. I think there is more than enough meat here for you to work with. I will let you decide on the format as to how this report should be organized. However, I think the first section of your report should include a review of the determinants of performance for Food4Less, and based on your conclusions in this section, you should also outline a plan of action for the next planning horizon.

That evening, Rick Wold returned to his hotel suite well past midnight. Having agreed to generate a first draft by early November, he knew he did not have much time to waste. He called room service for a double Chivas and laid out all the exhibits on his bed. "If we can't win this thing on style," he thought, "we sure will get them (owners) on content."

Questions for Discussion

1. Based on research findings, identify the key determinants of space productivity (sales per square foot).

2. To be able to better compete in the future, do you believe Food4Less should change its market positioning?

3. What additional services might the co-op provide to store owners to help them better compete?

Exhibit 1
Food4Less Consumer Research Study:
Selected Findings

A. Supermarkets Shopped

- One-third (33 percent) of Food4Less' regular customers shopped at a Shoprite store during the past 4 weeks, while one-quarter (25 percent) shopped at a Pathmark store.

- Thirty-five percent of Shoprite's regular customers shopped at a Food4Less store, while almost one-third (32 percent) visited a Pathmark store within the past month.

- Thirty-two percent of Pathmark's regular customers shopped at a Food4Less store, while 41 percent shopped at a Shoprite store.

- Over the past six months to a year there has been a slight drop in the percentage of Shoprite and Pathmark customers "occasionally" shopping at Food4Less stores.

B. Reasons For Store Patronage

- The major reason for customers to *shop at Food4Less regularly* continues to be *"convenient location."* The primary reasons for *shopping regularly* at Shoprite and Pathmark remain *"convenient location"* and *"price."*

- As in previous years, *high prices* continue to be the primary reason for *shopping at Food4Less only occasionally and not regularly*; however, "price" complaints appear to have declined since early 1985.

- *"Inconvenient location," "more familiar with another store," "pick up odds and ends," and "poor selection and variety"* are also mentioned frequently as the major reasons for *shopping at Food4Less only occasionally. "Inconvenient location"* and *"high prices"* continue to be the major reasons for *not shopping Food4Less at all.*

C. Store Ratings

- A comparison of the regular customers of Food4Less rating Food4Less "excellent" to the same ratings by the regular customers of Shoprite and Pathmark show that:

    - Food4Less continues to rate superior to both Pathmark and Shoprite in the area of *"convenient location."* Food4Less also rates superior to Shoprite and Pathmark in *"courteous/helpful employees," "clean store,"* and *"always having ad items in stock."*

    - Food4Less's ratings are lower than Pathmark's and Shoprite's on the following 7 of the 23 supermarket characteristics considered:

        * All needs under one roof
        * Large variety/selection
        * Advertised sales/specials

* Money's worth in fresh produce
* Good prices on private label
* Low everyday prices
* Low grocery prices

- Food4Less rates lower than Pathmark on the following eight supermarket characteristics:

  * Convenient store hours
  * Clean stores
  * Fresh produce
  * Good coupons (excluding doubles and triples)
  * Good quality private label
  * Always carrying items wanted
  * Money's worth in meats

- There is no statistically significant difference between the percent of excellent ratings of Food4Less vs. Pathmark and Shoprite on the following characteristics:

  * Pleasant shopping environment
  * Delicatessen selection/quality
  * Top quality meats
  * Quick checkout
  * Never running out of items wanted

Source: Consumer Tracking Study, Food4Less Stores, Inc., internal report, Spring 1985.

Exhibit 2
Market and Performance Assessment Project
An Operational and Financial Profile of Food4Less Stores

	Net Sales per Square Foot of Selling Area				
Operational Statistics	**All Stores**	**$450 or Less**	**$451-$600**	**$601-$699**	**$700 & Over**
Full-time employees per store	22.3[a]	15.3	18.3	23.8	29.9
Part-time employees per store	57.4	40.3	51.8	59.1	73.6
Weekly hours per part-time employee	22.7	22.2	23.8	23.2	21.9
Weekly hours per full-time employee	47.7	49.8	47.2	47.3	47.0
Annual rate of labor turnover	38.23%	43.69%	31.79%	40.41%	37.89%
Average hourly wage rate	$8.48	$8.27	$8.74	$8.51	$8.37
Selling area per store (square feet)	16,343	17,159	16,411	16,160	15,835
Gross leasable area per store (square feet)	21,991	23,750	22,328	21,468	20,814
Customer checkout counters per store	9.0	7.7	8.1	11.4	9.2
Customer parking spaces per store	171.9	230.0	183.9	144.8	139.5
Age of store	11.6	10.9	13.1	10.7	11.7
Years since last store remodeling	3.2	2.9	4.4	1.7	3.4
Store hours per day	16.1[b]	13.6	16.2	17.0	17.0
Store hours per week	109.3	92.7	110.3	115.8	115.7
Store Sales and Investment					
Net store sales per week	$189,347.97	$125,307.53	$165,213.14	$202,211.27	$247,854.57
Average inventory investment per store	$348,731.47	$317,339.07	$341,272.06	$354,628.26	$373,658.61
Fixtures, equipment, and leasehold improvements					
Net book value	$501,597.04	$236,028.40	$511,831.62	$642,797.67	$575,884.93
Gross book value	$928,176.09	$533,119.00	$939,492.35	$1,120,770.52	$1,089,313.11
Estimated size of transaction per customer	$16.34	$14.73	$15.92	$16.87	$17.46

[a] Read: An average Food4Less store has 22.3 full-time employees.
[b] Read: An average Food4Less store is open for 16.1 hours per day.

Exhibit 3
Market and Performance Assessment Project
Summary of Operating Results

	Net Sales per Square Foot of Selling Area				
Store Revenue and Gross Margin	**All Stores**	**$450 or Less**	**$451-$600**	**$601-$699**	**$700 & Over**
Net sales	100.00%	100.00%	100.00%	100.00%	100.00%
Cost of sales	77.63%	78.56%	77.51%	77.31%	77.33%
Gross margin	22.37%[a]	21.44%	22.49%	22.69%	22.67%
Store Operating Expenses					
Salaries and wages	9.29%	9.52%	9.97%	8.94%	8.75%
Payroll taxes and benefits	2.59%	2.54%	2.71%	2.59%	2.50%
Rent	1.08%	1.39%	1.06%	1.01%	0.94%
Utilities	1.53%	2.03%	1.67%	1.38%	1.17%
Advertising and promotion	1.76%	1.87%	1.71%	1.82%	1.68%
Other store expenses	3.87%	4.08%	4.09%	3.65%	3.68%
Total operating expenses	20.12%	21.43%	21.21%	19.39%	18.72%
Corporate overhead	2.11%	1.97%	1.94%	2.25%	2.26%
Total operating expenses and overhead	22.23%	23.40%	23.15%	21.64%	20.98%
Store Profitability					
Operating income	0.14%	(1.96)%	(0.66)%	1.05%	1.69%
Other income (expense)	0.60%	0.84%	.54%	0.49%	0.57%
Profit before taxes	0.74%	(1.12)%	(0.12)%	1.54%	2.26%
Estimated breakeven volume as a percentage of current sales	96.48%	114.61%	105.73%	94.21%	90.78%

[a] Read: An average Food4Less store operates on a 22.37 percent gross margin.

Exhibit 4
Market and Performance Assessment Project
Departmental Sales Contribution and Margins

	Net Sales per Square Foot of Selling Area				
Contribution to Store Sales	**All Stores**	**$450 or Less**	**$451-$600**	**$601-$699**	**$700 & Over**
Prepared meats department	15.33%[a]	15.27%	15.28%	15.31%	15.45%
Butcher	0.92%	N/A	0.40%	0.86%	1.23%
Produce department	7.75%	7.61%	7.38%	7.88%	8.09%
Frozen foods department	6.91%	6.97%	6.87%	6.87%	6.94%
Deli and appetizers shop	4.61%	4.88%	4.61%	4.74%	6.94%
Dairy products department	13.25%	13.65%	13.60%	12.55%	4.31%
In-store bakery	1.42%	1.24%	1.43%	1.63%	13.16%
Fresh fish department	1.35%	0.90%	1.25%	1.80%	1.41%
Wine and beer store	7.28%	N/A	9.08%	4.89%	1.26%
All other grocery	41.18%	49.48%	40.10%	43.47%	N/A
Gross Margin Performance					
Prepared meats department	21.45%[b]	20.86%	21.69%	21.23%	21.81%
Butcher	22.63%	N/A	22.74%	21.56%	23.65%
Produce department	31.38%	30.74%	30.10%	32.17%	32.44%
Frozen foods department	26.53%	27.81%	25.98%	25.65%	26.57%
Deli and appetizers shop	39.46%	37.37%	39.70%	39.48%	40.68%
Dairy products department	21.54%	20.36%	21.77%	21.14%	22.42%
In-store bakery	44.57%	45.64%	45.39%	42.75%	44.15%
Fresh fish department	22.63%	24.52%	22.50%	21.62%	22.97%
Wine and beer store	23.33%	N/A	26.40%	19.25%	N/A
All other grocery	19.42%	18.72%	19.57%	19.80%	19.48%

[a] Read: On average, prepared meats department contributes 15.33 percent of store sales.
[b] Read: On average prepared meats department generates a 21.45 percent gross margin.

Exhibit 5
Market and Performance Assessment Project
Population and Housing Profile in the Primary Trading Areas

Population and Household Statistics	All Stores	$450 or Less	$451-$600	$601-$699	$700 & Over
	Net Sales per Square Foot of Selling Area				
Population of the primary trading area	36,243[a]	44,467	28,975	37,771	35,712
Number of households in the PTA	12,599	15,688	10,000	13,163	12,291
Average household size	2.89	2.85	29.2	2.86	2.91
Proportion of 1-2 person households	49.41%	50.82%	48.26%	50.80%	48.39%
Proportion of 3+ person households	50.59%	49.18%	51.74%	49.20%	51.61%
Total number of families in PTA	9,435	11,400	7,590	9,871	9,352
Average family size	3.35	3.36	3.36	3.31	3.37
Proportion of married couples	80.65%	77.39%	82.62%	81.58%	80.52%
Proportion of nonfamily households	22.92%	24.54%	22.13%	23.000%	22.42%
Proportion of African Americans	12.34%	14.21%	10.50%	11.61%	13.17%
Proportion of Irish Americans	15.19%	13.76%	16.41%	15.48%	14.91%
Proportion of Italian Americans	15.32%	14.91%	13.82%	14.81%	17.39%
Proportion white collar	58.57%	53.84%	60.32%	58.61%	60.36%
Median household income	$21,100.29	$18,648.85	$22,276.64	$20,586.90	$22,186.04
Average household income	$24,304.43	$21,754.05	$25,655.76	$23,344.19	$25,639.75
Automotive vehicles per household	1.72	1.62	1.76	1.70	1.76
Median school years completed	12.52	12.31	12.64	12.49	12.60
Proportion completed college	32.60%	28.75%	35.76%	30.91%	33.79%
Rate of unemployment	6.79%	7.87%	6.22%	7.14%	6.26%
Housing Statistics					
Proportion of housing units					
Owner occupied	60.62%	52.83%	64.89%	62.40%	61.05%
Renter occupied	33.43%	39.93%	30.01%	29.47%	34.82%
Vacant	4.05%	5.27%	4.09%	4.05%	3.13%
Average housing value	$66,428.99	$60,223.30	$70,422.76	$63,629.38	$69,395.46
Average rent	$259.94	$242.25	$265.36	$249.48	$275.57
Proportion of households who moved to the trading area					
Prior to 1960	19.04%	16.76%	18.06%	19.60%	21.12%
During 1960-1969	20.73%	17.96%	20.38%	21.41%	22.50%
During 1970-1980	60.23%	65.28%	61.56%	58.99%	56.38%
Proportion of housing units built					
Prior to 1960	63.99%	63.64%	59.16%	63.10%	69.20%
During 1960-1969	21.00%	18.41%	22.69%	20.30%	21.86%
During 1970-1980	15.01%	17.95%	18.15%	16.60%	8.94%

[a] Read: The primary trading area for an average Food4Less has a population of 36,243 individuals.

Exhibit 6
Market and Performance Assessment Project
Competitive Market Structure in the Primary Trading Areas

PTA Competitive Market Structure	All Stores	$450 or Less	$451-$600	$601-$699	$700 & Over
	Net Sales per Square Foot of Selling Area				
Number of primary competitors in PTA	3.93[a]	4.45	3.35	3.90	4.11
Average distance from Food4Less (miles)	2.24	2.11	2.27	2.40	2.20
Average number of years in PTA	11.33	10.07	12.68	10.81	11.62
Average GLA of primary competitors (square feet)	22,387	24,450	25,515	20,630	19,599
Average weekly sales volume per store	$236,979.60	$273,072.55	$247,537.34	$223,170.07	$215,829.24
Estimated total retail square footage per household	11.14[b]	14.25	11.43	9.94	9.57
Estimated competitive retail square footage per household	8.78[b]	11.57	8.67	7.80	7.63
Food4Less vs. the Top Competitor					
Location	3.3[c]	2.6	2.8	3.9	4.0
Accessibility	3.5	2.8	3.4	3.7	3.8
Perceived prestige	3.6	3.2	3.4	3.9	3.9
Cleanliness	4.9	4.7	4.8	4.8	5.3
Availability of parking	2.9	2.7	2.6	3.1	3.0
Speed of customer checkout	4.2	3.7	4.1	4.2	4.7
Interior design	3.7	3.6	3.8	3.8	3.8
Displays	4.6	4.0	4.4	5.0	5.0
Store atmosphere	4.2	4.0	4.0	4.0	4.6
Store size	2.6	2.2	2.6	2.6	2.9
Assortments	3.2	3.0	2.9	3.4	3.4
Number of checkouts	3.0	2.4	2.9	3.1	3.3
Amount of advertising	3.5	3.3	3.4	3.5	3.6
Overall prices	3.3	3.0	3.4	3.5	3.2
Value for money	3.6	3.3	3.4	4.2	3.6
Weekly specials	3.5	3.1	3.6	3.7	3.4
Deli department	4.5	3.6	4.1	5.2	4.9
Bakery department	3.4	3.2	3.4	3.7	3.4
Produce quality	4.7	4.3	4.6	4.8	5.0
Meat quality	5.0	4.7	5.1	5.0	5.0
Quality of employees	4.3	4.6	4.1	4.3	4.3
Courtesy of employees	4.9	4.8	4.8	4.5	5.3

[a] Read: On average, there are approximately 3.93 "directly" competitive retailers in Food4Less' primary trading area.

[b] Note: In general, total retail space>competitve retail space>primary or directly competitive retail space.

[c] These are the average ratings given to Food4Less stores (compared to their key competitor in their PTA) by each store manager: A score of 1-2 indicates a "very unfavorable" rating...while a score of 6-7 is a "very favorable" rating for the Food4Less store in question.